Catching the Torch

Contemporary
Canadian Literary
Responses to
World War 1

CATCHING THE
TORCH

Neta Gordon

WILFRID LAURIER
UNIVERSITY PRESS

Wilfrid Laurier University Press acknowledges the support of the Canada Council for the Arts for our publishing program. We acknowledge the financial support of the Government of Canada through the Canada Book Fund for our publishing activities. This work was supported by the Research Support Fund.

Library and Archives Canada Cataloguing in Publication

Gordon, Neta, 1971–, author
    Catching the torch : contemporary Canadian literary responses to World War I / Neta Gordon.

Includes bibliographical references and index.
Issued in print and electronic formats.
ISBN 978-1-55458-980-7 (hardcover).—ISBN 978-1-77112-238-2 (softcover)
ISBN 978-1-55458-985-2 (pdf).—ISBN 978-1-55458-986-9 (epub)

    1. Canadian literature (English)—20th century—History and criticism. 2. Canadian literature (English)—21st century—History and criticism. 3. World War, 1914–1918—Literature and the war. I. Title.

PS8101.W37G67 2014   C810.9'3582821   C2013-905991-1
                                                 C2013-905992-X

Cover design by Blakeley Words+Pictures. Front-cover image: Detail of a Canadian Victory Bonds poster (*Buy Victory Bonds. Back him up!*), ca. 1917. Library of Congress, Prints and Photographs LC-USZC4-8047. Text design by Daiva Villa, Chris Rowat Design.

First paperback printing 2018

© 2014 Wilfrid Laurier University Press
Waterloo, Ontario, Canada
www.wlupress.wlu.ca

Every reasonable effort has been made to acquire permission for copyright material used in this text, and to acknowledge all such indebtedness accurately. Any errors and omissions called to the publisher's attention will be corrected in future printings.

No part of this publication may be reproduced, stored in a retrieval system, or transmitted, in any form or by any means, without the prior written consent of the publisher or a licence from the Canadian Copyright Licensing Agency (Access Copyright). For an Access Copyright licence, visit http://www.accesscopyright.ca or call toll free to 1-800-893-5777.

Contents

Acknowledgements   vii

Introduction
Contemporary Canadian First World War Narratives: Remembering Canada's Best Self   1

Chapter One
The Dead Speak: Considering the Use of Prosopopoeia in *Dancock's Dance*, *Mary's Wedding*, and *The Deep*   27

Chapter Two
The War and Concepts of Nation in Jack Hodgins's *Broken Ground* and Frances Itani's *Deafening*   57

Chapter Three
Abandoning the Archivist: Commemorating the War Insider and Outsider in the First World War Novels of Alan Cumyn and Jane Urquhart   85

Chapter Four
Other Canadians: The Representation of Alternative Versions of the Canadian War in *Vimy*, *Unity (1918)*, *Three Day Road*, and *A Secret Between Us*   119

Conclusion
Representations of the First World War and Wishing   161

Notes   173

Bibliography   195

Index   205

Acknowledgements

I would like to express my gratitude to the following individuals and organizations, whose guidance and help has made this book possible. First, my several research assistants, who have—over the many years I worked on this project—contributed their time, excitement, and hard work: Leah Bolan, Victoria Brzozowski, Leah Golob, Amanda Graveline, Alicia Robinette, Tanya Rohrmoser, and Cassandra Scavetta. I would also like to thank the Humanities Research Institute and the Office of Research Services at Brock University for their assistance over the life of this project, as well as my excellent colleagues (some past) in the Department of English Language and Literature: Rob Alexander, James Allard, Lynn Arner, Gregory Betts, Natalee Caple, Cathy Chaput, Tim Conley, Gale Coskan-Johnson, Martin Danahay, Adam Dickinson, Ann Howey, Leah Knight, John Lye, Mathew Martin, Angela Mills, Andrew Pendakis, Jackie Rea, Marilyn Rose, Elizabeth Sauer, Barbara Seeber, Angus Somerville, Sue Spearey, and Carole Stewart. A special thank-you to Sherryl Vint, for her savvy and encouragement (as well as her willingness to talk *Passchendaele* with me), and to Janet Sackfie—the department's Administrative Assistant—for her immeasurable support and kindness.

Earlier versions of my work on the First World War novels of Jane Urquhart and on Joseph Boyden's *Three Day Road* appeared in issues of *Studies in Canadian Literature/Études en littérature canadienne*, issues 28.2 (2003) and 33.1 (2008), respectively; many thanks to the editors and readers for this journal. Thanks also to the external reviewers for Wilfrid Laurier University Press, whose careful notes and suggestions most certainly contributed to the book's rigour, and to the wonderful team at the Press, including Lisa Quinn, Clare Hitchens, and Rob Kohlmeier.

To my family—Yel Seliger, Michael Gordon, Gilda Berger, Amir Gordon, Shira Brym-Friedland, Ben Friedland, Talia Gordon, Eytan Gordon, and Ruth Seliger—thank you for your enthusiasm for my work and for your love. To my children—Mina and Sasha—thank you for being so hilarious, inspiring, and brilliant. To my husband, Martin, thank you for being my favourite interlocutor, my very best friend, and my heart.

Introduction

Contemporary Canadian First World War Narratives: Remembering Canada's Best Self

The Effort of Collective Remembrance

In a review published in the *Globe and Mail*, Robert Wiersema initiates his discussion of four Canadian novels by defining a "condition" he calls "premise fatigue," which refers to a reader's want of enthusiasm for works whose basic setting is simply all too familiar. "The main symptom of the condition," Wiersema explains, "is this sinking sensation that comes upon the ardent bibliophile: 'Oh God, I just can't bear another…' Fill in your own blank: another earnest account of the atrocities on the other side of the world; another book about the Great War from a Canadian serviceman's perspective, etc."[1] While I do not pretend to be immune from the occasional bout of premise fatigue, my concern is not the condition nor its symptoms, but rather one of Wiersema's illustrations of an apparently outworn premise: the Canadian Great War novel. The review date of December 2005 provides a reasonable framework for Wiersema's assessment, for the Spring 2005 publication of Joseph Boyden's *Three Day Road*, a novel about the Great War from a Cree-Canadian serviceman's perspective, denoted a high-water mark of sorts to a decade fairly littered with new Canadian novels and plays about the First World War. The years between 1995 and 2007 saw the publication of Kevin Major's *No Man's Land* (1995), Guy Vanderhaeghe's *Dancock's Dance* (1996), Jane Urquhart's *The Underpainter* (1997) and *The Stone Carvers* (2002), Jack Hodgins's *Broken Ground* (1998), Kevin Kerr's *Unity (1918)* (2001), David French's *Soldier's Heart* (2001), R.H. Thomson's *The Lost Boys* (2001), Stephen Massicotte's *Mary's Wedding* (2002), Mary

Swan's *The Deep* (2002), Frances Itani's *Deafening* (2003), Alan Cumyn's *The Sojourn* (2003) and *The Famished Lover* (2006), Boyden's novel in 2005, Michael Poole's *Rain Before Morning* (2006), Vern Thiessen's *Vimy* (2007), and Daniel Poliquin's *A Secret Between Us*, published in 2006 and translated from French into English by Donald Winkler in 2007.[2]

The title of this study—*Catching the Torch*—alludes to the final stanza of the most widely known Canadian poem written about the First World War, John McCrae's "In Flanders Fields," in which voices of the dead charge readers to "Take up our quarrel with the foe: / To you from failing hands we throw / The torch."[3] Many of the tropes to be found in contemporary literary accounts of the First World War respond to images, concepts, issues, and dilemmas introduced in McCrae's poem, in particular the difficult question of what our debt to those war dead entails, especially as that debt inheres with the concept of collective memory. Jay Winter in *Remembering War: The Great War Between Memory and History in the Twentieth Century* draws attention to the work of Maurice Halbwachs, the early-twentieth-century French philosopher and sociologist who theorized the notion of collective memory. As Winter notes:

> One of the central premises of the work of Maurice Halbwachs is that social groups frame the memories they share. That is, when collectives come together to recall significant events, events which tell them who they are as a group, then they create something he termed "collective memory." And when they no longer form a group, or when life events intervene, and people age or move away or simply find other things to do, then the collective changes or disintegrates, and with it goes "collective memory." This sense of the socially constructed nature of "collective memory" is vital to historical study, since it precludes talking about memory as if it exists independently of the people who share it.[4]

As Halbwachs suggests in his discussion of the way remembrance occurs via comparisons among members of a social group, "other men have had these remembrances in common with me. Moreover, they help me recall them. I turn to these people, I momentarily adopt their viewpoint, and I re-enter their group in order to better remember."[5] When First World War historian Annette Becker writes of Halbwachs's idea that "memory is always an effort," she is referring to the effort made among the collective to construct coherent meaning out of a series of living memories, whereby even within the time frame when various individuals can still experience separate, vivid memories of an event or series of events, those memories can only be proclaimed as publicly productive—or even comprehensible—when they are filtered through the demands of a particular social order.[6] As Andreas Huyssen points out: "the past is not simply there in memory, but it must be articulated to become memory"[7]; in other words, even though it is "dependent on some past event or experience,"[8] memory occurs in the present.

In his study *The Collective Memory*, Halbwachs defines both "autobiographical memory" and "historical memory," going on to suggest the ways these concepts engage each other. Autobiographical memory is living memory based on personal experience, as in the sort of memories Winter and Becker are concerned with in their references to First World War participants; significantly, a determining aspect of autobiographical memory is that it is held "in common with other people only [...] by virtue of distinguishing [the individual] from others."[9] One's sense of an autobiographical memory is what sets one apart from the concept of the social group; thus, as Halbwachs argues, it is fairly limited because of the way individuals "must often appeal to others' remembrances to evoke [their] own past."[10] Furthermore, Halbwachs declares that the continued scrutiny of so-called personal memories over time will culminate in a sense of "lived history," whereby the past is understood as a historical time and space in which an individual's life was lived and that will be remembered with an ever-increasing sense of public or social context.[11]

Conversely, Halbwachs defines historical memory as the false "memory" of events that are known only indirectly: "these events occupy a place in the memory of the nation, but I myself did not witness them. In recalling them, I must rely entirely upon the memory of others, a memory that comes, not as corroborator or completer of my own, but as the very source of what I wish to repeat."[12] Halbwachs's point that historical memory depends on what a social group will "wish to repeat" is crucial in two ways. First, the idea of "wishing to repeat" brings to mind the sense that a group will work to continually and repetitively remember those aspects of its past that it finds useful or fulfilling or necessary in the present. Second, the notion of the "wish" suggests the way even historical, communal, and national remembrances have, at their core or as their impetus, something of the personal, something associated with desire. As Halbwachs asserts, "collective remembrances might be laid on individual remembrances, providing a handier and surer grip on them. First, however, individual remembrances must be present, lest memory function without content."[13] Thus, even historical remembrance speaks to individual need in terms of the way a living history must be vigorously "renewed" over time.

Furthermore, the term "remembrance" itself draws attention to the difference between personal memory and the idea of a living history, which necessarily entails a "wish to repeat." As Winter notes, the term "remembrance" takes into account "agency... [and] the question who remembers, when, where, and how?"[14] The term "reimagining," moreover, explicitly denotes the texts here under discussion as fictions. In his examination of the film *Saving Private Ryan*, Winter remarks on the absurdity of supposing that such a film will stir up the "memory" of the Second World War in audience members who did not personally serve a combat role in that war, thus raising the topic of how "film mediates the construction of individual and group memories."[15] He does so, however, without seriously considering the difference between, one the one hand, something like a documentary, and, on the other, films—like Spielberg's—that have more in common with historical fiction and drama. The works examined in *Catching the Torch* more or less explicitly thematize the way remembrance of the First World War in Canada is a second-hand affair, yet one we are compelled to "take up" and continuously rekindle.

A primary question informs this study: What accounts for the fresh and prominent interest among Canadian novelists and playwrights in remembering and reimagining Canada's participation in the First World War? In approaching that question, I will explore how contemporary writers have made use of the compelling myth that the Canadian nation was born in the First World War trenches, and the concurrent myth that a number of Canadian values were forged during the events of that war—values such as a sense of duty toward the just cause, a quiet, communal strength, a disinterest in ostentatious personal heroism, and a sense of pride that Canadian soldiers could be counted on to fight while remaining morally committed to mediation and peace.

Before we consider this literary corpus, a few comments are required.[16] My analysis of the plays *Dancock's Dance*, *Mary's Wedding*, *Vimy*, and *Unity (1918)* treats those works solely as dramatic rather than performance texts (for to consider the myriad productions of these plays over the last ten years would constitute another project altogether).[17] In his study *The Historical Novel*, Georg Lukács distinguishes between the historical novel and the historical drama, asserting that, whereas the historical novel represents a "totality of objects," the historical drama presents a "totality of movement."[18] Because of limitations associated with the genre, including how many personages can reasonably be expected to take part in staged action and dialogue, the historical drama necessarily presents the activities of figures to be taken as exemplars of dialectical historical forces at work.[19] Historical novels, by contrast, need not be organized around exemplary persons or cataclysmic events because they have more compositional breadth, though Lukács makes it clear that historical novels also depend on the idea of "totality," whereby every character and/or action contributes to the sense that historical forces are producing conflict and change.[20] This generic distinction is retained, for example, between Massicotte's *Mary's Wedding* and Itani's *Deafening*. The former is a one-act, two-hand play in which the war's effect is explored via the interactions of two lovers over the course of a single night; the latter is a novel in which the protagonist's separation from her husband during the war is set in the context of the protagonist's family, her schooling, her work in the community, and so on.

In the collective memory of Canadians, the First World War is a cataclysmic event of the type that Lukács argues is central to the historical drama and that is also central to the historical novels examined in this study. Significantly, one distinction Lukács makes between historical drama and historical novels disappears in the way contemporary Canadian authors have explored these myths. Lukács insists that only historical novels are able to take up the "everyday" point of view, by which he means the point of view of individuals who remain at a distance from sites of political power in any given historical conflict. Both the dramas and the novels examined here focus on the way the war was experienced—either on the battlefield or on the home front—by everyday Canadians, disregarding for the most part any discussion of political or even military objectives, and eschewing the perspectives of historically significant figures. Thus, according to these texts, it is the common infantryman or nurse or home front volunteer who best embodies core Canadian values. In fact, the very notion of the "common" Canadian exerts a homogenizing influence within representations of the national collective, one that contradicts Lukács's ideal of examining the divergent viewpoints making up the "totality of movement" of social forces.

My examination of individual texts is organized under four conceptual rubrics, with each chapter in turn dealing with the concepts of sacrifice, nation, commemoration, and unity. I begin Chapter 1 with an examination of McCrae's "In Flanders Fields" and the topic of the sacrificial narrative, not only because of the enduring legacy of that poem in current performances of collective memory, but also because of the way in which sacrificial narratives are set up to produce an affective response, in turn generating a framework for narratives about national progress, about commemorating the past, and about celebrating the notion of a coherent, collective national identity. I will consider the aggressive stance taken by McCrae's prosopopoeia—who declare "We are the Dead"—before considering three more recent representations of this type of spectral presence. Examining Vanderhaeghe's *Dancock's Dance*, Massicotte's *Mary's Wedding*, and Swan's *The Deep* reveals the trend in contemporary Canadian literature about the First World War toward muting the voice of the dead and thus quelling any anxiety that their potentially unruly presence might cause. Chapter 2 begins with an analysis of MacLennan's *Barometer Rising* for its portrayal of the nation being forged in an apocalyptic moment of fiery devastation, before moving on to readings of Hodgins's *Broken Ground* and Itani's *Deafening*, two works also concerned with the topic of forging the nation. Hodgins's earlier novel—published in 1997—signals its critique of the myth of the war's place within a narrative of national progress via the use of a postmodern aesthetic and a thematic exploration of desertion; whereas Itani's text—published in 2003—makes use of a realist aesthetic to fashion a comparatively conservative and idealistic national romance. Chapter 3's opening discussion of *The Wars* as an exemplary historiographic metafiction—one in which the figure of the archivist marks Findley's interest in the complexity of our relationship to the past—moves on to an analysis of the First World War novels of Alan Cumyn and Jane Urquhart, drawing attention to their representations of the figure of the artist and the way such figures are thematically linked, not to the question of the historical record, but rather to the practice of commemoration. In Chapter 4, the myth of the Canadian national collective is discussed, first in terms of how historians have broached the issue as it relates to the events of the First World War, and next via an examination of four literary texts: Thiessen's *Vimy*, which adheres most thoroughly to the idea that the First World War operated as a site for fashioning a collective Canadian identity; Kerr's *Unity (1918)* and Boyden's *Three Day Road*, texts that provisionally challenge the myth while still endorsing the national collective as an ideal; and Polinquin's *A Secret Between Us*, which engages the myth as a kind of trick, only to consider the way the idea of the national collective has become merely a matter of discursive convention.

In the following sections of this introduction, I will review extant literary criticism about Canadian First World War literature, paying close attention to criticism initiated by the publication of Findley's novel in 1977. The body of criticism rehearses a double narrative, one that forms an important context for the work of more recent authors—namely, war in general is condemned even while Canadian participation in *this* war is commended. Next, I will refine the idea of a distinctively Canadian collective memory of the war by briefly comparing Canadian myths regarding the war's meaning with myths associated with the British and the Australian experience; this will indicate that Canadian narratives about the war's constructive effect are discernible in their emphasis on representations of the collective duty of ordinary citizens. Finally, I will consider how recent Canadian literature that wrestles with the double narrative of the war's meaning does so in a contemporary cultural context of anxiety, one in which conceptions of the nation and of straightforward civic participation have become unstable.

Literary Criticism and Canadian First World War Literature

The first major, sustained critical analyses of English-Canadian historical fiction about the events of the First World War were, of course, the flurry of examinations of *The Wars*, a novel that, prior to the last two decades' publication of new Canadian First World War literature, constituted the alpha and omega of Canadian First World War writing. Aside from Findley's novel there had been, of course, Canadian historical fictions and dramas set—more or less—during or in the immediate wake of this series of events: in 1941, Hugh MacLennan published *Barometer Rising*, which has as its focal point the 1917 explosion of a munitions ship in the Halifax harbour; G. Herbert Sallans's *Little Man*, which opens with a description of the protagonist's experiences in the trenches before portraying his career as a newspaperman during the Depression, won the Governor General's Award in 1942; and between 1962 and 1973, Canadian humorist Donald Lamont Jack published three novels collectively known as *The Bandy Papers*, which narrate the madcap adventures of Bartholomew Bandy, a pilot in the Royal Flying Corps, whose war experiences mostly consist of irritating his superiors and of feats of heroic derring-do.[21] In 1978, John Gray and Eric Peterson mounted an enormously successful production of *Billy Bishop Goes to War*, a musical drama about the First World War flying ace; Anne Chislett's *Quiet in the Land* was first performed in 1981 and published in 1983, and Wendy Lill's *The Fighting Days* was first performed in 1983 and published in 1985.[22] It was the publication of *The Wars* in 1977, however, that sparked almost all critical interest in the subject of Canadian First World War literature, and even in the literature written in the decades immediately following the war. Eric Thompson's 1981 article "Canadian Fiction of the Great War" appeared in a special issue of *Canadian Literature* titled *Timothy Findley and the War Novel*. In that article Thompson, like many critics writing after him, culminated his analysis of the combatant literature produced by Canadians with a look to Findley's novel. He then made the paradoxical suggestion—again, often reiterated in later criticism—that *The Wars* represented the First World War more fully than combatant fictions, and that Findley somehow made more satisfying use of the gaps inherent in our understanding of the war than even those writers who were writing from first-hand experience in a culture still dealing with the war's immediate effects.[23]

Thompson's article was the first to provide detailed analysis of three examples of combatant fiction produced in the decades following the war: *All Else Is Folly, a Tale of War and Passion* (1929) by Peregrine Acland; *Generals Die in Bed* (1930) by Charles Yale Harrison; and *God's Sparrows* (1937) by Philip Child.[24] Though Thompson begins his article by sketching Canada's military exploits during the war and situates each combatant author, albeit briefly, in terms of his "real" military experience, his treatment of the novels depends on marking the disconnect between these representations of war and Findley's contemporary response. Thompson reverses his initial prioritizing of "first-hand experience of combat"[25] by suggesting that the work of war insiders ultimately transcends "hard-hitting realism" to become "emblematic,"[26] and he concludes his critique by iterating a logical contradiction that defines much extant criticism of Canadian First World War literature. On the one hand, he affirms that "it is not difficult to conclude that Canadian soldiers *earned* their fine reputation" on the battlefield;[27] on the other, he argues that, as is evidenced in both Canadian combatant fictions and in Findley's *The Wars*, our general cultural response to the war holds that it "proved to be the remorseless enemy of human hopes."[28] Such logic defines not only most critical responses to Canadian First World War literature, but also a good deal of Canadian First World War historiography and popular consensus regarding the war's cultural significance—namely, that Canada's participation and extraordinary accomplishment during that war simultaneously confirmed the young nation's coming of age and emerging importance on the international stage and, as a direct response to the trauma produced by the war, initiated a new belief in Canada's role and spirit, primarily and distinctively, as that of a peacekeeping nation.

Even more provocative is Cobley's treatment (albeit brief) of Harrison's novel alongside such international works as Henri Barbusse's *Le Feu*, Erich Maria Remarque's *Im Westen Nichts Neues*, Richard Aldington's *Death of a Hero,* and Robert Grave's *Goodbye to All That*. Cobley cites the dedication of Harrison's novel, to "the bewildered youths—British, Australian, Canadian and German—who were killed in that wood a few miles beyond Amiens on August 8th, 1918,"[29] as an example of the way it, like many other First World War narratives, strives to authenticate the commemorative impetus by privileging a sense of fiction-as-documentary. Cobley argues, however, that "commemorating the dead is therefore an attempt to alleviate guilt through the act of confessing one's own part in the war,"[30] and that such confessions often culminate in narratives that can "be seen as the source of a certain ideological complicity with the war."[31] Her examination of the way in which Harrison's protagonist adopts a fatalistic attitude toward the war—as the mechanistic war of attrition undermines any potential for achieving individual heroism or even ambition—leads to the argument that such depictions are not active anti-war protests, for "the war is indirectly meant to condemn itself through facts which are left to speak for themselves."[32] Because Harrison's novel is not set aside as a Canadian novel, Cobley does not comment on what might distinguish his attitude toward the war from those of his European and American counterparts,[33] and it is significant that Cobley, unlike many other critics, does not seek to rehabilitate the Canadian First World War experience as special or justifiable or even distinctive, except in her validation of Findley's novel as a more successful anti-war novel.

Jonathan Vance's examination of the postwar response to Harrison's novel is also interesting in that it reveals the difference between what readers in 1930s Canada wanted from a war novel and more current expectations. As Vance points out, though "recent scholars have debated endlessly the veracity of certain books, and contemporary readers [have] had the same difficulty in determining whether a book was intended as history or fiction," for many Canadian readers in the immediate postwar period, "the distinction was irrelevant... Any book that did not adhere to the accepted interpretation of the war [as socially productive] was a dangerous falsehood."[34] And, as recently as Susan Fisher's survey for *The Cambridge History of Canadian Literature*, the debate persists over which Canadian combatant-novels are more in keeping with the way we choose to remember our war. Coming full circle, Fisher's evaluation of the way Thompson privileges combatant novels—especially his attempt to show how *Generals Die in Bed* operates as "an accurate and damning portrait of the war"— recalls the post-war attitudes Vance traces in his study. Much as Canadian First World War general Sir Arthur Currie denounced Harrison's novel as "a mass of filth, lies... appeal[ing] to everything base, mean, and nasty" (Vance 194), Fisher asserts that Harrison's focus on "hideous injuries, visits to prostitutes, looting, and the killing of prisoners" amounts to a set of "misrepresentations" (Fisher 232–33).[35] What is significant in tracking the critical responses to Canadian combatant fiction is that doing so reflects the stakes of collective remembrance, as the circulation and recirculation of cultural texts either confirms or undermines a sense of living history. Thus, combatant novels are alternatively deemed too anti-war or not anti-war enough depending on whether the notion of being anti-war is considered socially productive.

In her review of Findley's *The Wars*, written in 1977 for the *Financial Post* (and reprinted in her *Second Words: Selected Critical Prose*), Margaret Atwood refers to the arrival of the novel as "a major literary event,"[36] declaring that "this is a book that deserves and should get both a literary audience and a wide popular one."[37] When Kevin Major's *No Man's Land* appeared in 1995, initiating the recent flood of Canadian literature about the First World War, Sandra Gwyn, reviewing for the *Toronto Star* wrote that "as a literary evocation of the Great War, *No Man's Land* belongs on the same shelf as David Macfarlane's [memoir] *The Danger Tree* and

Timothy Findley's *The Wars*."[38] Gwyn's move to compare Major's novel to *The Wars* is not unique: early reviews of Cumyn's *The Sojourn*, Urquhart's war novels, Itani's *Deafening*, and Boyden's *Three Day Road* all contain some version of T.F. Rigelhof's query: "Is [blank] going to supplant Timothy Findley's *The Wars* as the great Canadian novel about the First World War on college and university curricula?"[39] Thus, the extant criticism on *The Wars* forms a crucial context for the corpus under discussion in this study, especially in terms of the way Findley's novel has variously been marked as being about something other than war and/or something other than Canada's participation in that war. Just as the soldier-poetry of Siegfried Sassoon and Wilfred Owen has, to a large extent, framed the general cultural response to the First World War in Britain, the discursive field emerging in response to *The Wars* has not only reflected but also produced the contemporary Canadian response. As historian Tim Cook (somewhat glumly) remarks in *Clio's Warriors: Canadian Historians and the Writing of the World Wars*, "Timothy Findley's novel *The Wars* and the subsequent movie based on it have probably shaped a generation's thought concerning the Great War more than [G.W.L.] Nicholson's painstaking official history."[40]

In the mid-1980s, articles by Diana Brydon and Simone Vauthier examining the narrative strategies of *The Wars* were informed by emerging theoretical considerations that situated *The Wars* in a postmodern context. Brydon argues that *The Wars* "focusses less on the period of the first world war than it does on the relation of the researcher to his historical data,"[41] while Vauthier declares that "*The Wars* as a narrative [is] about narrative."[42] Such declarations have become fundamental to almost all subsequent discussions of the novel, as the presence of the historian or archivist figure marks a decisive difference between this kind of First World War fiction and combatant or even home front literature that does not explicitly negotiate the issue of temporal distance. One of the most fascinating moments in Vauthier's groundbreaking examination, however, occurs in her last paragraph, when she admits her own discomfort at being "unable" to "engage the novel as historical fiction," a discomfort that surprises her "since the referential approach is not one I usually favor."[43] Vauthier's revealing comment signals a conundrum that explains much of the critical ambivalence about examining (and probably writing) historical literature about war: there is always a lurking sense that such work must be scrutinized not solely, or even primarily, in terms of literary qualities but for an inquiry into the way historical events have been discursively reiterated.

In 1991, two full-length studies of Findley's work were published: Donna Palmateer Pennee's *Moral Metafiction: Counterdiscourse in the Novels of*

Timothy Findley, and Lorraine York's *Front Lines: The Fiction of Timothy Findley*. Palmateer Pennee's study focuses on how a postmodern approach to writing historical fiction—in particular, revisionist historical fiction— might be ethically problematic because the "counterdiscourse" is clearly also a construction and "writers of moral metafiction can only leave us with a choice of fictions, a choice of texts."[44] York, meanwhile, argues that all of Findley's fiction is about war, in that "war becomes a *means* of illustration in Findley as well as a phenomenon to be illustrated."[45] In a more recent article, Palmateer Pennee reflects on the novel's function as Canada's central, most formally innovative First World War fiction, arguing that this critical status itself tells the story of a nation's maturation and produces a blind spot when it comes to thinking critically about Canada's military and economic histories. In other words, the flourishing discussion about all the ways Findley's representation of war is associated with other concerns—concerns about gender relations, domesticity, sexuality, human and non-human animal relations, Canada's colonial heritage, and so on[46]—thrives in accordance with the basic, ahistorical premise that "war" (as an abstract category or a "*means* of illustration") is evil, insane, an absurd waste.

The basic tenet that war is evil, and that when writing about war one need not reiterate such a fundamental precept, is reaffirmed by even those critics of Findley's novel who wish to follow Thompson and consider what *The Wars* might have to do with Canada's concrete participation in a series of military events. Many seem to be struck by the same conundrum as Vauthier: they feel an obligation to affirm the relationship between *The Wars* and Canada's military record even while upholding Findley's ideological position. For many, Findley's writing of the war is part of a larger attempt by Western culture to account for the First World War as a catastrophic, dehumanizing series of events that called into question the idea that war could be associated with ideals such as personal courage and meaningful sacrifice. Tom Hastings, however, writing in the late 1990s, points out that Findley's take on the war depends perhaps too heavily on European frameworks to be held up as a specifically Canadian novel about the First World War. Hastings argues that *The Wars* relies on the myth of "the generational conflict"—a myth that informs British cultural remembrance of the war.[47] To confirm his point, Hastings draws attention to the work of Canadian military historians such as Ralph Allen, Desmond Morton, and J.L. Granatstein, who note that Canada's immediate political and cultural response to the war was favourable. Canada was granted the right to participate in the Versailles Peace Conference and join the League of Nations after the war; furthermore, the postwar social and economic boom transformed Canada into a modern industrial nation. Hastings's critical position is unusual in that he rejects the notion of "war as a *means* of illustration," finding it problematic that a contemporary Canadian novel, one that necessarily deals with the First World War from a position of remoteness, might remember what the war means to Canada according to European cultural myths.

Thus, a survey of criticism on Canadian First World War literature reveals various sources of anxiety and/or deliberation. Critics worry that attention to, for example, the aesthetic complexity of *The Wars*—or, conversely, the aesthetic conformity of works such as L.M. Montgomery's *Rainbow Valley* and *Rilla of Ingleside*—gets in the way of considering what such literary representations have to do with referential history.[48] Some critics have deemed it necessary to launch their literary analyses from the ahistorical premise that war itself is somehow un-Canadian, and that anything other than a clear-cut anti-war position in a literary work exposes what Cobley darkly labels "complicit[y] with war."[49] Other critics suggest that Canada's cultural memory is (or perhaps should be) distinctively affirming because of the way the war was affirmed in the decade immediately following the events. Especially compelling is Palmateer Pennee's suggestion that we have somehow become too comfortable with the myth of a "reluctant coming-of-age of one Canadian soldier [as it] encodes the story of Canada's initiation into the rights of nationhood."[50] In other words, because Canadians presuppose that those writing about the war do so from an anti-war position, they are free to both condemn the idea of war and to take satisfaction from its more particular rewards, whether in terms of political and economic gains or in terms of experiencing a sense of national distinctiveness and pride. Many of the literary texts examined in this study are informed by this central paradox. On the one hand, the war is remembered as cataclysmic for Canadians in the same way it is remembered as such by other Western cultures, in particular the British—the "reluctant coming of age" is a consequence of coming to terms with the death of ideals. On the other hand, the story of the Canadian soldier in the First World War is also the story of a productive, progressive "initiation" and, as such, is reimagined within a complicated framework of nostalgia for a time and set of events that might reify a set of constructive values (about, for example, community or duty or justice). The anxieties and deliberations of literary critics form a good part of the cultural context for the corpus being considered in this study, as each text wrestles with what kind of narrative about Canada's participation in First World War it is seeking to privilege.

Comparing Mythologies

To bring the cultural context for these recent Canadian reimaginings into further relief, it is helpful to compare the mythology that has emerged about Canada's participation in the First World War with the sorts of myths associated with, on the one hand, the British and European experience, and on the other, the Australian experience. Most contemporary Canadian representations of the First World War are distinctive in that the view of the war as a developmental stage in a plot of national progress opposes the view more common to British and other European representations of the war, which emphasize its function as the destroyer of innocence and of cultural beliefs in reason and the common good. As Vincent Sherry puts it in his introduction to *The Cambridge Companion to the Literature of the Great War*, the war "stands on the seismic line of divide between centuries...between Then and Now, Better and Worse."[51] In "Myths, Memories, and Monuments: Reimagining the Great War," Sharon Ouditt points out that the narrative of the "disillusioned subaltern" that Samuel Hynes outlines in *A War Imagined* "has come to typify the [British] story of war."[52] Ouditt acknowledges that the sheer force of that narrative is necessarily exclusionary, whereby even the most radical explorations of male sexuality and class consciousness in the work of such contemporary British authors as Pat Barker, Sebastian Faulks, and Kate Atkinson are still limited to a focus on men's stories of the Western Front, suggesting that because such powerful narratives as, for example, the generational conflict are "part of [the British] cultural landscape...we need them to be reinforced rather than dispersed."[53]

In his study *Battlefield Tourism: Pilgrimage and the Commemoration of the Great War in Britain, Australia, and Canada 1919-1939*, David W. Lloyd points out that there are various correspondences among the ways that British, Australian, and Canadian populaces experienced the war—for example, in terms of the way servicemen from all countries answered to the British command, in terms of the comparable ratio of causalities to total population suffered by each nation, and—most pertinent to his study of war memorials—in that "they were also similar because their dead were not brought home, but instead, with few exceptions, were buried in the country that they fell."[54] Lloyd goes on to argue, though, that because both Australia and Canada entered the war as Dominions of the British Empire, there are also distinctions to be made, especially in terms of the types of discrete national narratives that emerged as part of the practice of commemoration. Here again, Lloyd suggests that there are both similarities and differences in the ways the two young nations tended to memorialize the war experience. Lloyd argues that "in both countries...the war was perceived as a rite of passage to nationhood. Throughout the war and in the 1920s and 1930s political leaders, writers and journalists in these nations claimed that their men had not only passed the test of war, but had excelled to such a degree that they were the best troops not only in the British Army but in the conflict."[55] Robert Zacharias argues in his essay "'Some Great Crisis': Vimy as Originary Violence" that the sheer weight of discourse repeating the significance of the battle of Vimy Ridge to the project of Canadian national self-fashioning has produced a "logic [whereby]...every invocation of the national as a naturalized form of structuring society—from the national anthem to a tank with a maple leaf emblazoned on its side to the institution of Canadian literature—can be understood to be drawing on the authority gained by the violence of Vimy."[56] Though Zacharias goes on to suggest ways in which the myth of Vimy has been called into question, and ways that the reiteration of the story of Vimy operates to elide other violent episodes in Canada's history, he notes in his conclusion that works like *Three Day Road* and *The Stone Carvers* participate in a contemporary reaffirmation of the birth-of-a-nation narrative.[57] Indeed, this study will show that, despite various efforts to depict the material horrors of warfare—which include both the familiar degradations of the trenches and the overwhelming fact of death—the larger event of war is often portrayed as a site of cultural progression.

Another important distinction to be made with regard to the particularly Canadian—as opposed to British or Australian—mythology of the First World War is also gestured towards in the narrative of Vimy. As Zacharias points out, crucial to enshrining the narrative of Vimy as an originary moment is that "it represented a uniquely Canadian victory: the Canadian Corps that managed to take the ridge was fighting together for the first time, both literally and symbolically uniting men from across the country."[58] This notion of the war as a unifying influence is the primary thematic of Vern Thiessen's drama, *Vimy*. What might be added to Zacharias's analysis is the powerful and enduring idea that the soldiers who were fighting represented the "everyday" infantryman whose coming together was less a matter of military tactics than of natural/national inclination and ability. As a character in Thiessen's play puts it, "And I seen them. Waving at us. Wavin' from the top of Vimy. Wavin' like they were kids on a snowbank."[59] Lloyd argues that a survey of commemorative practice in Canada following the war indicates that Canadians "believed that they were a civilian force who had been reluctantly called to fight, but who had excelled despite their civilian backgrounds."[60] Here, what is important is the idea that, even as the war becomes situated as a site of originary violence, the uniquely Canadian narrative incorporates the notion of progressing *away* from violence, of learning from the experience of war that such violence is better left behind. Zacharias's analysis of the Vimy Memorial as commemorative—not of victory, but of the dead—is linked to the idea that popular Canadian discourse of the war articulates a dividing line, not between Better and Worse, but between Colonial Innocence and Worldly Experience.

Lloyd further points out that the commemorative practice of Canadians contrasts powerfully with that associated with constructing the myth the Anzac warrior. For example, Lloyd compares the way the 1936 commemorative pilgrimage to the Vimy Memorial focused on the experience of the bereaved: those in mourning were specifically distinguished, wearing blue berets, and "when the pilgrims arrived in France the first free afternoon was set aside for the bereaved to visit graves and memorials to the missing."[61] In contrast, the 1936 Australian pilgrimage to attend the Coronation of George VI was organized to "[emphasize] the achievements of Australian servicemen and the Anzac tradition," with men selected for the pilgrimage "who 'by their physique, discipline, bearing and appearance in England, will draw praiseworthy attention to themselves as representing Australia's best manhood.'"[62] As historian Alistair Thomson has argued, the discursive construction of the Anzac warrior—or "digger"—in literature and film depends on an ideal of outsize masculinity, physical bravery, and white superiority.[63] Literary critic Peter Otto has further argued that the narrative of the Anzac experience has provided the inhabitants of the Australian settler-nation with a sense of home and belonging, one that elides "Aboriginal narratives of dispossession and self-affirmation,"[64] while Donna Coates points out that Australian fiction by women confirms the myth of the "astral Anzac"[65] and their "mateship credo."[66]

In contrast to this set of narratives, the texts examined in this study insist on such distinctively Canadian values as tolerance of ethnic difference (though that difference is, to be sure, ultimately subsumed into the collective); the ability to do one's duty without complaint or arrogance; and the tendency to show moral as well as physical courage, especially—and paradoxically—in terms of decrying the horrors of war while still making use of its productive cultural effects. The "coming of age" of the Canadian national character occurs not *in spite of* a reluctance to participate in the war, but somehow *as a product of* that reluctance. The thematic emphasis on the Canadian soldier's, nurse's, or home front volunteer's generally grim attitude toward war, violence, and even the political machinations of the state thus becomes a context for celebrating a basis willingness to engage in civic service and to form community via that engagement.

Contemporary Canadian Reimagining of the First World War

In his conclusion to *Media, Memory, and the First World War*, David Williams speculates on why Canadians remain interested in engaging in acts of historical remembrance about the First World War:

> So how to account for such a vigorous persistence of the Great War in our cultural memory? Must we link it to "the birth of the nation," our national myth of origins that Canadians otherwise lack? (The "national" explanation doesn't begin to account for the strength of the British need to reimagine the Great War, not with a myth of origins reaching back to the Conquest, and even to the myth of Arthur.) Our own memory of the Western Front, by contrast, cuts against the grain of our contemporary myth of Canada as a peacekeeper, a myth that ignores the historical reality of our military traditions—a reality that clearly weakens the "national" explanation for our memory of the Western Front.[67]

Williams refers to the "vigorous persistence" of Canadian literature about the First World War; indeed, within the framework of his study, which investigates how changes in media affect the ways in which war experience and cultural memory can be represented, the use of the Canadian works *Generals Die in Bed* (1930), *Barometer Rising* (1941), *The Wars* (1977), and R.H. Thomson's *The Lost Boys* (2001) as proof texts suggests a consistent stream of interest on the part of Canadian writers.[68] What I have noted in my opening paragraphs, however, is not a consistent stream but rather a conspicuous rush of recent works revisiting this series of events after a relative dearth of new Canadian literary responses to the First World War in the two decades following the publication of *The Wars*. The marked flurry of works written between 1995 and 2007 reflects more recent awareness (and perhaps anxiety) among Canadian historical fiction writers and dramatists about a shift in collective memory, as the social collective known as "Canadians" is perceived to be shifting, at least in terms of how that collective responds to the series of indirect, historical narratives and images we have about the First World War and Canada's participation in that series of events.

The term "shift" does not refer primarily to a demographic shift, though I take Winter's point that "demography matters in our understanding of the cultural history of remembrance, and scholars who ignore the links between them do so at their own peril."[69] Susan Fisher helpfully notes that the "resurgence [of Canadian literary interest in the First World War] is partly a demographic phenomenon: the writers who came of age in the 1960s and 1970s are the last generation to have known the soldiers of the

Great War."⁷⁰ Though the 2006 Census reported that 36 percent of Canadians declared the British Isles as their ethnic country of origin and/or identity, making this the largest demographic ethnic group in Canada,⁷¹ that percentage does not compare to the numbers in the early twentieth century, when British Isles–born or ethnically identified Canadians made up 55 percent of the population.⁷² Thus, an increased interest among contemporary Canadian authors in the role of non-Anglo-Canadians during the war, such as is discussed in Chapter 4 of this study, is not surprising. Fisher also notes that the "resurgence" is "political: as Canada's military commitments and losses have increased, so has our interest in our military history."⁷³ Furthermore, recent attacks on the myth of the Canadian peacekeeper as opposed to warrior form an important context for a group of works that look back to a war that most Canadians are generally proud to have participated in, even if their notion of what constituted that participation is a bit hazy or overly simplistic. Leading the charge against the peacekeeper myth is military and political historian J.L. Granatstein, who laments the current "weakness of the Canadian military" and who pines for the time when "Canadians boasted they were always there in a pinch."⁷⁴ As a survey of the literary works examined in this study attests, the notion of being "there in a pinch" does indeed endure, in spite of a conflicting set of narratives about the futility of the war. Most works written since the mid-1990s, however, express a desire to make productive use of the war, even if simply to set ahistorical contemporary ideals—such as belief in duty, justice, or community—into a meaningful context of living history.

After commenting on the "vigorous persistence" of the First World War as a topic for literary reimagining, Williams goes on to dismiss the idea that Canadian interest in this series of historical events might have anything to do with "our myth of origins that Canadians might otherwise lack."⁷⁵ He justifies his dismissal via two paradoxical claims. In the first place, he argues that because British writers also continue to return to the topic of the war, Canadian interest cannot possibly have anything to do with a national myth of origin because the First World War is not part of the British myth of national origin. But why do we need to presume that two separate bodies of literature must respond to a series of historical events in the same way? To suggest that the Canadian and British experiences of the First World War were identical and should therefore hold an identical place in each nation's collective remembrance is illogical; so is the suggestion that the two nations must share a single myth of origin. As Williams himself argues in *Imagined Nations*, the power of language to "gather people into a profound sense of community" must be considered in the context of the particularities of history and culture.⁷⁶

Williams goes on to suggest that the myth of national origin must be rejected as a context for Canadian literary response to the First World War because "our own memory of the Western Front...cuts against the grain of our contemporary myth of Canada as a peacekeeper, a myth that ignores the historical reality of our military traditions."[77] Setting aside the problem of even talking about "our own memory"—as if current Canadian conceptions of an early-twentieth-century war might reasonably be considered to be coherent, unified, and straightforwardly related to "historical reality"—such an argument is based on the false premise that communities can only sustain one myth at a time about themselves and/or that, if several myths are operating, they cannot contradict one another. That Canadians might want to think of themselves as peacekeepers, while also believing in the special military part they played in the First World War, seems entirely reasonable and not even particularly incongruous. In fact, this "paradox" is sustained in most of the works examined, which represent the war as capable of producing a valuable and extraordinary context for Canadian moral and social development.

In her survey of many of the texts taken up in this study, Fisher's commentary highlights the way certain literary depictions of the First World War are more "anachronis[tic]" than others.[78] For example, she finds a scene near the end of Urquhart's *The Underpainter*, describing the lovemaking between Klara, a German-Canadian, and Giorgio, an Italian-Canadian, awkward. While, in the world of Urquhart's fiction, "their union under Vimy Ridge symbolizes renewal and reconciliation," Fisher argues that "in 1936, when the monument was unveiled, veterans and the bereaved would have found such a scene both preposterous and offensive."[79] While I do not dispute Fisher's observation that many recent literary texts about the First World War display contemporary sets of ideals, the purpose of this study is not to appraise those texts, for better or worse, regarding the degree to which they "[*project*] the attitudes of the present onto the war."[80] Such projection is not only inescapable, but also a key focus of analysis. After all, Urquhart's novel was not written in 1936. When we probe just how contemporary authors engage in the effort of remembering and/or reimagining the events of the First World War in their historical fictions, the desires, purposes, and anxieties that inform the effort become visible.

Furthermore, the activity of making productive use out of past events, specifically the war, is not solely a contemporary phenomenon. In *Death So Noble: Memory, Meaning, and the First World War*, Jonathan Vance explores how various forms of cultural discourse about the war emerging in the 1920s and 1930s performed the work of establishing a unified "social memory." He notes that studies of social memory often emphasize that "the dominant or collective memory of a society is not always (perhaps, even, not often) based on historical fact, but on a set of assumptions about what the past was like."[81] Thus, as he argues throughout his study, even those with direct memories of the war or wartime Canada were given to projecting particular views about war, about morality, or about nation, onto the developing narrative. Vance points out, though, that his aim is not to simply argue that "the myth of Canada's war existed to bolster social order."[82] Rather, he is suggesting that "in remembering the war, Canadians were concerned first and foremost with utility: those four years had to have been of some use. The war had to be recalled in such a way that positive outcomes, beyond the defeat of German aggression, were clear. In short, the mythic version existed to fashion a usable past out of the Great War."[83]

It is also important to consider the ways in which even what might be termed thematic "anachronisms" within the body of contemporary Canadian literature written about the First World War (and there are many) do not necessarily imply an abandoning or misuse of the idea of history. In her survey, Fisher also takes issue with Boyden's novel *Three Day Road*, because it depicts Xavier Bird's addiction to morphine, despite there being "no evidence that morphine addiction occurred among Canadian soldiers"; she also praises Major's *No Man's Land* for being a "sober and restrained account" of the battle at Beaumont-Hamel, one that signals its commitment to historical evidence by way of "photographs of the [Newfoundland] Regiment on the cover and back of the book."[84] I agree with Fisher that sorting through how contemporary authors make use of, and make reference to, historical records and archives reveals the extent to which the events of war are being referred to with an aim towards the ideal of accurate representation at the one extreme and the suggestiveness of metaphor at the other. Boyden's portrayal of morphine abuse, for example, though historically unproven is metaphorically rich, bearing in mind cultural associations that link morphine to forgetting, or even to the image of poppies so central to Canada's most famous war poem, "In Flanders Fields."[85]

Also compelling is Herb Wyile's argument in *Speculative Fictions: Contemporary Canadian Novelists and the Writing of History*, that historical fictions written by Canadian novelists in the 1990s (and, for my purposes, also in the decade following), while still "foregrounding that it is not possible to write about what is in the past without writing about how one writes about the past... for the most part convey that the past matters."[86] In this sense, literary texts that seek to remember the past are not exclusively, or even primarily, engaged in archival work that may be more or less meticulous. Rather, in confronting the national mythologies of the First World War, contemporary writers negotiate competing, pervasive narratives about Canada's involvement in the war. While one narrative emphasizes the nobility and courage of common Canadian soldiers, as well as the war's role in Canada's emergence as an independent and culturally distinct international power, another narrative emphasizes scandals of war profiteering, the costly incompetence of politicians and military officers, and the incomprehensible human toll of the war. Most of the works I consider look to the past to emphasize a nostalgia for the way the war provided a framework for national progress and for the forging of such Canadian values as a sense of duty toward the just cause, a belief in the strength of the collective, and a somewhat paradoxical pride that Canadian soldiers could be counted on to fight even while remaining committed to peace. Additionally, the recent iterations of a secure, mythic notion of national identity, one that is articulated via representations of straightforward civic and military participation, work to counter current anxieties about the stability of the nation-state, in particular anxieties about the failure of the ideal of a national "character."

David Williams asserts that the continued interest of Canadian writers in the First World War has nothing to do with the myth that our nation was born in the trenches. Daniel Francis states that "if a nation is a group of people who share the same illusions about themselves, then Canadians need some new illusions,"[87] which may very well be the case. That said, there is simply too much discourse—in history books, in the press, in literature, and in literary criticism—promoting precisely that myth about national origin for us to dismiss out of hand its current hold on Canadian imaginations. The question then becomes: What kind of Canada was born in the war, at least according to the new literary reimaginings of that series of events? In his conclusion to *Death So Noble*, Vance argues that for postwar Canadians, the

> legacy... [was] not of despair, aimlessness, and futility, but of promise, certainty, and goodness. It assured Canadians that the war had been a just one, fought to defend Christianity and Western civilization, and that Canada's sons and daughters had done well by their country and would not be forgotten for their sacrifices. To these great gifts, the myth added the nation-building thesis. By encouraging people to focus their thoughts on a time when the nation appeared to be united in a common cause, the memory of war could prove that the twentieth century did indeed belong to Canada.[88]

Unsurprisingly, this legacy has not been entirely sustained. Though most of the authors writing about the war to a much greater extent than Findley consider the specifically Canadian experience in the war, that focus has not resulted in a wholesale abandoning of the idea that many lives were destroyed due to the incompetence of military officers, the greed of war profiteers, and the stupidity of government officials. For example, Hodgins's *Broken Ground* critiques the failures of the Soldier Settlement Act, while Urquhart's *The Stone Carvers* and Cumyn's *The Famished Lover* both disparage the work of the Department of Soldiers' Civil Re-establishment in dealing with issues of veteran employment and pensions. Furthermore, the idea of "Western civilization" and a unified nation is interrogated, as works like Thiessen's *Vimy* and Boyden's *Three Day Road* consider the previously marginalized stories of francophone and First Nations participation, while *Broken Ground, The Stone Carvers,* and *Unity (1918)* explore the motley of immigrant communities on the home front who try to make meaning out of war. The idea that the war "had been a just one" is, in a certain way, countered with depictions of war activity—whether on the battlefield or in field hospitals—that almost uniformly portray horror, chaos, and the agonizing loss of life. Finally, many works—most explicitly Swan's *The Deep* and Poliquin's *A Secret Between Us*—confront the possibility that those who participated in the war may indeed be either forgotten or, at least, remembered in ways that have more to do with the needs of the living than the acts of the dead.

Yet despite the ways contemporary Canadian First World War fictions affirm the general Western narrative associated with the fighting of the war—that it was a futile, costly, dreadful military exercise—Vance's seemingly hyperbolic declaration about "promise, certainty, and goodness," also finds purchase. To be sure, the reconciling of competing narratives is often a delicate activity and sometimes a heartbreaking one, for authors and readers are faced with the impossible question: Was it—the horror, the chaos, the loss—worth it? Not one of the works I explore here culminates in pessimism or condemnation of Canada's participation in the First World War, including works like *Broken Ground, The Deep,* and *A Secret Between Us,* all of which suggest that narratives that depend on collective remembrance are doomed to recede in cultural importance, given enough time, because the collective will eventually choose to remember something else. Most of the works in this corpus might even be called optimistic in their intimations that the Canada that is born in the First World War is populated by those given to seeking love, healing, and a sense of hope and obligation toward community. Many of the narratives this volume examines rehabilitate the figure of the father and/or a conception of productive masculinity; many follow in the tradition of early-twentieth-century home front novels by women to consider the value of female work, in wartime and beyond; many explore productive ways to think about communicating across cultural and experiential divides; and most conclude with a look to the future (which is now the present) and a sense of promise that is decidedly free from irony. Thus, the remembrance of the First World War that has emerged in the past decade or so reflects a desire not to destroy the illusions Canadians have or have had about themselves, but rather to re-examine how those illusions about the war, with all its attendant horror and misery and loss, might offer a space for conceptions of the best Canadian self to emerge.

What I will be referring to throughout this study as a type of nostalgia for the way the First World War forged a sense of national character becomes a particular source of concern precisely because the very notion of such a thing is increasingly convoluted. Recent studies such as the essay collections *Trans.Can.Lit: Resituating the Study of Canadian Literature*, edited by Smaro Kamboureli and Roy Miki, *Canada and Its Americas: Transnational Navigations*, edited by Winfried Siemerling and Sarah Phillips Casteel, and *Shifting the Ground of Canadian Literary Studies*, edited by Kamboureli and Robert Zacharias, as well as monographs such as Kit Dobson's *Transnational Canadas: Anglo-Canadian Literature and Globalization*, Justin D. Edwards's *Gothic Canada: Reading the Spectre of a National Literature*, and Herb Wyile's *Anne of Tim Hortons: Globalization and the Reshaping of Atlantic-Canadian Literature*, all wrestle with the question of what constitutes, on the one hand, the nation, and on the other hand, a national literature in an age largely defined by postnational, transnational, and globalized movements of capital, culture, and communities versus the stable (albeit imaginary) notion of the national collective. Dobson, for example, sums up the argument of his study by asserting that "it is important to look beyond the nation (without forgetting that it's still there) in order to rethink, rework, and resist what global capitalism has meant for those excluded from the dominant within nation states,"[89] while Diana Brydon suggests in her contribution to *Trans.Can.Lit* that "writers and critics are rethinking relations of place, space, and non-place in ways that complicate understandings of where and how the nation fits. They are not transcending nation but resituating it."[90] In contrast, the literary return to the topic of Canadian participation in the First World War represents a type of rearguard defence against an increasingly shifting ground, whereby even Joseph Boyden's exploration of the way First Nations servicemen were marginalized during the war embraces the myth that the war transformed Canadians into a cohesive, collective force, "an army to be reckoned with, no longer the colonials."[91] Boyden's wish "to honour the Native soldiers who fought in the Great War"—in particular, Francis Pegahmagabow as "one of Canada's most important heroes"[92]—does not transcend or even resituate the concept of nation, but rather reifies it.

The curious embrace of the "promise, certainty, and goodness" of war and nation performed in these works—which seems so out of sync with thematic (and formal) trends identified by literary critics interested in examining the resituating of nation—is visible, for example, in the portrayal of the war dead. As discussed in more detail in Chapter 1 of this study, even the rhetorical figure of prosopopoeia, via which the dead become speaking figures in a text, tends not to disturb popular conceptions of the war as a productive space for defining the national collective. Such benign imaginings of the spectral presence run counter to what many critics have identified as a decidedly disruptive trope. In their introduction to *Unsettled Remains: Canadian Literature and the Postcolonial Gothic*, Cynthia Sugars and Gerry Turcotte reflect on the way "the construction of the Canadian nation as a homogenous and civil society...is belied by those peoples and cultures whose suppression made national consolidation possible and yet who remain as 'haunting' presences that challenge the national imaginary."[93] They go on to assert that the essays in their collection—in looking at varied instances in Canadian literature of the uncanny, the monstrous, and the haunted—"[examine] what has been silenced or forced to the sidelines in a national context and [are] therefore concerned with what emerges as uncanny reminders of that problematic history."[94]

The most obvious distinction between the texts under consideration here and the literary works interrogated in *Unsettled Remains*, as well as in works such as *Gothic Canada: Reading the Spectre of a National Literature* and Marlene Goldman's *DisPossession: Haunting in Canadian Fiction*,[95] is that, for the most part, Canadian First World War dead have not been "forced to the sidelines." There is no dearth of historical research on or popular knowledge about Canada's participation in the war, and the collective commemoration of that series of events—first as Armistice Day and then as Remembrance Day—has been a central feature of the public performance of a national collective memory since 1921. Thus, even texts that dwell on the horrendous human toll of the war—from Itani's *Deafening* to Urquhart's *The Stone Carvers*—do little to disrupt the established sense of what Goldman calls the "synthesizing ambitions of the nation-state...to create a unified national image."[96] In fact, those works that seek to rehabilitate the narratives of those left out of the first official histories of the war—the nurses depicted in Swan's *The Deep* and Urquhart's *The Underpainter*, the First Nations soldiers portrayed in Boyden's *Three Day Road* and Thiessen's *Vimy*, the soldiers shot for cowardice, represented in

Vanderhaeghe's *Dancock's Dance,* Hodgins's *Broken Ground,* and Polinquin's *A Secret Between Us*—all culminate in a move to simply enlarge the existing historical narrative, with the effect that the inclusion of such figures further "synthesizes" the dominant mythology of a unified collective.[97] Finally, even when the dead emerge as a potentially uncanny or disruptive presence, they are ultimately contained. As I will argue further in Chapter 1, the dead figures echoing McCrae's avowal, "To you from failing hands, we throw / The torch," are subsumed into a sacrificial narrative that is always retrospective and that takes comfort in a stable sense of the war's meaning as a site of uncomplicated national progression.

This recourse to stability derives from an attempt to manage anxiety about the increasing sense that, because of neoliberal interventions into state governance, the workings of the nation-state are increasingly occluded, at least in terms of the ways citizens might enact agency. In "Metamorphoses of a Discipline: Rethinking Canadian Literature within Institutional Contexts," Brydon posits a number of ways to "resituate the literary and redefine what is meant by literary study"[98]—ways that include an attention to matters of globalization, to the institutionalization of disciplines, to literature's putative social function, and to the concept that the "political will can be strengthened through literary engagements."[99] Here, Brydon is following up on the concept of "literary citizenship" as articulated by Donna Palmateer Pennee. In thinking about the relationship between post-colonial theory and pedagogy, Palmateer Pennee considers the "possibility that citizenship can be critically acculturated in a university literature classroom,"[100] so that even a course organized around the fraught concept of the nation offers the opportunity for instructors and students to "ask civic questions of state policies and inherited notions of nationalism."[101] Both Brydon and Palmateer Pennee emphasize that examining literature operates as starting point for active citizenship, whereby the exercise of critical reading models the procedure of socially productive and potentially interventionist civic participation. This critical interest in the possibility of enacting a "political will"—especially in the context of the "increasing social fragmentation" produced by "globalized life"[102] and the ways in which notions of civic engagement have become associated with "private" activities such as "volunteerism and personal management of the self"[103]—forms a context for works that depict the war as an opportunity for participation in a civic collective, via direct or indirect service to the military. Thus, in positing the relationship between the nation and its citizenry, the war is imagined as a metaphor for straightforward, active participation in the polis.

The texts I examine often hinge on the concept of participation—of service—and the character attribute most consistently marked as having something to do with a national trait is the willingness to "pitch in" on behalf of a community. While "community" is sometimes conceived in micro terms—for example, in the community of patients battling the flu in *Dancock's Dance,* or in the community of POWs bonding over a shared sense of brotherhood in Cumyn's *The Famished Lover*—the privileging of the military and/or home front collective becomes a laudable goal irrespective of, and sometimes in direct conflict with, any moral qualms about the activity of war. The attitude toward nation, then, is both optimistic and defensive, as the texts seek to answer complex questions about who is included in the polis, and about how national narratives are inscribed, by resorting to valorizations of "doing." In her contribution to *Crosstalk: Canadian and Global Imaginaries in Dialogue,* Brydon examines the controversy surrounding what she refers to as "the Hérouxville debates," in which she attempts to unpack "a local response to provincial, national, and global events, perceived through the town's understanding of national pressures promoting multiculturalism."[104] Brydon carefully analyzes both the Canadian media's hyperbolic condemnation of a town's "parochial" understanding of the concept of "reasonable accommodation,"[105] as well as the way the town's "code of conduct" points to "anxieties about identity, belonging, and agency in global times."[106] While Brydon is adamantly opposed to the content of the code itself—which originally included admonitions against female circumcision and the stoning of women in public, references that have since been removed—she does not resort to a blanket condemnation of the town's inhabitants; rather, she suggests, "at heart, these resistances [to cultural difference] may be linked to a certain notion of autonomy: the desire to control the conditions of one's personal and communal life, and the fear of losing that control to external forces."[107] The texts examined in this study are responding to the same anxiety about a lack of autonomy whereby, paradoxically, an "external force" such as a war provides a more comprehensible context for exercising agency than political and economic conditions produced by globalization. Thus, these texts are decidedly conservative in their imagining of the "political will," which in turn encourages a view of civic participation that promotes the collective by simply enlarging the category of the homogenous, and that imagines citizenship solely in terms of service to—rather than engagement with or challenge of—the progressive enterprise of nation.

Finally, the defensive manoeuvring found in many of the works examined in this study—which seek to condemn war even while commending appropriately Canadian war activity—also accounts for the move away from the explicitly metafictional aesthetic that is so visible in Findley's *The Wars* and in much of the Canadian historical literature written in the 1970s and 1980s. With the exception of Hodgins's *Broken Ground*, a relatively early text among the recent flurry, the works examined do not actively engage in the question of the veracity of the historical record, even when they seek to expand the borders of whose histories should be included in that record. In Section III of *Memory, History, and Forgetting*, titled "The Historical Condition," Paul Ricoeur draws attention to the differences between memory and history: on the one hand, "the problem of memory basically concerned *faithfulness* to the past." On the other, the challenge for the historian is "to exercise historical judgement in a spirit of impartiality."[108] Thus, the moral imperative of collective memory—that is, the imperative, as John McCrae might put it, of "keeping faith"—sets it at odds with history, as "the metamorphosis is underway that leads from history to the remembered, and then on to the commemorated."[109] The conflict between history and collective memory, whereby collective memory occurs in the present, electing what in the past it aspires to be "faithful" to, is visible in this corpus. Contemporary Canadian texts revisiting both the events and the ensuing narratives of the First World War turn to the compelling power of national myth more often than they do to the question of the historical record. While it is not always the case that certain myths are unquestioningly accepted, the influential idea that Canada's best self-as-collective came of age in the war—that it was forged on the battlefront and home front, as well as at sites of commemorative activity—more often than not emerges as a frontward-backward-looking wish.

1

The Dead Speak: Considering the Use of Prosopopoeia in *Dancock's Dance*, *Mary's Wedding*, and *The Deep*

"We are the Dead": Troubling Elegy and the Sacrificial Narrative

John McCrae's iconic Canadian First World War poem, "In Flanders Fields," uses the rhetorical figure of prosopopoeia—the impersonation of an absent speaker—in order to more forcefully stipulate a pact between "the Dead" and the living "you":

> In Flanders fields the poppies blow
>   Between the crosses, row on row,
>   That mark our place; and in the sky
>   The larks, still bravely singing, fly
> Scarce heard amid the guns below.
> We are the Dead. Short days ago
> We lived, felt dawn, saw sunset glow,
>   Loved and were loved, and now we lie,
>   In Flanders fields.
> Take up our quarrel with the foe:
> To you from failing hands we throw
>   The torch; be yours to hold it high.
>   If ye break faith with us who die
> We shall not sleep, though poppies grow
>   In Flanders fields.[1]

Since the poem's 1915 publication in *Punch*, after which it immediately became, in John Prescott's words, "*the* poem of the British army,"[2] the interpretation of what is meant by keeping "faith" with "the Dead" has fluctuated. Thus, the rhetorical figure of prosopopoeia is important to consider as it operates not only in McCrae's poem but also in more recent Canadian literary responses to the war in which the chief distance lies between the contemporary writer and the war dead he or she has chosen to impersonate. This chapter begins with an analysis of the way McCrae's famous poem has been deployed in current national performances that commemorate Canadian involvement in the First World War, suggesting that many of these choose to ignore or to contain the potentially unsettling voice of the dead. Next, I look at the way the voice of the dead has been incorporated into three contemporary works: Guy Vanderhaeghe's *Dancock's Dance*, Stephen Massicotte's *Mary's Wedding*, and Mary Swan's *The Deep*. While the reanimation of First World War voices in these texts functions to trouble the possibility of identifying with, commemorating, and/or elegizing a victim of war lost to temporal distance, the ghosts in this corpus, paradoxically, tend not to disturb the myth of a cohesive national character. Rather, the recourse to the prosopopoeiac voice serves to hide the dead behind a disfiguring mask, a fiction that approves of participation in the war as a productive site for articulating citizenship.

Dancock's Dance, first performed in 1995 and published a year later, focuses on the experiences of an officer, Lieutenant John Carlyle Dancock, who has been committed to the Saskatchewan Hospital for the Insane following the war. During the 1918 outbreak of influenza, Dancock must overcome his own demons and lead the patients in the hospital as they work to combat the spread of illness. In Vanderhaeghe's play, the potentially disruptive elegy for the dead soldier breaks down in favour of celebrating a fairly conservative code of masculine honour and the valorizing of duty. *Mary's Wedding*, another play, was published and first produced in 2002, and it continues to be produced throughout Canada and the United States. The action in *Mary's Wedding* all takes place within a dream space over the course of single evening, as Mary recalls her pre-war relationship with a young man named Charlie and gains access to Charlie's war experiences. Massicotte makes use of a counterfeit prosopopoeiac mask, burying beneath a fictional voice the historical personage of Lieutenant Gordon Muriel Flowerdew, who is a character in the play and whose actions during the charge at Moreuil Wood are cited as the historical anchor for the drama. Mary Swan's 2002 novella *The Deep* presents the story of twin sisters who drowned themselves on their way home from serving as nurses in France. *The Deep* is one of the most radical of the current crop of Canadian

First World War narratives in that it provisionally challenges the project of collective elegizing, representing dead voices that refuse to be placed in a sacrificial narrative. Even in Swan's narrative, however, the recourse to prosopopoeia indicates a desire to bury anxiety about the dead through a kind of affirming erasure. In all of these texts, what prosopopoeia usually produces—beyond a sense of apprehension regarding the space between the war dead and efforts of remembrance—is a confirmation of a stable code of national character, one that is associated with civility, as well as a confidence that the voices of the war dead need not trouble the Canadian mythology about the war. While there may be no way of constructing a totally unproblematic sacrificial narrative assuring us that the dead died "for something," these texts perform the ways that thinking about the dead may be linked to the idea of living for something, be it a sense of affirming the continuity of life, a sense of duty, or a sense of the civil collective.

Nancy Holmes's article "'In Flanders Fields'—Canada's Official Poem: Breaking Faith" provides not only a history of the poem's status in Canada but also an almost totally unprecedented and therefore much welcome literary analysis of it. She argues that "In Flanders Fields" has an "iconic status... [It is] English-speaking Canada's most well-known verse; most Canadians can probably recite a line or two from it if from no other."[3] Most current Canadian recitations of the poem, however, choose to keep the impersonating voice at arm's length, focusing on the first two stanzas—the ones reprinted on the Canadian ten-dollar bill—and avoiding the final stanza's charge that readers "take up our quarrel with the foe." The poem's message is thus commonly interpreted as a request that, as then-Governor General of Canada Adrienne Clarkson put it, "sacrifice" and "courage" be remembered and "inspire us to well and truly live."[4] Even since 2002, when Canada began committing infantry and special forces to the war in Afghanistan, the note sounded with regard to Canada's relationship to both First World War and more recent war casualties has usually emphasized the idea that "we must cherish the freedoms that so many died to protect."[5]

The centrality of McCrae's poem to current national performances of commemoration, generally associated as they are with a mandate for peace, reveals a troubling blind spot in the popular use of the poem. When the final stanza is invoked (and it is usually invoked pointedly), the standard next move is damage control, a frantic denunciation of interpreting such lines as proof that "In Flanders Fields" espouses pro-war sentiment. Such interpretive exercises disregard McCrae's own anti-pacifist convictions, which are readily and consistently observable in his post–Boer War and First World War writing.⁶ Even Holmes's otherwise careful examination of the poem—especially of the first two stanzas—ultimately seeks to contain the overt point of what she refers to as the "disappoint[ing]" final stanza.⁷ The prosopopoeiac speakers' pro-war imperatives are summarily dismissed as references to "petty quarrels and fairy tale foes...an Olympic torch in a relay race on the way to the Paris games. Even the ghosts in the last three lines could be seen as Halloween ghosts."⁸ Holmes concludes that McCrae's poem might productively force the contemporary reader to "ask if these tokens of remembrance are not deliberate strategies on the part of the federal government and militaristic segments of our society to re-instill simplistic devotion to nationalism at the expense of our more difficult humanitarian values and moral concepts."⁹ This claim, however, depends on her writing off the troubling final stanza as simply bad poetry. Holmes's apology is consistent with the popular conception of McCrae and his famous poem as executors of consolation for the noble sacrifices of the past that produced our better, peaceful lives, and with the consensus of reading McCrae's use of prosopopoeia as affirming our relationship with idealistic proxies who suffered constructively so that we should not.

My point here is not to disparage either John McCrae or his apologists, but rather to illuminate both the problem of associating such a poem with the genre of elegy and the danger of not interrogating the deployment of its sacrificial narrative, especially as that narrative has been recast over time. It is the aggressive stance adopted by McCrae's prosopopoeiae in particular, and the rhetorical trope of prosopopoeia in general, that can interrupt and problematize the logic of both elegy and sacrificial narrative. As Paul de Man points out regarding prosopopoeia, it is "the fiction of an apostrophe to an absent, deceased and voiceless entity...Voice assumes mouth, eye and finally face, a chain that is manifest in the etymology of the trope's name, *prosopon poien*, to confer a mask or a face."¹⁰ The voice of the dead, de Man shows, is always hidden in a figuring (and disfiguring) mask, so that, crucially, it is the mask that becomes the reality, creating the figuring (and disfiguring) fiction of the face behind it. This inversion in reality is why the use of prosopopoeia always indicates "the *threat* of a deeper logical disturbance,"¹¹ in that the very process of figuration producing the impersonating voice of the absent or dead also serves to deprive those absent or dead of their reality, their voice.¹² The "logical disturbance" invoked by the use of prosopopoeia by McCrae, as well as by contemporary Canadian authors who have used this trope, draws attention to the complex manoeuvring required for a community to make productive use of their dead.

The function of deferring to the voice of the dead in "In Flanders Fields" is decidedly unelegiac, admonishing against mere meditation and/or laying to rest, as shown by the warning in the third stanza that, if the "quarrel with foe" is not adopted, the dead "shall not sleep." As William Watkin clarifies in *On Mourning: Theories of Loss in Modern Literature*, the objectives of elegy—in terms of both its personal and its social function—are to help the mourning poet come to terms with his or her separateness from the dead and "relearn his subjective being."[13] In his guide to the genre of elegy, David Kennedy explains that "the elegist starts from a negative position. Positives, made into negatives by death, must somehow be made into positives again and have that transformation compensated for."[14] Thus, elegy requires that the distance between dead and living be marked: the elegist can then celebrate the fullness of his/her own capacity to be present in the act of mourning and—in speaking of the dead—find a way to put them away and to exult in the meaning of this process. The first two stanzas of McCrae's poem appear to invite meditation on absence and the logic of life, juxtaposing, as Holmes points out, the sensory wonder of living and loving with the noise of war and the stillness of death. The warning that McCrae's prosopopoeiae ultimately assert, however, precludes the course of putting the dead away, as the prosopopoeiac voice selfishly retains its hold on the living. The impersonating voice, which does not speak *of* the dead but *as* the dead, thereby inverting the negative space left by death into a positive mask, troubles the course of consolation. The dead are not a separate, distanced reality but a figured interruption that imposes on the present as well as on the power of the poet to assert a compensatory argument.

Though Holmes insists that McCrae's poem encourages its readers to be "haunted by doubt about the war's purposes and about who the victims are,"[15] she bristles at what she views as more egregious reclamations of the poem. She refers disapprovingly to Preston Manning's use of the poem "to bolster his militaristic argument, claiming that McCrae 'surely cannot rest' since Canada has declined to participate in the invasion and occupation of Iraq."[16] She calls Manning's allusions to "In Flanders Fields" a "distortion of the poem" because they "ignore history and conveniently add [a] new enemy."[17] Yet Holmes's own move—to casually dismiss McCrae's references to his army's military fight against the Central Powers as "petty quarrels and fairy tale foes"—also ignores history.[18] I agree with Holmes that Manning's attempt to recast the poem's references to "quarrels" and "foes" is problematic, but not because such efforts undermine the poem's "meaning." The attempt to read the last stanza of "In Flanders Fields" as a sacrificial narrative is problematic only insofar as such narratives are always subject to retrospective revision.

In *The Question of Sacrifice*, Dennis Keenan traces a genealogy of sociological, anthropological, religious, and philosophical approaches to the various ways that thinkers have tried to determine the social function of sacrifice. He argues that, in the first place, "sacrifice has come to be understood as a necessary passage through suffering and/or death (of *either* oneself *or* someone else) on the way to a supreme moment of transcendent truth."[19] In the second place, he suggests, "sacrifice joins people together in community and separates them from defilement, disease, and dangers."[20] Keenan's reference to the "passage through" that constitutes sacrifice shows that sacrifice is an event. It represents a transformation from one state of things to another, a transformation that, according to Andrew McKenna, "restores order" to a community "by restoring difference between the sacralized victim, arbitrarily chosen and the rest of the community, which is unanimous in its expulsion of violence."[21] What is important to note is that, while the "sacralized victim"—the one who experiences "suffering and/or death"—is singular, that victim is not necessarily individualized, but rather is "arbitrarily chosen" in order to fulfill the needs of the group.

Keenan (somewhat cryptically) begins his study with the statement that "sacrifice is sacrifice only as the sacrifice of sacrifice,"[22] by which he means that the one making a sacrifice cannot expect recompense for his or her offering. Paradoxically, "suffering and/or death" must occur meaninglessly in order to be given meaning as sacrifice, or as violence that does the work of "[expelling] violence." This means that the community served by the transformative occurrence always retrospectively defines sacrifice, designating the "transcendent truth" that they have no access to but that they are compelled to productively name. This is another paradox of the sacrificial narrative: because the sacrificial victim cannot know that the status of his or her suffering and/or death is sacrifice—because to know it as such would make that suffering and/or death a feature of a merely compensatory narrative as opposed to a sacrificial narrative—he or she also cannot know that such suffering and/or death occurs "on the way to a supreme moment of transcendent truth." The victim cannot know that truth, a truth only accessible to the sacrificial victim, until the sacrifice has been made. But sacrifice only becomes sacrifice after the fact of suffering and/or death, when the community names it as productively transformative. Thus, the "supreme moment of truth" is always, and will always be, transcendent, unreachable, postponed.

Thus, the sacrificial narrative is always retrospective and necessarily open to the type of recasting that Holmes laments, as the community continually attempts to rationalize such a narrative's tendency to "mimic *itself* in a gesture that infinitely postpones the revelation of truth."[23] The sacrificial narrative is always compelling, always repeating and repeated, because it is never sufficiently, conclusively productive. The community's incessant stake in the sacrificial narrative makes such a narrative coercive to the victim, perhaps doubly so, first, because the victim must actually, arbitrarily suffer, and second, because the victim has no knowledge or control over the way his or her suffering is then made *not*-arbitrary. This type of coercion is practised by those readers who want "In Flanders Fields" to be both an elegy, which responsibly marks and maintains the distance between the mourned dead and the consoled living, and a sacrificial narrative, one that helps banish Canada's historical collisions with military violence by categorizing that violence as transcendent.

The deployment of prosopopoeia, de Man argues, makes the impersonating mask the reality, whereby the dead become undead: they cannot be put away and cannot be put to use. The motives for a writer to raise the dead in this fashion are various. McCrae makes use of this rhetorical device in order to undermine the reader's attempts to take consolatory comfort in the distance between living and dead. This objective is made clear in the way the belligerent prosopopoeiac warning in the poem's third stanza overrides the nostalgic celebration of life, as well as in the suggestion perceptible in the first two stanzas that the dead know "[their] place." The prosopopoeiac disturbance in McCrae's poem is ultimately what makes us "both sympathize and recoil,"[24] and this disturbance also exists in Vanderhaeghe's *Dancock's Dance*, Massicotte's *Mary's Wedding*, and Swan's *The Deep*. The deployment of prosopopoeia in these works disturbs because it reveals the way the dead are out of place. However, the impersonating voice of the dead, as it figures variably in the contemporary texts, ultimately operates to hide the war. In *Dancock's Dance*, its use occurs as a form of temporary and containable haunting, as the prosopopoeiac mask the soldier takes on ultimately serves to generate identification with Dancock, the surviving officer, and with the ahistorical code of honour and duty he represents. In *Mary's Wedding*, the audience is encouraged to be morally instructed by the prosopopoeiac voice, as the dead soldier Charlie encourages his former lover to embrace life; problematically, however, the recourse to prosopopoeia in this play serves to conceal the historical soldier beneath the apparently instructive fiction. Finally, in *The Deep* the use of the figure shows a disruption in the project of collective remembrance and consolation, as the dead refuse to be placed in the context of cultural progression. Swan's novella indicates that the living ultimately make what they will out of the dead. Thus, each work signals the difficulty of acting out processes of remembrance, while simultaneously suggesting that going through such cultural motions allows the present moment to be informed by the fantasy of productive memory.

Becoming the Horror: Destabilizing Sacrificial Narrative(s) in *Dancock's Dance*

Vanderhaeghe's play, first produced at the Persephone Theatre in Saskatoon in 1995 and published in 1996, was the author's first foray into historical literature, a genre he took up more fully in the novels *The Last Crossing* and *The Englishman's Boy*. In an interview with Herb Wyile—included in *Speaking in the Past Tense: Canadian Novelists on Writing Historical Fiction*—Vanderhaeghe explains how representing the past provides a framework for his thematic explorations, asserting that the historical background for the fiction is simply a loose frame on which to hang an aesthetically satisfying, primarily imaginative creation. For his novel *The Last Crossing*, for example, the choice to focus on a "relatively unknown" figure like Jerry Potts allowed for "greater leeway ... because you don't have to struggle with something that's more or less set in stone."[25] His discussion of the historical research that went into writing *Dancock's Dance* is similar:

> There were enough gaps and it was open-ended enough that I thought that I could use that as historical material. When I'm writing fiction, I don't attempt to teach or instruct, or any of those sorts of things. What's always first and foremost in my mind is that a novel is an aesthetic experience, but because I always had an intense interest in history, writing about the past or circling historical questions interests me and fascinates me.[26]

Vanderhaeghe was drawn to the subject matter of *Dancock's Dance*, a play featuring a fictional First World War veteran, because of the "leeway" offered by archival material related to the North Battleford, Saskatchewan, asylum that is the play's setting.

Even more so than in his later historical novels, Vanderhaeghe's use of history in *Dancock's Dance* amounts to a gesture.[27] The play's loose historical frame is the story of the post–First World War outbreak of Spanish influenza at the Saskatchewan Hospital for the Insane, during which the inmates temporarily took over the running of the institution because the regular staff had fallen ill. While Vanderhaeghe is careful to catch the idiom and temporal details of his chosen historical setting, the characters in the play and its central plot are fictions that stand in relief. John Dancock, a former officer, is being treated by the hospital's Superintendent because of his psychotic response to something that happened "over there." In fighting his demons (personified in the ghost of a soldier, Vanderhaeghe's version of the prosopopoeia), Dancock simultaneously becomes protector of Rudy Braun, a patient of German descent who is terrorized by orderly Kevin Kennealy, and courter of Dorothea Gage, a voluntary patient. The narrative movement, thematic centre, and emotional impact of the play depend entirely on these fictional elements, though the historical locating of the fiction in a particular time and space produces crucial resonances with the mythology of Canadian First World War participation.

Vanderhaeghe is unimpressed by historical fiction that is transparently anachronistic, going so far as to propose that some overtly postmodern historical fictions "[come] closer to inhabiting the idea of the novel of ideas."[28] While acknowledging the ways in which questions of perspective and linguistic instability have influenced historiographic studies and the writing of historical literature, he asserts that "you have to have a foundational knowledge of some sort to even begin to talk about history and what history means and how it's interpreted. To even recognize the subjectivity of history, you have to have a certain amount of information."[29] Without the touchstone of "foundational knowledge," there is no possibility for historical literature to "establish connections,"[30] which, for Vanderhaeghe, is its decisive, bridging function. In *Dancock's Dance*, the interplay between history and fiction allows Vanderhaeghe to explore the "connection[s]" among concepts of honour, duty, and sacrifice, especially as they are associated with First World War and Canadian military mythology. It also allows a more general thematic examination of what traditional notions of honour have to do with displays of strength and weakness, both physical and moral. What is significant about Vanderhaeghe's deployment of a prosopopoeiac mask in the play is the way it undermines any attempt by the audience to read the First World War soldier's death in the context of a traditional elegiac and/or sacrificial narrative based on the premise that some die on the battlefield so that we can live. However, in exploring the way the mask can reveal the exploitative potential of such a premise, Vanderhaeghe ultimately promotes another sacrificial (and possibly elegiac) narrative, one that seeks to find solace in or to nostalgically mourn past conceptions of strength and honour. In this sense, the conclusive representation of Dancock as an anglophone gentleman, one whose "natural" leadership ability emerges in a time of crisis, inheres with what Daniel Coleman refers to as an ethos of "white civility," whereby the "regularly repeated literary personifications for the Canadian nation [mediate] and [reify] the privileged normative status of British whiteness in English Canada."[31]

At a very basic level, *Dancock's Dance* intercepts the traditional military sacrificial narrative, using a similar strategy to the one employed by (mostly British) soldier-poets who sought to condemn the political machinations of the upper-class statesmen who had sent the nation's sons to their deaths unnecessarily and without proper recognition of the real human toll of war. In Canada, the soldier-poetry of such authors as Frank Prewett and W.W.E. Ross is only now receiving critical attention; furthermore, as Jonathan Vance indicates via his analysis of the popular condemnation of Charles Yale Harrison's *Generals Die in Bed* in the years following its publication, the narrative of a pointless war death, familiar to British readers, has only found widespread purchase in Canada in the contemporary period. Vanderhaeghe's spin on the tale, however, is distinctive in that, in contrast to a text like Harrison's, or to such contemporary texts as *The Stone Carvers*, *The Sojourn*, *Deafening*, and *Three Day Road*, the war-insider at the centre of the plot is an officer. David Trotter points out that British military superiors were generally viewed as part of the problem of war:

> [British novels and memoirs] have a lot to say about the trials and tribulations of leadership, and of being led: but not much about the enemy, who are a nuisance, and frequently the cause of spectacular random destruction, but do not figure in the defining psychomachia. The term "strafe," ubiquitous in both, has reference rather more often to reprimands delivered by unsympathetic senior officers than it does to incoming artillery fire.[32]

It is significant that a central conflict in *Dancock's Dance* is between Dancock, the officer, and the prosopopoeiac ghost of a soldier in his company. Here, Vanderhaeghe draws upon a familiar plot construct only to challenge its more common thematic configuration; in doing so, he confirms a hierarchical social structure and the ideal of civility.

In the first pages of *Dancock's Dance*, Vanderhaeghe deploys familiar tropes of First World War literature in order to—at least provisionally—mark the text's alliance with the British soldier-poet narrative. When the Superintendent inquires why John Dancock is so friendly with Rudy Braun, a German immigrant, he and Dancock have the following exchange:

> DANCOCK: The German soldier did his duty. I did mine. He was an honest enemy (*Pause.*) I save my hatred for dishonest enemies. The ones who pretend to be your friend, then stab you in the back.
> SUPERINTENDENT: Ah, yes. Manufacturers who shipped rifles that jammed and lined their pockets with the profits. Politicians who promised the war would be over by Christmas, year after year after year. Teachers, clergymen... (*Beat.*) You see, I've heard you recite your roll call of scoundrels so often I know it by heart.[33]

This recounting of, in the first place, the commonality of those with frontline experience, no matter which side they were fighting for, and, in the second, the way such men were betrayed and misunderstood by war outsiders, is familiar not only to the Superintendent but to the audience as well.

Though it may have been the case that the first Canadian readers of *Generals Die in Bed* bristled at Harrison's representations of the hell of trench warfare, as well as his allegation that it made men into an ironic combination of fighting machine and amoral beast,[34] the prevailing response to these tropes has shifted with the passing years. Eric Thompson refers to Harrison as an "anti-war novelist,"[35] arguing emphatically that his novel shows that "[militarism] is the *real* enemy of the common soldiers."[36]

In rehearsing the now conventional position right off the top of his play, Vanderhaeghe raises a problematic corollary to conceiving the war as both "duty" and "enemy," one that Cobley addresses in *Representing War: Form and Ideology in First World War Narratives*. In assessing the significance of the way the generic conventions of the *Bildungsroman* and the picaresque collide in representative First World War memoirs or documentary-style narratives emerging immediately following the war, Cobley contends that "a narrative structure capable of mounting a critique against the horrors of the First World War is at the same time always also complicit with the condemned social order."[37] In other words, by recalling earlier, highly conventional narrative forms as a framework for presenting a radically "truthful" account of the horrors of war—forms from a time when belief in a humanist social order still held sway—the soldier-author signals his commitment to that order even as he proclaims its passing.[38] After getting his preliminary gesture toward the narrative of "the old lie" out of the way, Vanderhaeghe takes up the paradox of what it means to claim an anti-war position that concurrently maintains the stance that fighting a battle in the name of honour is somehow, transcendently, still worthwhile. In order to deal with this paradox he must both undermine the dead soldier's function as sacrificial victim in a now dominant anti-war narrative and rehabilitate the surviving officer, who, ultimately, stands for the meaningfulness of civic service: of "doing your bit."

Vanderhaeghe's disruption of the narrative that makes meaning out of the First World War soldier's sacrifice occurs via two related plotlines. In the first, Kevin Kennealy is depicted as a clear villain, a bully who uses his position of authority over Dancock to extort items of value from him, who mentally and sexually abuses Rudy Braun—justifying this behaviour by drawing attention to Braun's German heritage—and who refuses to nurse flu patients even when his services are required. In characterizing Kennealy in such stark terms, Vanderhaeghe draws attention to his thematic examination of honour versus dishonour. The author has acknowledged that an interest in notions of honour runs throughout his work, noting in his interview with Wyile that "honour, in my mind, is closely identified with a moral sense. So in some ways it's chivalric—this may sound trite, but, for instance, that the strong should protect the weak is honourable."[39] In the author's own terms, then, Kennealy is the personification of dishonour in that he mistreats those who have less power.

The characterization of Kennealy, however, is not a straightforward reproach of the way people in power behave dishonourably and thus in line with the narrative of "subaltern disillusion." Kennealy's speech patterns mark him as working class and probably Irish, and his actions are uniformly vile, troubling the idea of honour as an abstract value to which, ideally, all people will aspire. Kennealy's ethnic heritage is important to consider as it is set against that of Braun; though Vanderhaeghe does not specify whether Kennealy is English or Irish, the character's consistent references to Braun's "enemy" status, to the notion that he is "an undesirable alien,"[40] "the Hun,"[41] "the sauerkraut farter,"[42] and so on, set the context for Kennealy's identification with the Allied fighting forces, as when he asserts on the evening of the Armistice: "By the suffering Jesus, didn't we black old Kaiser Bill's eyes for him but good and proper."[43] In this way, Vanderhaeghe, somewhat anachronistically with respect to anti-German attitudes held in Canada during the war,[44] inverts "normal" conceptions of Canadian identity, casting the German immigrant as the true Canadian and making the thematic point that it is not who you are that matters, but rather how you behave.

Even more explicitly rendered than Kennealy's ethnicity, however, is his class, a rendering that comes into conflict with the abstract ideal of honour. In Scene 2 of the play, an exchange between Kennealy and Dancock reveals the way the lower-class orderly exploits his position of power over the upper-class patient:

> KENNEALY: *(Ingratiatingly.)* Ah well, but you're the lad with a heart of gold. Sympathy for all. Especially the poor working devil like Kennealy who has no choice but to do the bidding of mucky-mucks and uppity-ups.
> DANCOCK: Don't try it on me, Kennealy. I'm not going to bed at seven o'clock.
> KENNEALY: Ah, but don't you see? Neither of us has any choice in the matter. His nibs has laid down the law. It's going to be done easy, or done hard. So why don't you be the nice gentleman, put on your nightshirt and save us all some trouble?
> DANCOCK: Kiss my arse!
> KENNEALY: *(Over his shoulder.)* Mr. Cooper! Mr. Oswald! *(Pause.)* You know me, sir. Live and let live. *(Pause.)* There's still time to change your mind before the gorillas arrive.
> DANCOCK: Change your own mind.
> KENNEALY: Ah well, it's not my mind to change, is it? It's the Super's.[45]

By overemphasizing a false deference to class structure, whereby any distinction between the Superintendent of the hospital and the "mucky-mucks" is ignored, Kennealy makes it clear that he enjoys the incongruous power he has over "the nice gentleman," Dancock. The belligerence Dancock shows toward Kennealy in this scene, however, is not made to appear problematic. Throughout the play, the increasing despicability of Kennealy's actions, which culminate in the rape and beating of Braun, retroactively justify Dancock's contempt and confirm the rightness of a hierarchical social ordering. Thus, the highlighting of class identity comes into conflict with the representation of ethnic identity so as to suggest that, in some sense, the capacity for honourable action *is* inherently related to who you are. Though Braun is sympathetically portrayed as a victimized immigrant, it is Dancock, the upper class, clearly anglicized, and unduly mistreated officer, who emerges as the play's hero. As Coleman argues, "tropes" associated with personifications of the Canadian nation—here the anglophone First World War officer—"fuse the codes of personal morality, usually figured as the development of admirable character, with the codes for public citizenship."[46]

Dancock's status as hero, though, is not without its complications, especially as related to Vanderhaeghe's exploration of what it means to "die for" something. A second plot line in the play also interrupts the sacrificial narrative associated with "subaltern disillusion"; this one deals with Dancock in confrontation with the ghost of a soldier who was under his command, and whom he shot for refusing to go over the top during a battle in France. The soldier's appearance on the stage operates as prosopopoeia, in that the mask inhabited by the figure haunting Dancock has little to do with the man who was part of Dancock's past. The character is given no name or history, and his representative function is to haunt the living. He is not mourned, and his death cannot be put to productive use, as it is not really a particular man's death in war that is at issue. At issue, rather, is Dancock's status as a murderer and whether or not this status is in conflict with what is presented as his apparently natural (national) capacity for honourable action. By the time the audience finally learns why Dancock is being haunted, Vanderhaeghe has established the officer's credentials as defender of the harassed immigrant, courtly admirer of the morally upright woman, and instinctive and gifted leader in times of crisis, as Dancock is the one who rallies his fellow patients to care for one another during the flu outbreak.

Still, the scene in which the prosopopoeiac soldier finally confronts Dancock with his wartime crime enacts a resolute return to the very same sacrificial narrative referred to in the first scene of the play. As the soldier begins to re-enact the scene in the trench, Dancock recalls: "We officers had been warned. Of mutinies in the French army, in British labour battalions. Stamp out insubordination, we were told. Refusal of an order on the field of battle is an offence punishable by death."[47] Just as Kennealy claimed mere deference to the "mucky-mucks," Dancock initially clings to the idea that his role in the soldier's death was merely the result of a military system that defined them both. Later in the scene, however, Dancock admits his displeasure about the fact that his men felt no innate inclination to be led by him: "They should have thanked me. They might have gone forward out of... (*Blurts it*) out of regard for me!"[48] Thus, the soldier is apparently justified in naming himself as the familiar sacrificial victim of the soldier-authored narrative about "unsympathetic senior officers," declaring, "Someone had to pay when your men turned on you."[49]

That Dancock's victim refuses to stay silent, however, undermines his function in a sacrificial narrative. As Keenan points out, the sacrificial victim cannot name himself as such, for in doing so, the sacrifice ceases to be sacrifice. Because Vanderhaeghe's soldier figure does not signify a murdered man but rather a haunting mask, it succeeds in intruding on the process of mourning and ultimately becomes the horror it wants to stand for. The prosopopoeiac soldier becomes allied with the figure of Kennealy, as neither seem worthy of the kind of ultimate sacrifice made on the battlefield. As if Kennealy's behaviour toward his patients was not enough to make this point, Vanderhaeghe incorporates a scene in which the orderly drunkenly recites significant lines from "In Flanders Fields," including "If ye break faith with us who die / We shall not sleep, though poppies grow / In Flanders fields,"[50] though leaving out the stanza about how the living must "take up [the] quarrel with the foe." The ironic quoting of McCrae's verse by such a character is meant to challenge what the dead died for if the likes of Kennealy can adopt such words as his own; like Holmes, Vanderhaeghe wants to critique the way a sacrificial narrative can be co-opted.

The representation of the prosopopoeiac soldier, however, suggests that all attempts at a sacrificial narrative are potentially troublesome because they require the dead to stand for something and that something might come into conflict with, as Dancock asserts, the sort of "explanations [that] can be lived with."[51] The scene in which Dancock and the undead mask of the former soldier play out the moments leading up to the recollection of the murder indicates that, in life, the soldier was a coward, an insubordinate, a man so damaged by the horrors of trench warfare that he could no longer follow orders and participate in the fight. Even in this scene, and certainly throughout the rest of the play, there is no sustained thematic focus on what the soldier was in life, as reflected in the fact that he is represented as so utterly different in death. The undead mask becomes a new reality in which the soldier is the one who abuses his power over Dancock, just as Kennealy does. It is significant that, as is the case for Kennealy, the abuse of power culminates in a physical confrontation with homosexual implications. Kennealy rapes Braun by forcing him to perform oral sex while Braun is incapacitated in a hydrotherapy tub. The soldier forces Dancock to kiss him, noting that the kiss represents the "taste" of the "the devil's arse."[52] In *Dancock's Dance*, such homosexual acts of violence signify as assaults on more conventionally masculine conceptions of order and honour.

Despite the repeated references in *Dancock's Dance* to the sacrificial narrative of "subaltern disillusion," the play ultimately confirms the rightness of a traditional class structure as long as that class structure operates to fulfill a civil code of duty and honour, whereby the strong protect and provide leadership for the weak. This confirmation operates at odds with a prevalent contemporary sacrificial narrative; yet it also amounts to a rejection of the elegiac function of the war narrative. While it is certainly the case that Dorothea and the Superintendent encourage Dancock to put away whatever is haunting him about the war, there is little emphasis on mourning the dead. After forcing his lewd kiss on Dancock, the soldier disappears and Dorothea assures Dancock not only that he has gone, but that what she has seen of Dancock's crime "doesn't matter."[53] At the end of this scene, Dorothea also announces "(*Flatly*) Kennealy is dead,"[54] and neither character is even mentioned in the play again. The image from this scene that resonates until the end of the play is that of the phoenix bursting into flames and being reborn, as Dancock is when he accepts his role in a "natural" order of manly honour.

Thus, the recourse to prosopopoeia in *Dancock's Dance* ultimately works as a warning to the living not to let things become disordered, to keep at bay inversions in reality representing "the threat of a deeper logical disturbance."[55] Vanderhaeghe's use of the historical framework works merely as a backdrop for a thematic examination of codes of honour. That examination is mostly ahistorical, though the author may have in mind his idea that "certain older conceptions of masculinity...are valuable and would do very well to be integrated with newer ideas of what it means to be male."[56] The purpose of this ostensible historical drama, however, is not to remember the dead but rather to recall past events that serve as props to nostalgic notions of social order, for example as associated with "white civility" and the idea that productive civic participation is necessarily related to acts of moral leadership. Significantly in this play, as in several other works of contemporary Canadian First World War literature, the war is constituted in terms of a simpler—somehow better—code of lost ideals.

Mary's Wedding: An Elegy for a Fiction

In *Dancock's Dance*, the historical framework only tenuously connects to the First World War, as the Spanish influenza epidemic was thought to have been carried to Canada by returning soldiers. In contextualizing the fiction of *Mary's Wedding*, Massicotte denotes a particular soldier as the historical anchor. In the published version of the script, Massicotte prefaces the extended dream sequence that comprises the main action of the play, and that recounts the burgeoning love relationship between Mary and Charlie cut short by Charlie's death in France, with material relating to the historical figure, Lieutenant Gordon Muriel Flowerdew, who was awarded the Victoria Cross for leading a calvary charge at Moreuil Wood in March 1918, and who is referred to in the play as "Flowers." The prefatory material in the published version of the play includes a photograph of Flowerdew and a reproduction of a letter he wrote to his mother the day after the charge, which was also the day he died of the wounds he had sustained. Furthermore, the play's dedication reads "*For Robin. And the soldiers.*"[57] Thus, the paratextual material framing the play appears to clarify its performance as what Jay Winter would refer to as a personal "site of mourning," whereby commemoration might occur "on a much more intimate level";[58] indeed, *Mary's Wedding* is focused on the very private cost of war.

The ensuing plot of *Mary's Wedding*, however, locates the commemoration of the historical Flowerdew at a considerable distance from the emotional core of the drama, which hinges on Mary's dream meditation on and farewell to Charlie, who speaks with her in the voice of one already dead. Though it is Mary who first reveals to Charlie that he has died, Charlie leaves her with an appeal quite the reverse to that of McCrae's dead: "'Just love [your new husband] as well as you can and be happy...Don't forget. Just let go.'"[59] Mary's dream of the impersonated Charlie is at once idealized in the context of her own desire to affirm life's progression and necessarily limited to that context, the context of her imminent marriage. The dramatized impersonation of Charlie's desire and his perspective is compelling precisely due to its inaccessibility, its retrospective fictionality. Furthermore, as the prefatory emphasis on Flowerdew indicates ironically, the figure of Charlie is constructed as a surrogate figure at least twice more removed from the real: he is fictional, as is his lover, and he speaks from within her fictionalized dream space. In the performance of the play, the masking of Flowerdew is indicated not only by his relatively subordinate status in the plot, but also in that the character Flowers is played by the female actor who is also playing Mary. This cross-casting allows for a number of fascinating moments in which certain (homo)erotically charged interactions between Charlie and Flowers are controlled both by the sex of the actor playing Flowers and by the disappearance of the officer figure into a symbolic and performative surrogate.

While the prosopopoeiac mask envisioned by Massicotte is not nearly as aggressive as those envisioned by McCrae or Vanderhaeghe, the fact remains that it is a mask for the fictional figure as opposed to a historical one. In this way, Massicotte works to contain the "threat of a deeper logical disturbance"[60] that so concerns Vanderhaeghe in *Dancock's Dance*. In the prologue to the play, Charlie addresses the audience directly to indicate that the setting for the play is "the night before Mary's wedding. It's a July wedding on a Saturday morning in Nineteen Hundred and Twenty; two years after the end of the Great War, or as you might know it now, the first World War."[61] By referencing the audience's temporal location in the "now," the prologue introduces the ensuing drama as taking place not in some generalized distant past, but one that is explicitly located in the immediate post–First World War period, a location that is defined by both its remoteness from the present and its discrete place in the past. Setting up such a gap might be thought to introduce various dilemmas: how to achieve—or come to terms with the failure to achieve—a mimetic ideal; how to present history in a way that takes into account how that history has been discursively constructed; how to give a sense of the temporal moment to an audience with a vastly different cultural framework and no opportunity to draw on first-hand experience or memory.

In the second paragraph of the prologue, however, Charlie states, "So, tomorrow is Mary's Wedding, tonight is just a dream. I ask you to remember that. It begins at the end and ends at the beginning. There are sad parts. Don't let that stop you from dreaming it too."[62] Here, Massicotte absolves the audience (and his play) from being concerned with the problem of mimesis or a lack of memory. The drama has now been located within a dream space, and the audience is only responsible for "[remembering] that" via their own entrance into a dream space. Winter has argued that, in many representations of war, the "struggle against forgetting" emerges as an important theme: "What photographs, or plays, or poems, or letters provide are traces of a world that has almost vanished from both memory and history. The memory boom, therefore, may be understood as an act of defiance, an attempt to keep alive at least the names and the images of the millions whose lives have been truncated or disfigured by war."[63] The dream space that contains the action of *Mary's Wedding*, in functioning as the bridge between past and present, completely elides the immediate post–First World War location as well as the dilemmas of representing history. Thus, even though the published version of the play contains a photograph of Flowerdew, and even though his name inspires one of the play's characters, the elegiac mode of the play seems oddly misdirected, as Massicotte searches to find the language to mourn a fictional lover rather than a historical soldier. Charlie does not ask the audience to remember, but rather to dream.

Along with locating representations of the characters within an ahistorical dream space, Massicotte further undermines the play's commemorative function by conflating representations of love and war. In one scene, the action shifts between Mary and Charlie's tête-à-tête at her mother's tea and Charlie's experience of an artillery barrage, with the soundscape of a thunderstorm/artillery barrage used as the ground between the two scenes. In the context of Mary's dream, she is also present in both spaces, able to witness Charlie's fear and his vision of no man's land. Mary's presence in the war scene operates as a bridge for the audience to accept that they too are included in the experience of war being staged (just as they too are part of the dream). Such a figuring of the war scene is unusual, though not in terms of the tropes that are referred to: the noise, the mud, the chaos. Rather, it is unusual that such a scene would be presented as comprehensible to the war outsider. As Paul Fussell has pointed out, an overriding theme in much of the work of soldier-poets is the adversarial positions of war insiders and war outsiders: "even if those at home had wanted to know the realities of the war, they couldn't have without experiencing them."[64]

This thematic exploration of the gulf between those with and without first-hand war experience is explored in several contemporary Canadian texts, including Alan Cumyn's *The Sojourn*, Frances Itani's *Deafening*, the First World War novels of Jane Urquhart, and, as I will explore below, Mary Swan's *The Deep*. Often in such texts, the gulf is represented simply in terms of an inability to communicate, as in Itani's comparison of Jim's inability to write letters describing the front with Grania's inability, as a deaf person, to make herself understood to the hearing community, or in Swan's representation of a soldier's frustration at the girl who "wrote letters about missing him, asked questions [about his experience] he couldn't possibly answer."[65] The difficulty of writing letters back home is also broached in *Mary's Wedding*, as Charlie complains to Flowers that he can't write anything to Mary except concerning the mud. He responds to the officer's suggestion that he write what he feels with the question, "But how do you write that?"[66] Even here, however, the difficulty Charlie has is not describing the realities of trench life, but sharing his love for Mary. Mary's ability to witness Charlie's war experience, including his difficulties as a letter writer, eliminates the thematic of veteran estrangement. The eliding of this thematic futher curtails the sense that the difficulty for those at a distance to come to terms with war activity is really at issue.

The vacillating emphasis on the progress of the war and the progress of Charlie and Mary's love continues through the play, often in such a way as to undermine the horrors of warfare in an almost bathetic conflation. One such juxtaposition begins with a scene describing Charlie's participation in the Battle of Festubert, in which then-Sergeant Flowers tries to lead his men through the slaughter by offering an alternative to official orders. As Charlie reports to Mary, who is again a witness to the battle, "Right before we went over, Flowers passed an order down the line. Passed it man to man. Forget about the spacing. Forget about the even lines, you hear me?...Run, he said. You understand me? Run as fast as you can."[67] As Tim Cook explains in *At the Sharp End: Canadians Fighting in the Great War, 1914–1916*, the first attack at Festubert came on 17 May 1915, with troops "ordered...to thin out to five paces between men, and to advance in four skirmish lines of about 200 metres in depth."[68] The result was an absolute failure, as "men had been mowed down in straight lines by machine guns."[69] For the attacks that took place on 22–24 May, Cook reports that "infantry took matters into their hands," deciding on a "radical night assault." Canadian and British forces made a 600-metre gain during the Battle of Festubert, but at the "cost of 2,065 casualties,"[70] or four deaths per metre. After describing the battle to his witness, Mary, assuring her "that's the way it was,"[71] the scene shifts to that of Mary and Charlie meeting for a date, early in their courtship. When Mary admits that she had been worried Charlie would not show up, he assures her that he "practically ran the whole way."[72]

Later in the play, when the newly minted Lieutenant Flowers announces to Charlie that he has been placed in command of "C" Squadron (otherwise known as Lord Strathcona's Horse), he tells Charlie that the promotion feels "scary but good."[73] By this point in the play, this phrase has become a refrain, one that Charlie uses to describe the feeling of falling in love with Mary, and that both lovers repeat after they first kiss. The use of this phrase in both the context of war and the context of love confirms that Massicotte's juxtaposition of war scenes and courtship scenes is not meant to place the two sets of experiences in ironic tension with each other, but rather to link them in an almost metaphoric relation, whereby the audience is encouraged to consider the ground between love and war. It is certainly not the case that the burgeoning love between Mary and Charlie is conceived as a type of war, except to the extent that Mary's mother disapproves of her English daughter's attachment to a "dirty farm boy,"[74] and that Mary despairs at Charlie's decision to enlist. Rather, as indicated by Flowers's use of the phrase "scary but good" to describe his promotion to command, it is war that is conceived of as a type of courtship, especially in the sense that it is an initiation. The metaphor of war as courtship bolsters the prevailing myth that Canada as a nation was born in the war, and Massicotte makes explicit reference to this myth when Mary describes the success of the charge at Moreuil Wood: "You and the Canadian Cavalry Division stopped the German advance. Some say you saved the war."[75]

After a scene depicting Flowers dying in Charlie's arms (rather than at a Casualty Clearing Station, as history records), Massicotte includes an imagined letter from Charlie to Mary to juxtapose with Flowerdew's own letter to his mother, which is reproduced in the play's preface. The real letter certainly reveals a cruel irony or two regarding the disjunction between comprehending the First World War according to courtship formulas and confronting its actuality. For example, Flowerdew's opening, "Have been a bit busy lately, so I haven't been able to write," might be read as comically understated, considering the military significance and heavy human toll associated with the calvary charge at Morieul Wood, though of course, the irony of this opening, and Flowerdew's bland comments about the weather, dissipate when considered in the context of censoring directives governing communication with those on the home front. Flowerdew's final words, however, that he has "had the most wonderful experiences lately and wouldn't have missed it for anything,"[76] are more difficult to delimit and rationalize. The then-dying soldier may have simply wanted to offer some consolation to an imminently disconsolate mother; even so, the description of the bloody, casualty-ridden charge as one of many "wonderful experiences" is at odds with postwar condemnation of such romantic idealization—an idealization that is thought to have been sustained primarily by governments and the media. In fact, a persistent theme in Massicotte's play, as revealed by Charlie's shift in attitude regarding the relevance of Tennyson's "The Charge of the Light Brigade," critiques the paradigm of noble sacrifice for the good of Empire.

The fictional letter that Charlie sends after the charge contains none of the platitudes of Flowerdew's letter, emphasizing instead the pain of missing Mary and his fervent desire to return to her. What is significant about the revisions Massicotte has made according to what he deems suitable for a doomed soldier's final letter—which is ultimately voiced as prosopopoeia, for it arrives after his death—is what they reveal about the difficulty of elegizing the real in the face of a considerable temporal gap. Such an elegy, Massicotte's use of prosopopoeia suggests, is increasingly irrelevant not only because of the vanishing of mourners whose recovery of subjectivity depends on the process, but also because it is no longer socially productive within our present ideological attitude toward the war and its horrors. Flowerdew's rehearsal of romantic ideals associated with the war's purpose can no longer be remembered straightforwardly.

Yet even this gently ironic critique is not sustained, though not because the play gives in to the narrative of noble sacrifice suggested by the framing of the charge at Moreuil Wood. Rather, a critique of the war is not sustained because the play's real focus is on the irony that Mary's wedding is to go forward despite Charlie's death. The recourse to prosopopoeia, which ostensibly provides a conduit for mourning a soldier who died in the war, and perhaps for commemorating *"the soldiers"* mentioned in the play's acknowledgements, is a trick, as the historical subject can hardly be found beneath a fictional mask. The impersonating voice of dead Charlie Edwards, a fictional figure, operates as a substitute for that of the historical Lieutenant Gordon Muriel Flowerdew, in part because a productive elegy for the real soldier cannot be imagined as viable or even as interesting. The general idea promoted instead is that the war was productive for Canada (as it is for the dream lovers), because it taught Canadians how to live, boldly and with a sense of a new beginning. Furthermore, the figuration of the war as a kind of courtship suggests that participation in the First World War promoted a sense of duty toward community and national progress. Thus, the spectral figure in *Mary's Wedding*, far from disrupting a stable conception of memory, encourages the living to take comfort in the mere performance of remembering the dead, as such memory work provides rejuvenating comfort in the rightness of continuity.

The Deep: The Elusive Identity of the Dead

The structure of narrative focalizing in Swan's novella is similar to that found in Timothy Findley's *The Wars*, in that many sections are written as the fragmentary recollections of peripheral figures who provide a retrospective account to an unnamed researcher. In contrast to *The Wars*, however, sections of the text that directly concern the protagonists—twin sisters who leave Canada to work as nurses' aides near the Western Front—are focalized not as impersonal, indirect, past-tense speech, which places emphasis on the interventions made by Findley's researcher into the interpretation of Robert Ross's experiences, but as personal speech voiced prosopopoeically. Though the very first section of *The Deep* reveals that the twins have already died, their "we" account of their war work is simultaneously ghostly and immediate. Despite this haunting effect, however, the grounds for Swan's deployment of prosopopoeia differ from Vanderhaeghe's, whose concern for the way the dead might interfere with the work of reconnecting with older ideas manifests itself in the dismantling of the prosopopoeiac mask, as well as from Massicotte's, whose overriding interest in an ahistorical story of love cut short by loss results in the creation of a false prosopopoeiac mask with nothing of the historical behind it. Rather, Swan is concerned with the failure of consolation, especially the failure of the elegiac mode or sacrificial narratives that attempt to place catastrophe within a narrative of progress. In this sense, Swan's recourse to ghostly figures appears to have more in common with the unsettling spectral figures examined in works such as Sugars and Turcotte's *Unsettled Remains* and Goldman's *DisPossession*, as Swan becomes one of several "Canadian writers [who] have been led to conjure, and indeed channel, the crowded landscape of ghosts and monsters that circulate above, around, and within the parameters of the Canadian nationalist project."[77] In the end, however, Swan's narrative of the First World War dead does little to dismantle the mythology of the war as a site for national self-fashioning, as her dead simply fade into an obscurity behind their mask. Further, their spectral presence is shown to be produced by a personal loss rather than by any violent overdetermination of how to make meaning out of the nation's participation in war.

As it does with McCrae's dead, Swan's use of prosopopoeia depends on a shared sense of identity; though, unlike the motley whose shared war experiences lead them to voice their grievances as a collective, the twins in *The Deep* are a "we" in the sense that the two sisters share an entirely fused sense of self, a sense that predates their war experience. The twins' uncanny habit of speaking as "*we*," recalled by Mrs. Moore, who oversaw their work in France, is similarly remembered by their headmistress from school, Miss Ann Reilly: "They replied politely to anything I asked, whichever one answered speaking in the plural. I'd quite forgotten that, but I remember how it struck me at the time. The way they never spoke together, but there was no hesitation, no collision, conversation flowing so easily from one or the other so that the effect was of talking to a single person."[78] Like Miss Reilly, Mrs. Moore supplements her recollection of the twins' use of the plural by noting, "I'd forgotten that."[79] The irresolution between remembering and forgetting in the two reports reflects Swan's interest in the problem of how remembrance works, for example, in terms of sorting through how different individuals recall similar events. Swan is also interested in why things are remembered or forgotten, and how the practice of remembrance occurs as the result of some kind of prodding or insistence, whether individual or cultural.

Winter argues that the very term "remembrance" denotes an act and "helps us avoid the pitfalls of referring to memory as some vague cloud that exists without agency."[80] Furthermore, Winter, following Halbwachs, uses the term "historical remembrance" to explain the phenomenon of a cultural prodding: "'historical remembrance' [is made up of] acts and practices of groups of people who come together to remember particular historical incidents and upheavals. The focus here is on forms of remembrance triggered by what men and women consider to be major events which have touched their lives in significant ways. If they did not think so, they would not make the effort of remembrance."[81] The format of *The Deep* raises the question of who is behind the procedure of bringing together the various recollections contained in the narrative. Unlike *The Wars*, Swan's novella does not individualize the archivist figure and thus does not explicitly engage with the question of how history is discursively produced. The absence of this figure reflects the text's thematizing of the slippage between the particular and the collective need, as well as its concern with the point at which a private memory (or lapse in memory) is reconfigured due to cultural provocation or due to the needs of a collective. It is the *collective* that fixes the twins in the context of a progressive cultural narrative, though Swan's metafictional attention to this process does not disrupt the mythology of Canada's originary war. In fact, the reifying recollection is ultimately marked as productive, as the collective participation in story making is what gives the twins' death a meaning that transcends the personal. In this sense, Swan implicitly signals her nostalgia for narratives that can be massaged into meaning, even narratives associated with war, rupture, and suicide.

The narrative fragments the make up *The Deep* reflect that those who remember the twins find it psychologically productive to do so, especially with respect to the uniformity of their "we" identity. Their brother Marcus, who blames his mother's illness and death on the twins, remembers them "whispering, heads together. The sound of a couple of snakes."[82] In contrast, the family caregiver, Nan, who had "been with [their mother] Miss Alice since she was a girl,"[83] and thus feels a certain responsibility for the twins, has a different interpretation of the whispering, "as if no one else mattered at all. But there, they only had each other all those years."[84] In almost every account given of the twins, they are thus marked as insiders to their own situation and, for better or worse, as divided from others. Unlike the identity of the spectral figures who, as prosopopoeia, destabilize the public narrative and "haunt the nation/subject (from without and within) [until ...] finally being heard,"[85] the twins' fused identity collapses into itself. Thus, Swan's depiction of the war participant's voice, like Massicotte's, does not inhere with the conventional trope of lamenting the gulf between war insider and outsider. However, whereas in *Mary's Wedding* the goal is to imagine a way of traversing that gulf so as to promote a plot of progress, in *The Deep* the gulf is simply besides the point: the twins express no interest in "finally being heard," while those who labour to make sense out of their deaths are valorized for desiring a culturally productive brand of remembrance.

The juxtaposition in *The Deep* of sections detailing the recollections of others about the twins and their own accounts reveals Swan's misgivings about constructing a materialized memorial, a process presupposed by elegy and at least provisionally attempted by Massicotte in the prefatory material to *Mary's Wedding*. In Swan's work, the externally motivated, retrospective focus on the material record is shown to be not merely limited to the context of sentimental idealization, but also a somewhat self-interested and fatuous displacement of core war experience, as what the twins lay emphasis on bears little relationship to what is subsequently construed as significant. Like the photographs taken during the twins' residence at school, the "proof" or "record" of a time and space may "[invite] one to understand certain things"; such "things," however, are not "recogniz[eable]" to the one apparently contained in the material record.[86] In other words, the photographs and letters left behind by the twins, which include the letter sent to their father from a nursing station near the front, and the "War Book" the twins themselves construct out of fragmentary impressions of Europe, meant to "give someone an idea of how it was,"[87] do not manifest themselves as an alternative, more trustworthy and knowable story of their experience. Rather, the twins assert that even "if we could string [such fragments] all together," such a narrative would remain inaccessible to "even the closest person."[88] The psychic space the twins inhabit during the war is likened to a dream space, a world in which "familiar objects, even faces, become mysterious, remote."[89]

However, whereas Massicotte's use of the dream space provides an emotional proxy for secondary would-be mourners hampered by temporal distance, Swan's dream space is construed as inaccessible to anyone but the dreamer. Swan's rejection of the elegiac imperative as it relates to the mourner's attempt to identify with the experience of the dead culminates in her challenge to ritualized memory work that is meant to offer consolation and a sense of meaningful subjectivity to the mourner. No amount of narrative memory work or material memorialization on the part of the mourner can truly function as identification; the contract McCrae envisions, whereby mourners "take up" the life-function of the dead, is shown in Swan's text to be untenable. Just as the twins refuse to take part in a sacrificial narrative, the attempt to make collective, consolatory meaning out of their deaths is shown to be a retrospective endeavour produced by the needs of the living rather than by the remembrance of the dead.

Swan's pessimism regarding the possibility of a legitimately elegiac narrative as a means of accessing history relates to her focus on the efforts and experiences of women doing war work. Much of the postwar material collected by the unnamed researcher adds up to a narrative of commemoration that posits shifting constructs of gender as a framework of meaning for the twins' war work and their death. Accounts by Miss Reilly, for example, emphasize her sense that the decision to go to France ensued from an education that produced "a generation of women proud of their minds, secure in their worth, who believed in truth, in beauty, who would spread that belief by their very existence."[90] Miss Reilly's words raise an issue that has been of increasing interest to historians and cultural critics dealing with the First World War, and one that Donna Coates comments on in "The Best Soldiers of All: Unsung Heroines in Canadian Women's Great War Fiction." Making reference to the literary work of women writers during the war and immediately following it, Coates describes the way women "write themselves into the discourse of war"[91] by portraying women "in action."[92] Other contemporary Canadian works that have taken up the issue of women's war work (whether overseas or on the home front) include Jane Urquhart's *The Underpainter* and *The Stone Carvers*, Frances Itani's *Deafening*, and Vern Thiessen's *Vimy*, while works such as Kevin Kerr's *Unity (1918)* and *Dancock's Dance* show women "in action" as nurses during the postwar flu epidemic. Coates argues that the early-twentieth-century war novels by the likes of Francis Marion Beynon, Grace Blackburn, and Lucy Maud Montgomery ultimately operate "in subtle ways, as pleas for peace, instructions on how to avoid war";[93] in the more contemporary period, the women's pacifist stance has been dealt with more explicitly in Alan Cumyn's *The Sojourn* and Ami McKay's *The Birth House*.

The twins themselves, however, never validate this narrative and seem disinclined to allow the meaning of war work to be extrapolated beyond immediate sensations that cannot be reconfigured. They are as much a part of the war machine as anyone or anything and refuse to participate in the rhetoric of moral righteousness or even of progress. Like Sainte Germaine—who chose to commit suicide rather than be forced into marriage—they would rather escape than be taken captive, even by a narrative that would see their work as shedding light on "women's capabilities."[94] In fact, it is in a letter to Miss Reilly that the twins gesture toward the narrative of women's progress, and then reject it, ultimately asking "if we did the right thing by coming here, by being part of it."[95] Even the forward-thinking Miss Reilly acknowledges that "what they told me was not what I myself believed... So much for all those fine words about confidence and identity. I failed them, and now they're dead."[96] In many ways, the reference to the twins as "unsung heroines" of the war fails precisely because they refuse to consider nursing as in any way meaningful with regard to the way they have changed: the rupture in identity that Swan presents is only incidentally related to war work.

Regardless of the fact that many of the recollections, both of others and of the twins themselves, recognizably refer to the specific historical site of the First World War, Swan's critique of the possibility of the materialized memorial to fix the consolation process is echoed in the way she presents the war as symbolic. In *Dancock's Dance*, the historical anchor of the patients taking over the Saskatchewan Hospital for the Insane allows Vanderhaeghe to explore the relationship between codes of honour and traditional forms of masculinity, while in *Mary's Wedding*, even the explicit references to the historical referent of Lt. Gordon Muriel Flowerdew are overwhelmed by Massicotte's interest in writing an elegy for a romance rather than for a soldier. The copyright page of *The Deep* notes that the work is "based on an actual historical incident, [but] all individuals and events in this accounting are fictional,"[97] though nowhere in the book is it specified what the "actual" incident was, or how one might distinguish between the "incident" and the "events."[98] One might presume that the incident in question is the story of a suicide (or perhaps two suicides) by drowning off a boat returning to Canada from Europe following the armistice, in which case the fictional accounting that the narrative presents works to make sense of the suicide(s). Like *The Wars*, then, *The Deep* might be said to examine how the horrors of the First World War lead the war insider to madness.

Also like *The Wars*, Swan's novel appears to explore the relationship between military and domestic conflict, as many of the recollections provided by those who knew the twins comment on the devastating toll their birth had on their family. If the twins did not already recognize that, in being born, they eventually caused the death of their mother, other family members—in particular their brothers—make it clear to them. The text insinuates that at one point, James and Marcus tried to drown the twins in an outdoor fountain. Furthermore, the twins' attachment to their father, whom they imagine as a (singular) prince who might save them from the dismal household,[99] is connected to their encounter with Hugh, a soldier they meet at their nursing station. Like their father, Hugh "didn't ever play that tedious game of trying to tell us apart... As if together we were too much for them, as if the only way they could deal with us was to divide, to diminish us."[100] In a section titled "In his study the Father closes his eyes," however, the narrator affirms that Mr. A can tell his children apart: "Esther, with a slightly higher arch to her eyebrow."[101] Thus, the deep structure of the novel is a failed family romance, whereby the twins are unable to let go of their fantasy of a father-prince who will be able to save them without compelling them to function as two fully adult, distinct women.

Swan contrasts the way the twins are framed by the individual perspectives that produce remembrance with the prosopopoeiac narrative, by which I mean the sections of the novella spoken from the point of view of the dead twins. In this narrative, the "we" stands for the fantasy of a coherence of memory, as the twins assert: "We were not together every minute of our childhood, every minute of our lives, although most, perhaps. But there must have been times when one of us was in a room but not the other. When only one of us saw something, heard something, was spoken to. But we don't remember anything like that. This is something you have to understand, if you are to understand anything."[102] The address to "you" in this passage locates the interlocutor and suggests that there is indeed a specific impetus for gathering the recollections, which is someone's attempt to "understand" why the twins leapt into the ocean on their way home from France. This "you," like the "you" whom Charlie addresses in the prologue to *Mary's Wedding*, exists at a temporal distance from the events being recollected, drawing attention to the active mechanisms of collective memory.

The temporal distance implicitly marked between the "we" and the "you" reaffirms the strong temptation to read the twins' use of the plural as marking their position as war insiders. In his review of *The Deep*, Jonathan Vance suggests that Swan "take[s] up the modernist interpretation of the Great War as fundamental rupture in the lives of individuals and nations."[103] However, unlike McCrae's dead or the category of war insiders Fussell describes, the twins are not a "we" because their experience in the war has made them a separate unit, nor does the war itself cause a sense of modernist disillusionment. Rather, it is during an occasion only incidentally associated with their war activity that the catastrophic rupture of their "we" identity occurs. On a rare outing they take with Hugh, one of the twins sleeps through a conversation shared by Hugh and her sister: "On the drive we slept; it was completely dark. I woke once and the two of them were laughing at something I hadn't heard."[104] Just before this scene, Hugh has taken the twins to the cliff of Sainte Germaine, named after a young girl who committed suicide rather than allowing herself to be taken as a pretty conquest of Attila the Hun; the three discuss "whether it took more courage to live or to die, in such a situation."[105] When Esther realizes the implications of the fact that Ruth has fallen asleep and that "Hugh was talking to *me*,"[106] she decides to pursue the potential romance, lying to her sister so that she can try to see Hugh alone.

Though Hugh declares that "one should always choose life,"[107] once the rupture of identity has taken place, the twins choose suicide to cope with their loss. Swan makes an explicit comparison between the effect of the war on the human condition and the twins' despairing sense of being disconnected; in a section called "Teacup," the twins describe the restless, angry mood of the men after the armistice, asking, "Was this the new world?"

Likewise, for the twins, "between us there was a strangeness... We were no longer whole; we couldn't imagine how we would ever be whole again."[108] Like Sainte Germaine, however, the twins do not consider suicide to be an act of courage or noble sacrifice, but rather an "escape." Thus, the rupture that occurs is not represented as even related to the experience of war, which sets the historical events within a primarily symbolic framework. In this sense, Swan's novella is unusual in its refusal to name the war as a site of national origin, in that it produces both the breakdown of an (albeit limited) collective identity and a sense of despair. The text does affirm a sense of nostalgia, however, by diminishing the complexity of the twins' spectral presence to their part in a romance plot. In this way, Swan avoids troubling the mythology of the war as productive and indeed commends the activity of those who seek to make the death of the twins retrospectively meaningful in the context of a narrative of progress. Despite the representation of rupture, Swan portrays such an occurrence as deeply personal, while—paradoxically—the "violent, synthesizing ambitions"[109] of those who recollect are portrayed as a type of recovery.

The final, short section of *The Deep*, titled "After," repeats selected sentences from the novella's first section, also entitled "After": "Here there are two tall windows and the gauzy white curtains lift and fall like a breath, like a sigh. The sounds that reach us are muffled, and we wonder if someone has died."[110] The image of the breathing curtains suggests the veil between the living and the dead that the twins exist behind, in a space where they have only a vague sense of time's movement and where they may not realize that they (and not some others) have died. The "muffled" sounds that reach the twins have by this point in the text been retrospectively defined as the various acts of remembrance performed by those involved with the twins before the war, during their service in France, and in the hours preceding their suicide. While these assorted recollections reflect the attempts of the living to make sense of the dead—of their experiences and choices, of their function within larger sacrificial or elegiac narratives about family, the role of women, or the war—such attempts are shown in *The Deep* to be entirely disconnected from the way the dead make sense of themselves via their prosopopoeiac mask. Thus, like *Dancock's Death* and *Mary's Wedding*, Swan's novella is ultimately about the way the living compel the dead to be what they need them to be, a necessary step in the creation of an elegiac or sacrificial narrative.

In looking at the way the voice of the dead has been incorporated into three contemporary Canadian First World War narratives—Vanderhaeghe's *Dancock's Dance*, Massicotte's *Mary's Wedding*, and Swan's *The Deep*—it is clear that all three undermine attempts to construct closed elegiac and/or sacrificial narratives. Thus, these texts disturb the stable concept of the sacrificial hero, especially as he or she might represent the "best" of Canada, for this concept is shown to depend too heavily on what is unrecoverable and what must be replaced with fiction. Yet all three works ultimately affirm the living community, one that stops worrying about whether or not the dead sleep and one that is able to affirm those ideals that may or may not have anything to do with the activities or desires of the dead. In relation to the problem of how Canada should or can remember the First World War, the recourse to the figure of prosopopoeia in these works reveals that though there is no such thing as dying for something—as sacrificial narratives must necessarily postpone their meaning—there *is* such a thing as living for something, whether that be a sense of masculinity, a sense of intimacy and forgiveness, or a sense that the living are only obligated to remember whatever it is that will give them peace. As contemporary Canadian literary responses to the First World War, these works participate in the move to consider the very act of engaging in cultural performances of remembrance as socially productive, not so much to explore an obligation to history, but rather to extol the ideal of taking comfort in a set of powerful and containable fictions.

Thus, the recent deployment of prosopopoeia constitutes a shift away from attempts to problematize the process of historiography, so prevalent in the Canadian metafictions of the 1970s and 1980s, as well as a movement toward nostalgic celebration of the way fictions of the past allow it to be usable in the present, especially a present at risk of exhausting the cultural myth that Canadian First World War soldiers sacrificed themselves so that others might learn to avoid the horrors of a pointless war. In recuperating the notion of the war's function in a history of progress—a move that is ironically coupled with narrative acts that once again bury the voices of the dead—these contemporary texts avoid confronting the uncanny and instead seek to allay anxieties about senselessness, especially in the face of increasingly complex attitudes towards civic participation.

2

The War and Concepts of Nation in Jack Hodgins's *Broken Ground* and Frances Itani's *Deafening*

Forging the Nation

In the Part One of *Imagined Nations*, David Williams provides a dense genealogy of theories of nationhood, focusing on how "the mode of communication and the form of community have been linked in relations of mutual dependence."[1] He argues that even distrust in the concept of nation cannot overwhelm "language's power to mediate the nation...to gather people into a profound sense of communion."[2] Williams's genealogy provides a useful framework for the comparative analysis of Hodgins's *Broken Ground* and Itani's *Deafening* and the way each text works through the relationship between the First World War and the myth of the birth of the Canadian nation. Published in 1998, *Broken Ground* represents the lives of the settlers of Portuguese Creek, a section of land on Vancouver Island given to First World War veterans. The motley community, whose attempts to farm the unforgiving land are mostly disastrous, is almost destroyed when a forest fire sweeps through the area. The immediate and long-term effects of the fire are explored, often in juxtaposition with the memories of one settler's—Matthew Pearson's—wartime and postwar experiences. The basic "plot" of *Broken Ground* is difficult to summarize, as Hodgins's representations of Matthew's wartime experiences, and of life on the settlement before, during, and after the forest fire, are often achronological and always highly mediated, as particular incidents are recounted from varying, usually second-hand perspectives. *Deafening*, published in 2003, focuses on Grania O'Neill, a deaf woman born on the day of the Great Fire of 1896 that destroyed much of Deseronto, Ontario, who grows up in neighbouring Belleville and whose husband Jim joins the war effort as a stretcher bearer. After describing Grania's childhood and school years, in particular her experiences at a school for the deaf, the novel moves between representations of Jim's wartime experiences and scenes of life on the home front and the effect of the war on those in Canada. Thus, in comparison to *Broken Ground*, the plot of *Deafening* operates primarily as a straightforward *Bildungsroman*, recounting the story of Grania's childhood, her schooling, her wartime work on the home front, and her relationship with Jim; Jim's experiences overseas are juxtaposed with scenes set in Belleville in a way that maintains a sense of strict chronology.

Hodgins's novel—one of the earliest texts in the corpus under consideration, and one of the most overtly critical of Canada's First World War myths—represents the war as morally problematic, ultimately suggesting that the ideals of inheritance and progress are potentially unrealizable in its wake. Hodgins, for the most part, holds the paradigm of the essential nation in contempt as the diverse community of soldiers on the settlement can rarely find common cultural ground. Furthermore, *Broken Ground* explores stories of various kinds of desertion in order to interrogate whether the First World War can operate within a narrative of emerging national unity. Even in Hodgins's critical model, however, the work of rehabilitating the father figure and of community building is endorsed, as *Broken Ground* explores the uneasy development of the cultural nation, the ideal of which is social consensus over time. Thus, to connect back to Williams's point, the cultural nation that Hodgins imagines manifests itself in the work a community does in collating its most socially productive stories about itself, even if those stories are geared toward reception rather than truth telling. Itani's coming-of-age narrative—published five years after *Broken Ground*—invests heavily in the myth of national progress; it renders the events of the First World War only temporarily threatening because they disrupt the normal pace of familial continuity, an ideal that is chiefly exemplified in the marriage of Grania and Jim. Itani constructs the war insider—Jim—as embodying the national spirit and representing such Canadian character attributes as dutifulness, loyalty, and decency, all of which are made manifest as part of his war experience. An examination of Itani's representation of the way the war is figured as a necessary stage in the development in a national romance, despite temporary threats to familial continuity, reveals *Deafening*'s reimagining of the war as straightforwardly socially productive. In avoiding entirely some of Hodgins's more trenchant critiques of the narrative of the moral "rightness" of the war,

Itani's text functions as one of the most conservative reaffirmations of Canadian First World War mythology.

In his brief discussion of ancient peoples and the media they used to inscribe their sense of nation, Williams notes that the people of ancient Israel wrote the history of their covenant with God on a hard-wearing "leather roll," contending that "the durability of the medium thus helped to underwrite the messianic promise, preserving God's covenant with his 'nation.'"[3] The lack of detail provided in the Table of Nations and elsewhere in Genesis regarding the sorts of physical or cultural characteristics that might distinguish each nation puts into greater relief what ultimately sets the Nation of Israel apart: simply, God chooses to set the Israelites apart, a fact underscored by the narrative's eventual focus on a single family rather than all humanity. The parameters of genealogical nationhood are here plainly but powerfully defined to include the promise of land, the promise of familial descendants, and the promise of blessing, which might be defined as the promise of *promise*. While biblical scholars have debated whether Abraham somehow merits God's selection or whether this choice is arbitrary, it is the choosing and articulating of such clear parameters that has maintained an imaginative grip on Judeo-Christian culture, making the genealogical or progressive nation a relevant paradigm for the analysis of contemporary novels concerned with nation building.

Canadian authors have sometimes stressed the feature of promise inherent in the blessing of the chosen nation, even after examining the way nation is threatened by the genealogical crisis. MacLennan's *Barometer Rising* inverts the familiar biblical genealogical crisis of childlessness in its portrait of Neil Macrae, who not only is unaware of the status of Jean as his daughter, but also is himself a kind of orphan: as his lover and cousin, Penny, explains, "his mother died when he was born...and his father could never fit into this menagerie, so he stayed away from us as much as he could."[4] Neil's uncle Geoffrey Wain tries, unsuccessfully, to eliminate him from the family, first by sending him away to be educated, and then, more seriously, by fabricating a story about Neil disobeying orders on the battlefields of France so that Wain can save himself from official military censure. The final image of Neil and Penny travelling by railway toward Prince's Lodge to collect Jean, however, confirms MacLennan's reliance on the conceptual vigour of the genealogical nation, as the reconnection of the single family and the implied persistence of their narrative—their line—reveals the promise of "a great country mov[ing] into its destiny."[5] Both Hodgins and Itani make use of the paradigm of the genealogical nation in service of exploring how two communities deal with the effects of the war, whereby representations of familial crises and/or continuity, and of practical and/or imagined inheritance, reflect the author's attitude toward the concept of national promise.

The final segments of *Barometer Rising* also point to a second approach to the idea of nation that Williams surveys: the essential or romantic paradigm. In this paradigm of nationhood, it is the artist who is best capable of expressing the spirit of place, the *genius loci*. In German Romantic Johann Gottfried Herder's model of the *Volk*, a people's distinctive character both merges with and emerges from the vitality of place, and the articulation through art of the nation's spirit is a crucial objective of this as well as an inevitable consequence. Though Neil Macrae is not an artist-figure, MacLennan writes him as a man with a necessary vision, as one of "the generous ones who had believed the myth that this was a young man's country."[6] At the end of the novel, Neil has ceased his wanderings—his interlude as a social outcast and ghost—and will claim not only his family's continuance but also the place he springs from. Neil meditates on how Canada might develop into a distinctive nation, no longer "ham-strung" by its relationships to England and America, but comprising a "new order."[7] MacLennan invokes the romantic paradigm of nation, which insists on a communion with the materiality and spirit of place, in the final line of the novel: "[Neil] heard in the branches of the forest behind him the slight tremor of a rising wind."[8]

Williams is dismissive of the concept of the romantic nation, labelling the idea of the "unified *Volk* [as] nothing more than a sentimental myth," and insisting that "only idealists and ideologues are likely...to take as fact the cultural fiction of a unified *Volk*."[9] Williams's pronouncements are, to be sure, valid; it is doubtful that any contemporary cultural or political critic would persist in claiming the political relevance of Herder's model. In his introduction to *Worrying the Nation*, however, Jonathan Kertzer argues that "the romantic basis of national literature...continues to enchant and plague us."[10] Nation, Kertzer asserts, is, in the first place, "an old word used to describe a slippery idea"; while ideally, nations are straightforwardly constituted by a group of people who can assert the essential distinctiveness of their own national character and who feel a natural bond with others of the same nation, in practice every nation is an "invention...[that] requires constant ideological tinkering...Citizens must continually be reminded...of what they are supposed to know in their bones."[11] Williams may well assert that the very idea of an essential national character is a "myth"; however, myth as a product of imaginative energy is something that has long proved to be an amazingly powerful, even dangerous, motivator.

Kertzer notes that in their assertions of an essential character, nations are prone to "volatile inconsistencies."[12] In order to draw on the power of mythical unity, the nation must exert homogenizing force, suppress diversity and opposition, and then pretend that sameness is natural. The metaphor of family bonds—inherited from the genealogical paradigm—is used to reinforce the myth of the essential nation, and this amplifies the sense that to deviate in cultural practice or belief from established and enforced parameters of nationhood is to enact a painful breach of confidence, a personal betrayal for which a response of outrage, reprisal, and/or ostracism is entirely appropriate. Kertzer notes that "modern nationalism engenders, or is engendered by, a new conception of history," whereby "basic unit[s] of historical activity" become developmental stages in the "life" of the nation. The nation is thereby personified, granted a "character";[13] its individual progress and interaction with other nations is made narrative, and that narrative is implanted and cultivated so as to edify, to validate, and to inspire. While much criticism of contemporary Canadian literature wrestles with the problem of how to approach the very idea of a national literature, especially given the increasing significance of "postnational, transnational, and globalized contexts,"[14] the emphasis in Canadian popular culture on the war's function as a necessary stage in the "life" of the nation and as a crucible for the nation's "character" informs the way Hodgins and Itani apply the paradigm of the essential nation.

Hodgins, following a pattern perhaps familiar for Canadian writers, presents the attempt to realize the essential nation as a fraught, possibly misguided, and ultimately failed venture, while Itani produces a hopeful, though problematically naive, national romance. This oppositional reading of Hodgins's and Itani's' representations of nation is both amplified and troubled by Kertzer's assertion that for every attempt to expose the moral failings of the nation with regard to the political treatment of a particular marginalized group, a necessarily parallel attempt is made to affirm, on behalf of that group, those cultural values that can only be realized in the context of an idealized nation.[15] Hodgins's ironic portrayal of social fragmentation cannot help but express a desire for an ideal community that recognizes the cultural value of the marginalized and that achieves a sense of cohesion. It is in this sense that Hodgins's novel—though often critical of myths associated with the national collective—expresses a desire for the unifying gesture promised by the mythology of Canada's First World War experience. Itani's hopeful romance, however, moves even further away from the complex inquiry into the relationship between history and fiction that informs the writing of a historiographic metafiction such as *Broken Ground*, and toward a less self-conscious appeal to a stable sense of collective memory. Thus, Itani's text exemplifies the increased nostalgia for a more straightforwardly identifiable sense of a culturally cohesive national community over the course of a decade in which stable conceptions of the nation are increasingly threatened. As Daniel Francis suggests in *National Dreams: Myth, Memory, and Canadian History*, "in the age of anxiety, it is not surprising to find nostalgia flourishing... There is consolation in nostalgia, the glance behind to a better time when the world seemed to make sense."[16] In Itani's fiction/fantasy, the world of the First World War, though temporarily chaotic, is a space in which the ideal of community service and perfect, profound communication might manifest itself, and in which a mutually tolerant national community might develop.

Desertion Stories in *Broken Ground*

In *Rewriting Apocalypse in Canadian Fiction*, Marlene Goldman cites *Barometer Rising* as a "relatively straightforward apocalyptic [narrative]," one that can be said to reflect the developmental plot identified by Canadian historians: "*Barometer Rising* dramatizes the Halifax Explosion of 1917 (the most devastating explosion before Hiroshima) as a momentous, apocalyptic event necessary if Canada was to leave behind its past as a British colony and move into the future as an autonomous nation."[17] It is not surprising that in making use of traditional apocalyptic features, MacLennan's novel is structurally targeted toward its apocalyptic climax: the restricted time frame of the novel is in keeping with the apocalyptic narrative's obsession with imminence, while the climax itself occurs toward the end of the novel, with only the ratifying of a new elect national community comprising the novel's dénouement. In contrast, the 1922 fire that ravages the fictional settlement of Portuguese Creek is depicted at the centre of Hodgins's novel as a false climax described from various, sometimes conflicting points of view. His subversion of the apocalyptic narrative, however, is not contrived in service of honouring the non-elect or condemning a failure of humanity; rather, it operates as an almost comic critique of the attempt to create and uphold any myth of a nationally unifying originary event.

In keeping with Hodgins's broader goal of examining the failures of various kinds of authority, including the authority implied by an omniscient narrator, several voices from the settlement provide recollections of the fire toward the end of the first and longest section of the novel, titled "Voices from Portuguese Creek: 1922."[18] Even for these recollections, however, Hodgins is unwilling to grant the stamp of authenticity usually associated with autodiegetic narratives. In the third section of the novel, "A Helmet for Bees: 1996," the narrator, octogenarian Charlie MacIntosh, reports that "Voices from Portuguese Creek" was based on a collection of interviews made by "a local fellow twenty years before...[who] wrote it up the way he imagined we might have told it if we had told it all at once quite soon after the fire."[19] Hodgins's emphasis on the multiple levels of mediation used in the description of the fire is important not only in terms of marking his novel as a historiographic metafiction, but also because it undermines an important characteristic of the standard "grammar of apocalypse,"[20] whereby the narrative of catastrophe and revelation is imparted via "divine revelation... [in which] the human recipient of the revelation is normally presented as a famous hero of the past... [so as to] lend authority to the writing."[21]

In a further attempt to destabilize the meaning of the fire, Hodgins positions its representation at the structural midpoint of the novel, so that its function as an allegorical veil works in reverse. The central image of the burning logging train racing toward the settlement, "[turning] the railway grade into a sizzling fuse that was bringing the fire down out of the hills as fast as any reel of Black Clover cord could have done,"[22] brings to mind the fuses and dynamite used by the community of Returned Soldiers to try to break apart huge tree stumps left behind by loggers on the plots of land granted to them as part of the Land Settlement Act. Most of the soldiers accept the land grant with the intention of establishing farms on the Vancouver Island settlement, though it soon becomes clear that the soil cannot support crops and that the ground yields little but stumps and stones. In the first section of "Voices from Portuguese Creek: 1922," a young Charlie MacIntosh describes a miscalculation with fuse and explosives that leads to the death of his father, and also reports on the appearance of a man who "entered the settlement on horseback from the wrong direction."[23] The man Charlie speaks of is Wyatt Taylor, who turns out to have developed a talent for using explosives during the war, and who will eventually be partly responsible for driving the burning logging train down from the hills. Charlie's reference to "the wrong direction" is a crucial interpretive signal, as Hodgins intends that the metaphorical link between the First World War and the settlers' war with the land be read backwards: it is not the case that war experience—or even expertise—proves a productive framework for subsequent experience, as in a traditional developmental plot. Rather, the settlers' failure with the land operates as pathetic parody of war, especially as such activity might function to forge a community.

The description of the fire itself makes use of highly apocalyptic language and imagery; as Tanner Pearson declares, "this was the end of the world roaring up towards us."[24] After losing his daughter, Elizabeth, to the fire, Matthew Pearson wanders through the devastated settlement and expresses his anguish in apocalyptic terms that might also reference his war experience: "I have been left behind to find my own way out through the kingdom of the dead past young hemlock and white pine and alder as naked and pitiful as the bones of the dying who cry for help."[25] Hodgins's ultimate strategy, however, is to drain the apparent apocalypse of its meaning, as the second half of the novel contains various comic iterations of the fire scene that undermine its originary utility. In "A Helmet for Bees: 1996," Charlie recalls that, during a party that takes place once rebuilding has started, the settlers tell stories about the fire, and "before the night was over they had begun, some of them, to remember themselves as figures in a ridiculous comedy, scurrying around like frightened mice trying to save their hides."[26] In later years, Charlie reports, Matthew Pearson decides to make the fire "an important part of the [school] curriculum... [inviting] a different group every year of folk competing to relate the most thorough, dramatic, hair-raising, or comical version of the great disaster."[27] Finally, the fire becomes the climax of a movie made by the great-grandson of one of the settlers, a structural choice Charlie finds predictable, though disappointing. In this way, Hodgins signals his impatience with a developmental reading of the past, and of the war. With his subversion of the apocalyptic narrative, however, Hodgins draws attention to the question of why the First World War retains its special status within our national narrative, and what the social function of revisiting the past via collective remembrance might be.

One of the novels Wyile examines at length in *Speculative Fictions* is Hodgins's *The Invention of the World*, published the same year as *The Wars*, in which "Hodgins parodies and foregrounds the limitations of the traditional historical novel and raises important concerns about historiography in general and oral history in particular."[28] As analysis of Hodgins's representation of the settlement fire indicates, similar challenges to the traditional historical novel are demonstrated in *Broken Ground*. As is the case in *The Invention of the World*, the foregrounding of acts of oral narration and historiographic activity—such as those of a grandson of an original settler who compiles "Voices from Portuguese Creek," and Jeff Macken, who puts together the feature film about the fire—demonstrate what Wyile describes as a "recognition of the impossibility, not of telling the story, but of telling the true story."[29] After seeing the film, Charlie MacIntosh—whose memoir comprises the final section of the novel—wonders "what affect this movie would have upon future accounts of the War's survivors and the fire of '22. Was this the 'true' story we were witnessing now in this world of popcorn and rustling candy wrappers? Would it *become* the true story, erasing from our memories the versions we'd heard a thousand times from those who'd been there and from those whose parents had been there?"[30] Ultimately, though, Hodgins's novel concedes that the "true" story is less significant than stories that provide a means for social cohesion.

The relatively cohesive community of Anglo descendants that Itani focuses on in *Deafening* (examined below) contrasts with the motley of Returned Soldiers whom Hodgins portrays in *Broken Ground*. As an American immigrant to the settlement, Al Hueffner, declares, "'I thought I was moving to a country where everyone's the same...I figured you'd all be English, but you're everything else *except*!'"³¹ The diverse cultural heritage of the settlers is highlighted early in the novel when the artificial community tries to deal with its first death. Once it becomes known that Ellen MacIntosh has resolved not to have a funeral for her husband, the women of the settlement gather together to register their pique and assert their own opinion about how to properly mourn the dead: Arlette Martin insists that, in the tradition of French-Canadian Catholics, the community should "'sit up all night with the body,'" while Anya Korsakov recalls wistfully that "'if this was Russia, my mother would make a sad dance.'"³² In focusing on the community's diversity, Hodgins demonstrates his misgivings about the paradigm of the essential nation and its reliance on Herder's conception of the unified *Volk*. The settlers take pride in their cultural diversity, and also consistently display an antagonistic relationship to the land, denying any sense of union with a *genius loci*. Hodgins alludes to two of the most familiar thematic contexts for Canadian literature—Northrop Frye's concept of our "garrison mentality" and Margaret Atwood's notion in *Survival* of an alien and hostile Nature—in order to mark the settlement as a microcosm for Canada. After listening to each woman of the settlement lament separate mourning practices, Johanna Seyersted teasingly suggests that they light Mac's body on fire, as in India; when she is reproached by Nell Richmond, who scolds, "'We're not talking about India...We're talking about *here*,'" Johanna probes, "'And where is that?'"³³ Later in the novel, she again articulates a paraphrase of Frye, and also Atwood, declaring that "'this place scares some of them half to death. They don't even know where they are.'"³⁴

Hodgins constructs an ironic metaphor whereby the tree stumps the settlers are so desperate to remove—and that keep the artificial community from becoming a viable economic interest—are stubbornly connected to the land in a way that the settlers are not. In particular, Hodgins describes a tree stump on Matthew Pearson's lot: "This one was taller than the others, and twisted, with jagged spikes thrust from the top—a tree that had probably fallen when cut only halfway through. Some poor logger may have been killed by the kick. Its giant roots were half-exposed, curled around boulders as though refusing to budge, like a wisdom tooth wrapped around your jawbone."³⁵ Like the tree stump, the organic development of each settler's life has been violently severed by the war, the "kick" of which has left its ugly mark on all of them. And while each settler might assert a "half-exposed" allegiance to the cultural "roots" that have been relinquished, such roots are of little benefit in their new settlement. Like wisdom teeth, old cultural roots crowd in and may ache; yet because without force they "[refuse] to budge," making room for healthy growth triggers even more pain. Anchored though the tree stumps are, the settlers believe these traces of the original landscape must be removed before the new community can take root.

The absent sense of a *genius loci* in Portuguese Creek also becomes evident in the descriptions of Matthew Pearson's late night explorations of the settlement, during which he finds the remnants of a sawmill, built by a logging company not to be used but only "to fulfil the requirements for a timber license." Like the settlement of Returned Soldiers, the bogus sawmill is "a ruin without ever having been anything else, a thing of the past in a place that had no past."[36] Here, Hodgins alludes to the war as a problematic common denominator for the community and for Canada. Vance argues in *Death So Noble* that, in the decades immediately following the war, popular discourse asserted that "the Great War could breathe life into Canada, giving birth to a national consciousness that would carry the country to new heights of achievement."[37] Hodgins, however, proposes the rival case that, for the Canadian soldier, "it would be healthier...to behave as though there were no 'before' and 'after'—nothing beyond the trenches and the countryside we could see from the fire step whenever we wanted to have our heads blown off."[38] Even though members of the Portuguese Creek community have the war in common, this "before" only produces the "sleepless nights [that send Matthew Pearson] to the abandoned sawmill...[searching for] the past, the future, the heart and soul of the village."[39] Matthew Pearson's failure to find "the heart and soul of the village" in a ruin from the past is thus contrasted with the dynamic community that is created simply as a result of telling and retelling stories about the past that are increasingly divorced from the notion of "truth."

Like *The Wars*, *Broken Ground* is explicitly concerned with debunking the popular Canadian myth of the First World War's moral merit, though Hodgins's interest in the war's effects diverges from Findley's. Throughout *Broken Ground*, the Returned Soldiers—for example, Matthew Pearson—make it clear that serving in the war basically amounted to "'[being] taken for a fool...[as w]e're still trying to figure out what we're supposed to have accomplished.'"[40] Charlie Sullivan is even more pessimistic, demanding, "'What will happen when the men who got so good at writing lies for this bloody war start selling their skills to others?'"[41] Hodgins's desire to challenge the myth of moral development is emphasized by the novel's abrupt shifts in temporal setting and focalization, as well as by the self-reflexive attention to the problem of plotting: after watching the film made by "young Macken," in which the fire becomes the narrative's climax, Charlie realizes that, as is the case for most makers and consumers of popular narrative, "[Macken] was more interested in the disaster than in the recovery that followed."[42] In this way Hodgins distinguishes his primary concern from that of Findley: while *The Wars* focuses on the madness of war itself—on its horrifying and dehumanizing events, which eventually make Robert Ross insane—*Broken Ground* represents the "recovery," such as is possible, of the Returned Soldiers. Despite Hodgins's rejection of the developmental myth of the war, despite his seething reproach of certain political decisions made by Canadian statesmen during and after the war, and despite his general distrust of the essential or romantic attitude toward nation that comprehends shared history as an inspirational focal point for community, his interest in "recovery" results in a surprisingly hopeful narrative about the forgiveness that might follow betrayal, and the renewal that proceeds from loss.

In writing his memoir, Charlie admits to his own practice of fictionalizing the past:

> I can take advantage of an opportunity I could never hope for as a newspaperman—to add to what I remember seeing and hearing myself, and to what I've been told by others, the products of my own imagination. Old age has encouraged me to assume that I can know now what I did not know then—that is, what other people were thinking or feeling even when they kept it to themselves... Knowing, after all, that mine is only one more voice amongst many.[43]

Hodgins chooses Charlie to be the main purveyor of the novel's narrative, the voice that provides a retrospective account of the settlement's recovery from the fire. Charlie reports on other stories that have circulated, as for example when he situates "Voices from Portuguese Creek" as a well-meaning, though necessarily distorted, written attempt to capture oral narrative. Charlie further acknowledges that his disappointment with Macken's film, which emphasizes the love triangle among Nora Macken, Wyatt Taylor, and Johanna Seyerstad, stems from his belief that "everyone was the main character in his own version [of the story]."[44] This self-reflexive moment in the novel raises a question: why is Charlie's "version" the one that Hodgins highlights?

Charlie himself states that, even in his own story, it is Matthew Pearson who is "something of a main figure."[45] The focus on Matthew reveals as a recurring theme in the novel the problematic relationship between fathers and their families, especially in terms of the way men become deserters. Charlie comes to view Matthew as an ideal father after he loses his own to the accident with explosives. When Matthew returns to France after his daughter Elizabeth dies in the fire, Charlie suffers a second loss of a father figure. The focus on Charlie's "version" allows Hodgins to explore a genealogical crisis that occurs "from the wrong direction," whereby fathers become absent before their role in passing on the nation's promise has been fulfilled. He then relates this to the problem of counting on the past to determine the shape of the future. Charlie's function as a mediator of the past thus indicates Hodgins's exploration of the way that stories of national character, cohesion, and development must necessarily occur in the present, whereby references to the past are simply productive deployments of narrative.

The issue of rootlessness—of the failure of the community of returned soldiers to establish a link to the concept of the genealogical nation or the romantic nation—is explored by Hodgins in his varied representations of desertion. One of the stories the narrator imagines in "Voices from Portuguese Creek: 1922" is Matthew Pearson's tale of a Canadian soldier, Hugh Corbett, who is shot for desertion during the war by his military unit because he misses a particular battle, identified by Hodgins as the "attack on Hill 70."[46] As historian Tim Cook explains, the Battle of Hill 70 was a significant Canadian victory in that "the Canadian Corps had revealed how to carry out a minor operation that successfully ground away the enemy's morale, killed his troops in greater numbers, and assisted with the overall British strategy of attacking along multiple fronts."[47] Cook's point throughout his description of the Battle (or battles) of Hill 70 emphasizes the way Canadian infantrymen learned how to survive a war of attrition, whereby the goal became simply having the tenacity to remain in a battle long enough that the enemy quit first. Hodgins's reference to this particular military episode functions as a noteworthy context for the tale of Hugh Corbett, as it pits what Cook refers to as the "unpalatable"[48] concept of attritional warfare, whereby the 10,000 casualties suffered by the Canadian Corps during a relatively "minor operation" were considered acceptable mostly because the Germans had suffered even more, against the concept of the individual soldier's experience.

Unlike Guy Vanderhaeghe's portrayal of the prosopopoeiac mask that covers over the figure of an unnamed, cowardly soldier, Hodgins's depiction of Hugh is complex. As the narrator explains, even Matthew's wife Maude—who insists that her husband tell the story of Hugh in order to justify her sense of "indignation"[49] at the injustice of army policy—does not fully understand to what extent Matthew's experience with Hugh undermines the notion of war as a productive national enterprise. The events related to Taylor include the description of a report that, after complaining of headaches the day before, Hugh "wandered off in the wrong direction and ended up, a few hours later, at the nearest field hospital complaining of his aching head. And not at all sure how he'd got there."[50] The reference in this report to "wander[ing] off in the wrong direction" resonates sharply with Charlie MacIntosh's early remark that he first saw Wyatt Taylor coming into the settlement from "what seemed like the wrong direction," as well as with the various ways the genealogical line from father to son is undermined in the novel.

Hodgins's representation of Hugh's "crime" of wandering off also functions as a keen censure of a Canadian military policy during the war, as evidenced by Matthew's recollection of the way "Private Berry, who had a way of knowing peculiar facts unknown by the rest of us, announced that Hugh Corbett was the twentieth Canadian shot for desertion since the start of the war."[51] Hodgins too is interested in "announc[ing]" details about the Canadian experience of the war that are generally "unknown by the rest of us," in order to trouble the myth of the war's moral merit. Cook notes in *Shock Troops: Canadians Fighting the Great War 1917–1918* that it was the policy of the entire British Expeditionary Force, with the exception of the Australian Corps, that the penalty for desertion was death,[52] and asserts that "the execution of soldiers at the front remains one of the grimmest legacies of the war."[53] Hugh's tale is picked up again in "A Helmet for Bees," both in terms of Matthew's attempt to come to terms with his own role in the episode, discussed below, and in the depiction of his meeting with Hugh's parents. The Corbetts have received a letter from "Frederick Bond, care of the Record Office," whose report that their son has been shot for desertion begins with the phrase "'I have the honour to inform you—.'"[54] The name of the Record Officer registers with sickening irony here, as *Broken Ground* questions what sort of national "bond" is possible in light of such an act.

When Matthew relates the story of Hugh to Wyatt Taylor at his wife's behest, he admits that he "could not go straight to what [she] wanted of me," as the narrative notes again the impossibility of pursuing the tidy plotting of events so necessary in a developmental plot. Matthew reflects that his take on Hugh's story had "a thousand roots to feed it."[55] What Matthew cannot tell Maude or Wyatt (but what might somehow be imagined by the unnamed voice behind the fictionalized recollections in "Voices from Portuguese Creek") is the wider context of Hugh's story of a hapless "crime" and horrifying punishment. Matthew ruminates on the parts of the narrative that, presumably, cannot be told because they are too grotesque, as Hodgins explores the gulf in communication that exists between war insiders and war outsiders. Hours before Hugh's absence is noted, he is "sprayed" by the remnants of a man who has been killed beside him: "there were grey and pink bits of blood and flesh on Corbett's forehead and in his hair."[56] Hugh's physical response to this experience is continual retching and the repeated motion of wiping "his hand...down across his face."[57] Hodgins, however, is interested in more than the likelihood that Hugh's "wandering" is a consequence of trauma. He is also concerned with how Matthew, the company's officer and a familiar face from home, contends with the incident. Matthew knows that Hugh is distressed that his childhood friend Donald is also missing; he knows that Hugh, like other young soldiers, "counted on [him] to keep them safe from harm."[58] In a representation of the officer figure that is diametrically opposed to that of Dancock in Vanderhaeghe's play, Hodgins explores Matthew's ambivalence about his role as a father figure, a teacher, and a military leader.[59]

Matthew himself becomes a type of deserter: after the settlement fire and the death of Elizabeth, he returns to France and spends several months working on a farm belonging to Elizabeth's grandparents. Though Maude proudly shows his letters to the other settlers, the women in particular have little patience for Matthew's absence, noting that "one of these days it's gonna hit her, he's just another husband that didn't come home."[60] Matthew justifies his continuing absence from the settlement by stating, "I am still here because I still believe that this is the greatest good I can do for you. Selfishness would have me race home."[61] Matthew's desertion of his wife, and of his community, is thus linked to his sense that he has failed to inhabit productively the leadership role expected of him in the war; this is made clear by the way that thoughts of Hugh Corbett return to him. Matthew recalls not only that Hugh was "shot for desertion and then himself deserted, left behind in foreign soil," but also that in the hours leading up to the execution, Hugh explained to him that he had wandered off to try to find Donald; as Hugh complains, "How could I tell them that?...If they knew what I meant they'd take it as reason enough to shoot me."[62] In portraying the interruption of Hugh's love for Donald (whether homosexual or platonic), Hodgins indicates his rejection of a developmental narrative that would bury the love relationship beneath the national romance.

In the final section of "A Helmet for Bees," depicting Matthew's return to the settlement, he tells Charlie the story of Hugh:

> "They stood deserters up against walls like this to shoot them, Charlie," he said. "Did you know that? It didn't matter if you hadn't meant to desert...What they shot you for was this—you behaved as though you lived in a different world from the others and deserved a separate peace...You'd acted as if you were the main character in the story and

other people could wait until you'd found your own happy ending...I think we should stand in front of blank walls like this in order to ask ourselves if we have deserted anyone today, including ourselves."[63]

The story of Hugh Corbett is meant to operate as a crucial historical touchstone in *Broken Ground*, through which Hodgins can raise the spectre of a particular military policy that troubles a desire by contemporary Canadians to make claims about the moral merit of the war in their remembrances. In this regard, it is interesting to note how often this plot emerges in contemporary representations of the war (for example, in *Dancock's Death*, in *Broken Ground*, in Alan Cumyn's *The Sojourn*, in Vern Thiessen's play, *Vimy*, and, as a parody, in Daniel Poliquin's *A Secret Between Us*). As the Historical Notes of Thiessen's play mention, "twenty-three Canadians were executed by their own men during the Great War for desertion, cowardice or other military crimes."[64] While one could argue that this number is insignificant in relation to the 61,000 Canadian First World War deaths, clearly the idea of these types of executions has resonated powerfully, especially as contemporary writers seek to amplify a narrative that condemns the First World War's particular horrors, or—more generally—the horror of war.

More so than in any other contemporary Canadian literary response to the First World War, though, the idea of "desertion" also functions as a thematic anchor in *Broken Ground*, as Hodgins also criticizes attempts to straightforwardly associate the remembrance of the war with the ideal of the genealogical nation or the romantic nation. Matthew Pearson's identity as a failed father figure undermines any attempt to consider the war in the context of national promise; when it comes to Hugh, to Elizabeth, to his son Tanner, and even to Charlie—all attempts to teach, to lead, or to keep them safe seem to occur "from the wrong direction." The reference Matthew makes to the "blank walls" that deserters stand against reflects the novel's insistence that there is no inherent connection between a community and a place, no genuine manifestation of *Volk*. However, as W.H. New points out, "the site of *contra-diction* [in the novel] is not simply a burden, but a challenge,"[65] a challenge to continually assess and reassess how individual narratives necessarily overlap and become community narratives. Like the story of the settlement fire, the First World War is a set of stories that will continue to be told and retold. Hodgins's novel asserts that it is the obligation of members of a diverse community to continue to "ask ourselves" what such tellings leave out or leave behind.

Thus, one of the most significant images in *Broken Ground* is that of Donald McCormack, survivor of the war, beloved friend of Hugh Corbett, broken, voiceless member of the community at Portuguese Creek who must wear a mask to cover his mutilated face. During the first viewing of Macken's film version of the fire, Donald interrupts the proceedings, first by making unintelligible noises and, finally, by throwing his mask into the crowd and forcing them to look at the "collapsed hole" of his destroyed face.[66] The narrator Charlie concludes that Donald's distress arises from his realization that Macken's version of events does not include him, that Donald "must have thought that someone had erased him from his own life."[67] Hodgins contends that the narrative of the First World War that Canadians tell about themselves can potentially "erase" those uglier episodes that, because they are so ugly, become incomprehensible and faceless. Yet it is only via the moment of showing Macken's film—via the attempt of the community to tell its own story—that the opportunity arises for Donald to throw off his mask and share "this calamity [that] had been amongst us all these years without our seeing it."[68]

In *Speculative Fictions*, Wyile asserts that it has been the general trend of contemporary Canadian historical fiction to "[find] and [tell] the stories of those left out of traditional history."[69] Furthermore, the emphasis on representing those communities Goldman might refer to as "non-elect," and on confronting, as Wyile puts it, "the role of representations of the past in the construction of social, political, cultural, and, not least of all, national discourse,"[70] often produces parallel experimentation with formal features of traditional historical fiction. Thus, Hodgins's desire to problematize established myths about the Canadian First World War experience manifests itself in the use of various postmodern tools for mounting his challenge. Hodgins's novel—one of the earliest examined in this study—is often critical of the notion that the First World War can be recalled as having moral merit, as the state's actions toward a soldier like Hugh Corbett, or toward the settlement of Returned Soldiers, prove to be morally reprehensible. Despite the embedded critique of the state, however, *Broken Ground*'s inquiry into the activity of national self-imagining culminates in the idea that it is only through the effort of collective remembrance that the cultural nation can come to grips with itself. Thus, the cultural narratives of Canada's participation in the First World War retain their paradoxical status in the development of the national imaginary. The meaning of historical events—their moral merit or social utility—is thus mediated by the community, which will refine the stories it tells about itself in response to the needs of the present. Writing in 1997, at the tail end of the period during which, as Wyile argues, the stories of those left out of the "traditional history"[71] were prevalent, Hodgins's attitude toward narrating the war highlights the way in which reiterating stories of "calamity" makes visible the existence of suffering.

Itani's *Deafening* as a Coming-of-Age National Romance

The image of fiery devastation as it is associated with the features of the apocalyptic plot and the forging of nation is also used in Frances Itani's 2003 novel *Deafening*, though here the apocalyptic narrative is written not as a climax or false climax, but as a type of preamble. "The fire story," a fictional account of a historical fire, is recast in almost mythic terms as a buttress for "the name story," an account of the protagonist, Grania's, birth.[72] The prefiguring allusions to the Great War set within this tale of the so-called "Great Fire" establish this mythic plot as an interpretive framework, allowing Itani to write the war as part of a romance of a national community forged by disaster. Itani uses accounts published in the *Deseronto Tribune* and *Napanee Beaver* of the 1896 fire that destroyed a large section of Deseronto, Ontario, and many of the details she includes in her description appear in such historical documents. For example, the narrator of Itani's novel insists on the connection between "the story of Grania's birth and how she came to be named, the day of the town fire, the Great Fire, 1896, Monday the twenty-fifth of May, the end of the holiday weekend that celebrated Queen Victoria's birthday."[73] The report of the fire in the *Deseronto Tribune*, dated 29 May 1896, similarly begins by noting the ironic timing of the fire: "May 25th, 1896 the day set apart for the loyal observance of the anniversary of the Majesty's birthday will long be remembered by the people of Deseronto as one of the most disastrous in the established history of their fair town."[74] Itani also calls attention to the small town's status as part of the lingering British Empire, noting that the date of the fire was "the end of the holiday weekend that celebrated Queen Victoria's birthday,"[75] and indicating that the town's population was made up of immigrants from places like Ireland and Scotland.

What Itani explicitly adds to the historical context is Grania's "name story," which is constructed to mark the "Great Fire" as an apocalyptic episode that culminates in "revelation": as Mamo reflects, Grania's birth represented "the miracle of new life in the midst of destruction."[76] Grania, whose infant lungs "did not seem bothered"[77] by the smoke of a scene of "transformative catastrophe,"[78] is not quite the resurrected embodiment of her grandmother, but does represent a new version of Mamo, her hair "as red as [Mamo's] own when she'd been a young woman."[79] Grania inspires fervent love and hope for the future in Mamo, as she is given the Irish name "*Gráinne*," meaning "love," though Mamo chooses to "spell it the English, the Canadian way."[80] Thus, Itani inverts the conventional plotting of the apocalyptic narrative to lay emphasis on redemption before dwelling on devastation.

Only after the name story has been narrated does Itani backtrack to describe Mamo's trek through the burning streets of Deseronto, where the narrative records her observations of, on the one hand, the upheaval of ordinary lives, simply shocked and shifted by the catastrophe, and, on the other, an instance of earthly evil. In making note of the shifted ordinary—of one man's tragicomic effort to save a plate of boiled potatoes[81] and of one woman's distress over the ruin of her plum preserves and gooseberry jam—Itani engages with a First World War grammar that documents the effect of destruction on the everyday and that provides an amoral framework for observation. Mamo's observations of the shifted ordinary, however, give way to an image with clear apocalyptic resonance:

> Three drunken men...were crammed into a wide rig and, with horrible cruelty, they were whipping and forcing a pair of horses down a narrow street between rows of burning houses. The fear of the animals was terrible to see, and men and women shouted, trying to stop the drunken men...On her way home, retracing her steps through the streets, she was not surprised to come upon one of the horses, dead.[82]

The familiar tropes used in this depiction of earthly evil are set in opposition to the description of the trek back to town made by Grania's father. Unlike the drunken men, Grania's father "would not force the horses" down the road until the fire and thunderstorm had passed, and he arrives home to "a newly arrived, newly named daughter and a town half-gone."[83] Itani's emphasis here on a cycle of destruction and renewal mitigated by references to ordinary goodness is repeated throughout the novel, so that by the time the war scenes are introduced, they have already been given meaning as preceding an almost mundanely anticipated community rebirth. Itani's war narrative is a romance of the ordinary, a celebration of communal decency and its relationship to continual national progress.

Itani's novel, published five years after *Broken Ground*, displays only residue of the postmodern attitude and aesthetic that had dominated Canadian historical fiction for at least two decades. Furthermore, unlike many contemporary Canadian historical fictions concerned with the politically and culturally marginalized, *Deafening* focuses on the Anglo-Canadian, middle-class, central Canadian community, whose ideals have tended to shape popular expressions of postwar commemoration. As the detailed acknowledgements of her novel show, Itani has carefully and thoroughly researched the period and communities she wishes to represent, and her generic mode is unequivocally realism. Like the myriad producers of Canada's postwar myth of a distinct and unifying national spirit, however, Itani's concern for how gulfs in communication can and should be traversed in service to the nation's "life" ultimately produces a narrative that must be understood as a hopeful, though naive, national romance. The novel brings together three conventional plot patterns to underscore Itani's thematic focus on the developing "life" of the nation: the *Bildungrsoman*, the modern romance, and the war story. Though it is Grania's *Bildungsroman*, the story of her experiences as a deaf child growing up in Deseronto, Ontario, at the beginning of the twentieth century, that encompasses the other two plots, analysis of her romantic partner Jim's story of his experiences as a Field Ambulance worker on the First World War battlefields, as well as of the home front, reveals most vividly Itani's nostalgic desire to stage a return to the stability of mimesis, and to a mythically coherent and morally unproblematic narrative about social unity and national progress.

In the fourth section of *Deafening*, "1917–1918," Itani represents how Grania's family and community endure many hardships that were typical for those waiting at home: Grania hoards letters from Jim, attempting to stifle her fear for him; her sister Tress's husband Kenan returns from the battlefields maimed and traumatized; her brother Bernard, who is physically unfit to serve, is "pinned" as a coward by a self-righteous anti-pacifist; an underage Patrick finally manages to enlist, to the anguish of the family; and Grew, a close family friend, is informed that his son, Richard, has been "*killed in action.*"[84] Itani includes in her depiction of life on the home front a letter from Richard's platoon lieutenant that Grew receives a month after the official telegram:

> I must tell you that I have known your son from the time he enlisted. In losing him I have lost one of the best men from my platoon, and I am very sorry. Both officers and men desire me to say how much we miss him. You may be extremely proud of the fact that he was always ready to do his duty and that he was willing to sacrifice his all for the cause. He died nobly and in service of the Empire and his King. I am able to say positively, from witness reports, that he was killed by a sniper's bullet while on night patrol in No Man's Land, and that he died instantly. I know it will relieve your worries that he did not suffer at the end. You should also know that one of our Canadian boys managed to kill the sniper almost immediately. It is most unfortunate that we were unable to recover your son's body. Shortly after that episode, the area came under heavy fire and we were forced to remove ourselves to another location.[85]

So conspicuous in this letter is the rhetoric of duty and Empire that, particularly in light of the customary self-awareness of most contemporary historical fiction, it is tempting to read the excess of cliché as ironic. Itani, though, frames the inscription of this letter with a scene in which Grania photographs young Patrick kitted out in his new, ill-fitting uniform, thus undermining attempts to read against the grain of sentimentality. As Patrick poses awkwardly for the camera, Grania asks to be told the name of the song Grew played on the piano the night he learned of his son's death. Patrick answers "with care... [it] was 'The Irish Laddies to the War Have Gone'";[86] so ending the chapter, Itani undercuts an ironic reading, as her reference here (as elsewhere) to such popular responses to the war clearly approves the sentimental. If the rhetoric of duty and Empire makes Itani "angry," as Grania admits to being, particularly at "the endless poems by patriotic citizens, many of them women,"[87] it is an anger represented and associated with personal fear and grief rather than with political discontent or a more generalized critique of war.

Itani's chief concern with the war's effects on individual lives and community spirit is in keeping with her desire to make use of the genealogical paradigm of nation, whereby the repercussions of war must be managed in such a way as to materially preserve the promise of social, and thus national, continuity. Itani demonstrates her inclination to portray the war as an instance of genealogical crisis by writing her modern romance—the love story of Grania and Jim—without engaging a complex plot logic of desire thwarted and realized, but rather in the context of material progress. It is not that Itani is unconcerned with whether Grania and Jim love each other: on the contrary, the scenes portraying their expressions of affection and physical desire for one another are among the most feelingly written in the novel and operate crucially for the novel's thematic exploration as to the value of intimacy. Importantly, however, the love story, which commences in the second section of *Deafening*, is contiguous with Itani's representation of ideal social progress and the war that threatens this ideal. Thus, the love story operates allegorically, as Itani considers Jim's participation in the war—or Canada's participation in the war—as a moment of crisis for the nation, one that has the potential to impede its realization of the promise of promise.

When Jim is introduced into the narrative, he is immediately marked as a future soldier, his "'joining up'...neither a question nor statement—perhaps something of both."[88] In fact, Jim's temporary absence from the community because of the war is almost the only plot dynamic Itani introduces as a potential threat to the modern romance; otherwise, the courtship and marriage of Jim and Grania proceed without much of a hitch. Even the potential dilemma of Grania's deafness is given short narrative shrift: Grania's initial avoidance of Jim, because he is hearing, is retrospectively described a few scenes after the narrator reports that "he had been part of her life for more than eight months now."[89] Her mother's apparent apprehension regarding the match is briefly noted, but in the scene immediately following, Grania, now married, ruminates that "in two weeks, her own husband, Jim, would leave."[90] Later still in the narrative is a succinct account of a family debate about whether Grania should delay the wedding until after the war, even though her refusal to submit to this plan has already been established and the wedding party and the lovers' brief period of living together as husband and wife have already been described. As in her plotting of "the fire story," Itani's plotting of Jim and Grania's love story is organized so that small disruptions to the otherwise chronological impetus of the novel make plain Itani's confidence in the ideal of social progress, as well as her position that the main threat to national continuity is not a crisis of desire, but a crisis that puts at risk the material arrangement of home and the fulfillment of genealogical promise.

Providing a social context for Jim and Grania's love story are other portrayals of courtships and marriages; in keeping with the genealogical paradigm, matters of familial continuity and the stability of community are crucially related to idea of national promise. The story of Tress and Kenan represents perhaps the gravest repercussion of the war that Itani entertains. As a child, Tress announces that she intends to marry Kenan, and, as is the case in Jim and Grania's love story, no narrative pause is given with regard to the dynamics of desire; several chapters later, the narrator simply refers to Kenan as "Tress's husband...gone [to war]."[91] After learning that Kenan, badly injured, is on his way home, Tress rents an apartment for them containing "an empty room for a child,"[92] which remains empty long after Kenan's return. Further along the continuum that gauges the war's effects against the potential for social renewal is the story of Grania's brother Bernard and Kay, a "kind" girl whom, as the narrator reports early on, Grania had known and liked in childhood. Kay reappears in the narrative's fourth section, dressed in mourning for her husband who was killed in battle; unlike Tress, however, Kay conceived before her husband went overseas, leaving her with a young, now fatherless, son. Bernard is unable to serve in the war because of a weak lung, and in his story, Itani reveals her underlying sense that, whatever "anger" one might feel in response to the personal and social toll taken by the war, the campaign itself retains a moral merit so absolute and inherent that it requires no articulation. While the "pinning" of Bernard, who is suspected of being a pacifist and therefore a coward, is condemned, the issue of moral objection to the war on the grounds of pacifism is never seriously engaged. Bernard stays home only because he is not physically fit enough to enlist, which suggests that Itani is less concerned about reflecting on pacifism as a legitimate response to war than she is about criticizing those who make judgments based on (false) appearances. This simplifying of the grounds for Bernard's standing as a man not made absent by the war allows for the straightforward re-establishment of a genealogical line, as Bernard, an upright, hard-working member of the community, is an appropriate new mate for Kay.

Most optimistic is the story of Fry, Grania's best friend from school, and Colin, who is also deaf. Colin is also "pinned," though unlike Bernard, Colin repeatedly tries to enlist, patently confirming both his moral integrity and the novel's tacit approval of active participation in the war. Towards the end of *Deafening*, Fry happily signs to her friend that she and Colin are expecting a baby. Finally, the portrayal of Mamo's death, though not an expression of familial continuity, can also be read as a manifestation of Itani's valorization of a genealogical paradigm of nation. In a scene that inverts and bookends the narration of "the fire story," which describes "the miracle of new life in the midst of destruction,"[93] Grania is pulled from her convalescent bed to witness the town's celebration of the declaration of the armistice, just prior to learning of Mamo's death. Though Grania is devastated to lose Mamo, the death is situated so as to suggest both the end of a developmental stage in the nation's "life," and a return to a social situation inclined toward continuity.

The story of Grew's son, noted earlier, represents the darkest social effect of the war for those on the home front, though here too Itani strictly confines herself to considering personal as opposed to broader cultural effects. A significant feature of the letter Grew receives, however, draws attention to the novel's representation of the battlefront, as Richard's platoon lieutenant describes the death and his unit's response. Perhaps surprising in a work that contains so many detailed and grisly scenes of the physical effects of trench warfare, the sentence "one of our Canadian boys managed to kill the sniper almost immediately" is the novel's sole mention of specific violent action taken by a Canadian soldier. Except for this highly mediated representation, Itani does not depict Canadian soldiers killing anyone. Even here, she obscures the image of killing within a morally simplistic plot of just retribution. While there are periodic references to particular battles that the Canadian army engaged in, the language used to describe military action is euphemistic and detached: "*the now famous battle of Langemarck where the Canadians so distinguished themselves*";[94] "counterattacks by our Canadians near Hooge on the thirteenth have been successful in taking back the trenches";[95] "Vimy Ridge, almost a year ago... A great Canadian victory";[96] "Cambrai taken on the ninth. The Canadians, the Royal Naval Division to the south, everyone was so strong."[97] While maintaining the brevity of such comments, Itani takes pains to refer to specific battles, marking the progression of the war not in terms of violent action, but rather in terms of ground won and time spent as the Canadian army matures and comes of age.

As it happens, among the thirteen Canadian First World War texts examined closely in this study, only two—Alan Cumyn's *The Sojourn* and Joseph Boyden's *Three Day Road*—are to a large degree situated in a battlefield setting, though even in both those works the idea of distance is crucial.[98] As the title, *The Sojourn*, indicates, a large part of Cumyn's narrative concerns Ramsay Crome's leave in London, while the framing narrative of *Three Day Road* is about Xavier Bird's journey back to his community and through memory. In plays such as *Mary's Wedding* and *Vimy*, the representation of battle is highly stylized: both Stephen Massicotte and Vern Thiessen, respectively, consider the ways in which military exploits become usable within personal and cultural narratives. In Jane Urquhart's novels *The Underpainter* and *The Stone Carvers*, in Mary Swan's *The Deep*, and in Kevin Kerr's *Unity (1918)*, war experience is only ever related or imagined after the fact; while—as in *Deafening*—Daniel Poliquin's *A Secret Between Us* represents such activity as an interlude within a narrative chiefly concerned with the home front and an expanded examination of particular Canadian communities in the early twentieth century. Like Hodgins's *Broken Ground*, Guy Vanderhaeghe's *Dancock's Death* and Cumyn's *The Famished Lover* include sections that portray the war, but they are mostly set back in Canada during the postwar period. Thus, Itani is not unusual in her attempt to figure Canadian participation in the war without confronting the murky territory of the moral merits of killing; this facilitates her ability to retain a nostalgic attitude toward these events.

In her descriptions of trench life, Itani is, however, comprehensive, portraying with gruesome, terrifying, and heart-rending detail the filth and horror that surround Jim and his unit. Itani's object in enumerating such familiar trench war indignities as the relentless lice and treacherous mud, the constant barrage of noise, the ever-present sight of body parts, human agony, fear, and death is to depict war as an absolute nightmare, as hell. In her dedication of the novel to "*the nine and a half million who died serving their countries,*"[99] and in certain scenes that echo Harrison's *Generals Die in Bed* and Findley's *The Wars*, such as one in which a team of German stretcher bearers help Jim and Irish with their own wounded, Itani confirms her abhorrence of war *in general* and her conviction that German soldiers were equal victims of its madness. Even in this intention, however, Itani makes no attempt to challenge the rhetoric of duty and sacrifice that saturates the letter Grew receives. Furthermore, the description in the letter of the way "one of our Canadian boys managed to kill the sniper" undermines the novel's overt stance that Germans were not the enemy. In sections of the novel dealing with Jim's experiences during the war, Itani makes use of what Cobley describes as "autodiegetic narratives," in which "a 'marked' narrator [tells] his own story" and "[concentrates] almost exclusively on everyday occurrences...pointedly [refusing] to comment on wider historical, political, philosophical, or psychological implications."[100] Repeatedly, Itani refers to the war as "a great, moving, humming machine,"[101] rejecting a more ideologically inflected course of condemnation while confirming a self-congratulatory narrative about a "reluctant coming-of-age."[102]

Jim is portrayed as suffering in the war, though because Itani constructs Jim as a Field Ambulance worker as opposed to an infantryman or machine gunner, she avoids the prospect of having to depict him taking explicit violent action against the enemy. In his contribution to *The Cambridge Companion to the Literature of the First World War*, David Trotter provides a survey of British combat novels that appeared in the decades following the armistice and asserts that the regular portrayals of "suffering" in these works derive from a goal on the part of middle-class writers to highlight the "adaptability" of the British soldier, and the "belief that the maximum of individual adaptability will ensure a minimum of collective change."[103] In other words, a soldier-protagonist's character trajectory primarily entails his "suffering" *in* the war as he "suffers" *through* it.[104] The soldier's mere survival, which constitutes the sum of narrative expectation, is a matter of adapting to horrific conditions, commonly depicted as a series of accumulating set pieces; attempts to transcend such conditions or oppose their source go unrepresented. Trotter asserts that British narratives of "adaptability"[105] do ultimately emphasize the damage, often psychological, done to individual men. As Sharon Ouditt contends, contemporary British novels revisiting the "established myths" of Britain's Great War have tended to "reinforce" the narrative of damage done to "the brave, innocent white male."[106] For Itani, however, the narrative of suffering, while making use of the same set pieces found in British combat novels, does not culminate in a portrayal of damage.

After his first shift collecting and transporting the wounded, Jim writes to Grania, "I have begun my work in this war."[107] Itani deploys familiar trench tropes and, at points, mimics the style and narratological features of the "documentary war accounts" that Cobley analyzes.[108] For example, Jim's response to the sight of body parts littering the floor of the dugout is detached, just like that of "the authors of autobiographical narratives...[who] adopt an objective and distanced stance towards their own experiences,"[109] and the trench scenes are narrated in accordance with a strict chronology, in order to "reinforce the illusion of authenticity."[110] Jim insists, though, that he does his "work" in the war because "*This is our war, too,*" because he feels he is "*needed.*"[111] Like Richard's platoon leader, Jim expresses the rhetoric of duty to Empire; even more significantly, he is constructed by Itani as an emblematic figure, a personification suited to a national romance. Despite his "suffering," Jim remains a static character whose coming of age in war parallels his nation's and occurs as an inevitable rite of passage. When Grania first meets Jim, he is working as an apprentice to Dr. Whalen, a young man learning the practice of medicine from his elder; Itani notes that Grania "saw *earnest* in his eyes."[112] Jim's "work" in the war brings him into contact with every customary horror, yet he remains morally steadfast: he is loyal not only to Grania, but also to his stretcher partner, Irish; he makes no comment one way or the other about the "Self-Inflicteds;" at the *estaminet*, he neither drinks to excess nor gets into a brawl, but rather entertains his fellow soldiers with sentimental, wholesome tunes; he doesn't loot or dip into the morphine he administers to others; even his grief-induced madness after Irish's death is brief. In the final chapter of the novel, when Jim returns, Grania again notices Jim's eyes: "Eyes that were earnest, but old."[113]

The dominant "earnestness" of Jim remains unchanged, though now his "*old eyes*" must be accounted for. Grania thinks to herself, "he is different,"[114] as Itani plays with the idea that a gulf now exists between Jim, the war insider, and Grania, the outsider. On the battlefield, Jim had concluded that "no one at home would ever know. Because what was happening was impossible to be told."[115] However, the gentle suggestion that Jim "is different" cannot be construed as an assertion that he is "damaged." Grania's comprehension of his difference is, after all, compared to the way she became different from her own family: "It was like returning from the land called *School*. Only this time, Jim was returning from the land called *War.*"[116] Jim has "old eyes" because he has been educated in another "land"; he is "different" because his education, much like Grania's, has mandated the forging of an exclusive community. The novel's final image of Jim and Grania embracing in front of a train continuing its "cross-country journey"[117] not only recalls the final image in *Barometer Rising*, but also suggests that the lovers will find a way to communicate across the divide, to be again united, unified. Thus, Itani much more so than Hodgins privileges the idea that past experiences bequeath a necessary foundation for progress, and that something like the lessons to be found in the First World War—lessons about work, about loyalty, and about decency—operate as a kind of foundational wisdom in a progress-oriented narrative.

Itani, like Hodgins, makes use of the paradigm of the genealogical nation to represent the war as a crisis threatening the promise of the future.

For Itani, the events of the First World War are threatening because they disrupt the normal pace of familial continuity and social progress, in the same way that illness might. However, because Itani does not seriously question the war's moral value, the crises engendered by war can be managed. To reinforce the view that the experiences of Canadians during the First World War were a necessary stage in the budding "life" of the nation, Itani by and large keeps to a chronological structure, ending her novel with the declaration of the armistice and Jim's return to his wife, so as to emphasize the idea of stability in the war's meaning. Itani's thematizing of the First World War as an impediment to ideal moments of intimacy—moments that, in *Deafening*, operate as sites for productive community building—indicates her conviction that efforts of remembrance must ideally be forward looking and predicated on finding sites of commonality if they are to usefully serve a conception of nation. Thus, her text fits squarely among the most conservative of contemporary Canadian First World War narratives, texts that seek to rehabilitate the idea of a stable national history and an easily identifiable national character.

Kertzer points out that though the current popular critical stance is to "reject nationhood as a viable conceptual tool,"[118] the ideal of nation retains its power because it is adaptable to any number of political configurations, and because it continues to inspire "passion."[119] Kertzer's point that a narrative of nationhood is "protean"[120] and might be adapted to suit any political requirements or conditions has particular relevance for an examination of how Canadian authors have responded to the mythologizing of the First World War in terms of its role in nation building. Regarding the function of war for our collective remembrance, the main distinction between Hodgins's take and Itani's relates to their differences when it comes to weighting the horrors of the war against its potential value as a means of forging a unifying national narrative. Hodgins's novel, written in 1997, toward the beginning of a decade of Canadian First World War reimaginings (and thus perhaps more closely linked to the period when the historiographic metafiction dominated English-Canadian fiction writing), explicitly articulates a skeptical view of apocalyptic, originary national events and stable national narratives. He challenges the myth that Canada's participation in the First World War was a morally righteous national undertaking, as shown most emphatically in his rendering of the tale of Hugh Corbett, shot for desertion by the Canadian military. He also registers discomfort with concepts such as the *Volk* or a *genius loci* in his representation of the failure of the transplanted community of returned soldiers to develop a productive relationship with the land settlement of Portuguese Creek. In *Broken Ground*, the community is forged only as a function of cultural reiteration, as evidenced by the thematic/aesthetic foregrounding of the process of storytelling, which—like acts of national storytelling—ultimately covers over as many horrors as it claims to articulate. What is important to note, however, is that even in Hodgins's critical view, the cultural nation is formed by the ideal of communal activity, of a sense of participation in the process of national reiteration. While it may be the case that the way the settlers deal with the land and the fire becomes a pathetic parody of war, the communal retelling of the fire episode once again renders action as heroic and productive.

Thus, Hodgins articulates the need for community members to register their service to the nation, and it is this need that accounts for the increasingly nostalgic view of the war expressed in such works as Itani's *Deafening*, published five years after *Broken Ground*. Itani's novel is determined to advocate a clear-cut narrative of progress, whereby the First World War functions as a set of events that impel the nation to come of age and to articulate more firmly its essential qualities. After reimagining the apocalyptic fire story as a preamble for various narratives of individual, romantic, and community progress, Itani considers the grief brought on by the war in entirely personal as opposed to political terms, so as to avoid any fraught consideration of the war's moral merit. This avoidance continues in her representation of the war insider who, in the first place, is never put into the position of carrying out violent action against the enemy and, in the second place, remains essentially unchanged by his war experiences: as a personification of Canada at war, Jim is represented as a stable model of dutifulness, faithfulness, and earnestness. Furthermore, Itani's representation of Grania and Jim's romance—their promise to each other even across the gulf of hearing versus deafness—signals her belief that it behooves the contemporary Canadian to remain confident that the gulf of time, as well as the gulf between community insiders and outsiders, can by managed by remaining committed to hope and trust in the ideal of communication.

3

Abandoning the Archivist: Commemorating the War Insider and Outsider in the First World War Novels of Alan Cumyn and Jane Urquhart

"Post"-Historiographic Metafiction

In *Dubious Glory: The Two World Wars and the Canadian Novel*, Dagmar Novak enumerates three classes of Canadian fiction about the First World War. The first class includes the idealistic and heartening works written during the war years, such as Ralph Connor's *The Sky Pilot in No Man's Land* (1919) and Basil King's *The City of Comrades* (1919). These are greatly indebted to the romance tradition and have a tendency for uncritical patriotism toward Canada and—to an often greater degree—England. Such work has prompted little critical response except regarding its reflection of Canada's political naïveté and literary crudeness.[1] The class of "realistic" Canadian war fiction, written in the late 1920s and 1930s by First World War combatants, has received more attention. In his article about Peregrine Acland's *All Else Is Folly* (1929), Charles Harrison's *Generals Die in Bed* (1930), and Philip Child's *God's Sparrows* (1937), Eric Thompson asserts that, in each, the literary protagonist is identified with the combatant author, especially as the protagonist's status as a hero is based primarily on having simply endured the horrors of war. Harrison's novel is examined also in Evelyn Cobley's *Representing War: Form and Ideology in First World War Narratives*, an extended analysis of combatant fiction the central argument of which denies the simple correspondence between historical referent and literary text, as well as the objectivity of reproduction by the war insider. The third class that Novak indicates is made up of only one work: Timothy

Findley's *The Wars*, published in 1977. For Novak and Thompson, writing in the 1980s, and Cobley, writing in 1993, Findley's novel represents a mature stage of Canadian First World War writing and not just because it was, at the time, one of the only contemporary works to take up the subject. In it, according to these critics, the traditions of romance and realism are combined;[2] the "drama of *personal* heroism" is more explicitly articulated;[3] and the self-consciously constructed documentary format serves to undermine the potentially misleading truth claims of combatant fiction.[4]

Cobley, who is interested in the way combatant fiction falls short of succeeding as convincing protest literature, reads *The Wars* as a more trustworthy anti-war tract than those written by war insiders; Findley's experiential distance from the war itself keeps him from unwittingly diluting his novel's ideological position in an attempt to exonerate the combatant. Cobley's analysis of the way the figure of the archivist in *The Wars* highlights the novel's self-consciousness—its position that "all truth claims are necessarily suspect"[5]—is not new. As noted in the introduction to this study, many critics, including Lorraine York, Martin Kuester, Diana Brydon, and Simone Vauthier, have pointed out that the complex form of Findley's novel—its juxtaposition of archival fragments collected by a researcher and scenes that an anonymous narrator constructs about Robert Ross's life—serves to undermine the distinction between fact and fiction and disclose how meaning is ideologically assembled. In turning away from the figure of the archivist, a figure so important to examinations of *The Wars* as a historiographic metafiction, both Alan Cumyn and Jane Urquhart signal their relative disinterest in sorting through the problem of how to confront a historical record. Rather, Cumyn's *The Sojourn* and *The Famished Lover* and Urquhart's *The Underpainter* and *The Stone Carvers* depict the figure of the artist. Cumyn's novels are about the Canadian soldier-artist, especially as he is distinct from British representations of the soldier-poet, in that Ramsay Crome affirms his war work as duty and uses art not as a kind of "truth-telling" tool but as a means to privately confirm the brotherhood of subaltern soldiers. Urquhart explores the work of commemorative artists, representing them also not as "truth tellers" but as meddlers in the lives of war insiders. Both authors thus promote the idea that war insiders have a private narrative, one that they either wish to protect from outsiders, or to forget.

Alan Cumyn's First World War novels, *The Sojourn* and *The Famished Lover*, were published in 2003 and 2006, respectively, and feature as their protagonist Ramsay Crome. Set during the first half of the war, *The Sojourn*'s opening few chapters relate Ramsay's experiences as a private on the front lines at Ypres; the bulk of the novel recounts his experiences during a ten-day leave in London, during which he stays with his British relatives and falls in love with his cousin Margaret; finally, in the last chapters, Ramsay returns to the front lines in time for the disastrous battle at Mount Sorrel, and is captured as a prisoner of war. In *The Famished Lover*, Ramsay is home in Montreal after the war, married and trying to eke out a living as a commercial artist; the narrative is interspersed with his recollections of his experiences in a German POW camp, as well his musings about the passion he retains for Margaret, who is now also married. In both of Cumyn's novels, Ramsay's status as a soldier-artist recalls the figure of the British soldier-poet, especially as that figure is reimagined in Pat Barker's *Regeneration* trilogy, though Cumyn's attitude toward the war differs from the standard British position. Jane Urquhart's First World War novels are not connected by a shared protagonist, but rather by a shared thematic concern with commemorative artists who are war outsiders. *The Underpainter*, published in 1997, focuses on Austin Fraser, an American painter who spends summers in Canada, where he meets, among others, George Kearns and Augusta Moffat, both of whom participated in the war and who met in an asylum for shell-shocked patients. Augusta is a morphine addict and, after a night during which she explains to Austin the horrors of her nursing experience, she overdoses; upon discovering her body, George also commits suicide, leaving Austin to ponder his responsibility for these deaths and for representing the war insider's experiences in art. The protagonist of *The Stone Carvers*, published in 2001, is Klara Becker, a young woman whose first love affair is cut short when the young man enlists and goes missing in action. Klara and her brother Tilman, who lost his leg somewhere in battle, travel to Vimy after the war in order to work as sculptors on Walter Allward's famous memorial. In these reimaginings of Canada's participation in the First World War, and more importantly of the disconnect between war insiders and outsiders, both authors suggest that public, commemorative practice should concern itself with the building of shared, necessarily emblematic—as opposed to historically accurate—narratives.

For Cobley, the "temporal and emotional distance from events"[6] is what allows Findley to avoid the prospect of complicity with the war agenda—a complicity that marks the novels of First World War combatants. By "complicity," what Cobley means is that, in their narratives, combatant authors like Charles Harrison, Ralph Hale Mottram, and Siegfried Sassoon unconsciously reveal their desire to somehow preserve the ideals they believed they were defending. For example, Harrison's recourse to such features of autobiographical-documentary as the impersonal focalizer and excessive description of the quotidian aspects of life at the front reveals his conviction that facts may be counted on to speak objectively and that liberal human agency was not accountable for or subject to war.[7] Harrison's framing of *Generals Die in Bed* as a memoir/memorial counteracts the thematic that war is absurd with one that doggedly stresses the purpose of fighting and dying for *something*. Thus, for Cobley, narratives that may have been intended as anti-war tracts, and that are commonly viewed as such, ultimately function as defences of war or, at least, defences of preserving continuity with a past tradition, and she remains suspicious of their embedded exonerations of the dutiful soldier. Cobley argues that because *The Wars* is not invested in the sorts of historically determined defensive postures that might try to conceal political or literary ambivalence, its anti-war stance is more genuine. She values Findley's foregrounding of narrative reconstruction, his suspicion of truth-claims, and his effort to de- and re-contextualize violence.[8]

The marking of *The Wars* by Cobley and others as a culminating Canadian First World War novel is also significant because that novel has emerged as one of the central proof texts of Canadian historiographic metafiction. As Andrea Cabajsky and Brett Josef Grubisic note in their introduction to *National Plots: Historical Fiction and Changing Ideas of Canada*, "the current wave of criticism on Canadian historical fiction began over two decades ago with the publication of [Linda] Hutcheon's 'Canadian Historiographic Metafiction' (1984–1985), which links changes to the narrative forms of reflexive historical novels to larger changes in Canadians' historical self-understanding."[9] In her *The Canadian Postmodern: A Study of Contemporary English-Canadian Fiction*, Hutcheon discusses the work of Findley, examining in particular *Famous Last Words* (1981) and *The Telling of Lies* (1986), as well as, to a lesser extent, *The Wars*. Hutcheon draws attention to the narrator's description of photographs and transcripts in *The Wars*, arguing that such descriptions reflect "the novelist's own self-consciousness either about distancing, the marking of absence...or about the fact that this 'evidence' is many times removed from any historical 'reality.'"[10] Other critics, including Brydon and Vauthier, had anticipated Hutcheon's discussion of the novel's narrative self-consciousness and representation of history,[11] but Hutcheon linked *The Wars* and Findley's other works (as well as several other Canadian novels written in the late 1970s and 1980s) with the category of "historiographic metafiction," which she defined as

> historical novels...[that are] very metafictional in their attention to the processes of writing, reading, and interpreting. They are both self-consciously fictional but also overtly concerned with the acts (and consequences) of the reading and writing of history as well as fiction... [Historiographic metafictions are] a critical counterpoint-

ing or dialogue between the 'texts' of both history and art, done in such a way that it *does not deny the existence or significance of either.*[12]

Hutcheon's conception of postmodern literature is not so radical as to do away completely with the touchstone of history or, as Cobley might have it, to reject as dishonest older representations, either literary or historical, of the past. Though Hutcheon admits that "[the] phenomenon does betray a loss of faith in what were once the certainties, the 'master' narratives of our liberal humanist culture... that loss need not be a debilitating one. In postmodern literature... it has meant a new vitality, a new willingness to *enter into a dialogue with history* on new terms."[13]

Depending heavily on Hutcheon's work, Martin Kuester picked up on the analysis of the Canadian historical novel in *Framing Truths: Parodic Structures in Contemporary English-Canadian Historical Novels*, using *The Wars* and *Famous Last Words* to discuss the category of "metafictional histories," and declaring that "Timothy Findley is without a doubt one of the foremost contemporary Canadian writers of 'fictive history.'"[14] Kuester's reading of *The Wars*, however, moves away from Hutcheon's ideal of "dialogue," focusing instead on the way the parodic elements of Findley's work reveal *The Wars* as "a historical novel about the inhumanities of war and the casualties it inflicts on human beings and nature, as a novel, too, which 'implicitly claims that it illuminates the past better than history' by showing how life (human and animal) is really affected."[15] Kuester's use of the phrase "really affected" reflects his sense, like Cobley's, that Findley's version of the First World War is not only accurate but also constructive, especially in the way the novel apparently counters attempts to "suppress the disturbing memory of an aberrant violence."[16]

More recently, two other book-length surveys of Canadian historical fiction have cited *The Wars* as a characteristic historiographic metafiction. In *"Trading Magic for Fact," Fact for Magic: Myth and Mythologizing in Postmodern Canadian Historical Fiction*, Marc Colavincenzo focuses on such novels as Rudy Wiebe's *A Discovery of Strangers*, Michael Ondaatje's *Coming Through Slaughter* and *Running in the Family*, Susan Swan's *The Biggest Modern Woman in the World*, Gwendolyn MacEwen's *Noman's Land*, and *The Wars*. In his introduction, Colavincenzo outlines his project to investigate how in the process of "deconstructing and demythologizing history... [such works] also [give] history a mythic twist by working with preexisting myth, by including the legendary, the magical and the unlikely in [their] treatment of history, and by making the ordinary extraordinary."[17] It is the idea of "making the ordinary extraordinary" that frames Colavincenzo's analysis of Findley's novel, which ends with a reading of Robert Ross's freeing of the horses. This act, Colavincenzo argues, is simple, not major, almost banal, not heroic in any standard sense of the word. But this is the point. Robert does not go out and win the war or a battle single-handedly. His act is the type of act which an ordinary soldier and human might be capable of. The novel portrays a possible human reality behind questionable official history, raising Robert above the ordinary through the context of his action.[18]

Colavincenzo concludes his study by suggesting that contemporary reimaginings of history that end up mythologizing fictional moments force one to rethink the "limitations, contradictions, and biases" of "history itself,"[19] because of the way previously marginalized histories are given power and because the "truth value of myth...speaks to something deeper in us."[20] Setting aside Colavincenzo's odd characterization of "standard" accounts of the First World War—none of which, as far as I know, make claims that any one person "[won] the war or a battle single-handedly"—it is clear from his analysis that his praise of Findley's novel depends on the idea that "official history" is "questionable." It is difficult, however, to determine what exactly Colavincenzo means by "official history," for his study does not refer to a single historical work on the events of the First World War, or to any other series of events from Canadian history. Suffice it to say that to an even more striking degree than Kuester or Cobley, Colavincenzo's privileging of Canadian postmodern historical fiction rejects Hutcheon's concept of dialogue between contemporary fictions and other types of discourse "that does not deny the existence or significance of either."

Herb Wyile's *Speculative Fictions: Contemporary Canadian Novelists and the Writing of History*, which examines many of the same works as Colavincenzo's study, is by far the most attuned to the idea of dialogue. Wyile introduces Hutcheon's work on historiographic metafiction to frame a discussion of the way "contemporary fiction about history and historical subjects has...increasingly represent[ed] the past not 'as it really was' but as it is being constructed by some interpreting agent."[21] Wyile does not go as far as Kuester in terms of marking contemporary fictions as necessarily taking up a parodic view of "official" history, though he raises the issue of the way writers of historiographic metafiction reveal a "scepticism about objectively representing the past, the recognition of the mediation of the past in historiography and fictional discourse, and the struggle to find an appropriate form for addressing historical and historiographical issues."[22] Again, Wyile turns first to *The Wars* to examine these issues, asserting that the novel "has been widely and rightly recognized as a ground-breaking historical novel in Canada because of its deheroicizing of the traditionally heroicized role of Canadians in World War I, but more so because of the metafictional strategies that Findley deploys in the novel to denaturalize the presentation of history."²³ Significantly, the ensuing examination of the novel focuses on the issue of metafictional strategies and has very little to say about deheroicizing, as if it is to be taken for granted that countering traditional history in this way is unproblematic and worthwhile.

Wyile returns to the issue of contemporary fictions' relationship to extant, traditional history in the conclusion to his study. Here, he argues convincingly that the novels he has examined—which are all written after *The Wars*, during what Wyile sees as a slightly differentiated period—though sometimes judicious in their attitude toward traditional history, do not reject out of hand the idea of a stable historical record. Novels such as Urquhart's *Away*, Vanderhaeghe's *The Englishman's Boy*, Margaret Atwood's *Alias Grace*, and Wayne Johnston's *The Colony of Unrequited Dreams*, Wyile suggests, "come across as less profoundly sceptical about historiography, less concerned with fracturing and interrogating retrospection, and largely, if somewhat ambivalently, rooted in historical verisimilitude and an engagement with (rather than abandonment or disruption of) the historical record."²⁴ Cabajsky and Grubisic further note that, for many of the critics whose work is included in *National Plots*, the issue of "the social role of historical fiction" is taken up via "a shared vocabulary of responsibility,"²⁵ whereby the critical move is to examine how authors of Canadian historical fiction have sought to consider our complex relationship with the recorded past, as opposed to simply disparaging the record. Interestingly, Wyile notes that during the writing of *Speculative Fictions*, Jack Hodgins's *Broken Ground* (1998) was published; thus, almost every contemporary Canadian reimagining of the First World War discussed in this study, including Cumyn's and Urquhart's novels, belongs to what might be termed a post-historiographic metafictional period, or at least a period when authors began to signal a distinctive interest in dialogue with the past, a dialogue that, paradoxically, seeks out a sense of stability rather than ambivalence and flux.

In *The Underpainter*, Urquhart moves away from self-reflexivity with a narrative that is focalized through a single, realistically conceived persona. Urquhart does not create a postmodern pastiche out of the documents she refers to in her acknowledgements, which include both historical studies and such primary source material as letters from Canadian soldiers, Rockwell Kent's autobiography, and the writings of Robert Henri.²⁶ Rather, she has used her research for "inspirational purposes" and has changed "recognizable places and events...to fit the shape of the narrative."²⁷ Likewise, in *The Stone Carvers*, the historical figure of Walter Allward "is used in the text in a purely fictitious manner."²⁸ The acknowledgements sections of Cumyn's novels tell a similar tale: Cumyn has consulted many historical works, as well as national archives and the Canadian War Museum, but insists that both novels are "work[s] of fiction."[29] Cumyn also points out that for both *The Sojourn* and *The Famished Lover*, he made use of "family history and mythology,"[30] in particular the memoir and family history of Philip Arthur Cumyn and a letter of condolence sent to his family upon the death of one of his great-uncles.[31] Even more significant than what each author has to say about her or his approach to historical research and the way such research is incorporated into fiction is the fact that neither incorporates into their fictional work moments of self-reflexivity on the process of historical research, or on the complex process by which historical, public figures are made into characters in their novels. Though both authors acknowledge the time they personally have spent in the archives, they do not textualize the archivist figure, thus moving even further away from the formal marking of metafictional self-consciousness of novels written in the heyday of Canadian postmodern historical fiction and remarked upon by critics responding to that work.

The abandoning of the textualized archivist figure and of other indicators of metafiction in the First World War novels of Cumyn and Urquhart is related to a desire to express an attitude toward the war in particular, and toward history in general: one that seeks to "convey that the past matters."[32] This is not to suggest that either novelist wants to glorify the war by ignoring the numerous historical accounts of the battles, the causalties, or the political scandals associated with the war (as it happens, counter to the way Kuester and Colavincenzo characterize "official histories" of the war, Tim Cook shows in *Clio's Warriors: Canadian Historians and the Writing of the World Wars* that though "the official historians were indeed petitioned and pressured…they fought against writing 'court history' that would simply please their political and military masters.")[33] Cumyn's depiction of the battlefront portrays all manner of horror and loss, and in her interview with Wyile, Urquhart refers to the war as "a terrible tragedy, massive."[34] Still, each author also wants to explore how that series of events, now so entirely remote, overwhelming, and incomprehensible, might have the potential to speak to contemporary ideals in a way that implicitly confirms the war's productiveness. While Cumyn returns to the subject of the First World War in order to meditate on a narrative about masculine ideals and a Canadian concern with being on the right side of history, Urquhart considers the way the experience of loss can become a catalyst for intimacy and the building of community. Each novelist entertains a sense of nostalgia for a particular approach to history, whereby participation in the war and the cultural work of remembering that participation via the writing of historical fiction helps tell Canadians something about who they are and, thus, provides a welcome sense of stability in an uncertain world.

In contrast to representing the archivist, the First World War novels of both Cumyn and Urquhart depict the artist. Cumyn's artist is a soldier-artist and, as shown below, Cumyn draws upon the familiar figure from British First World War literature of the soldier-poet. British literary and cultural critics have looked at the poetry of Wilfred Owen and Siegfried Sassoon and the art of Paul Nash and C.R.W. Nevinson, as well as contemporary British literature about the war, in terms of the function of the war insider as "truth teller." Cumyn's representation of the soldier-artist in *The Sojourn* and *The Famished Lover*, by contrast, focuses on how the private circulation of art among soldiers is associated with the confirmation of a vital masculinity that is, paradoxically, best expressed in the war situation that brutalizes the individual man. Urquhart, who more so than Cumyn signals her discomfort with postmodern approaches to history that favour the war outsider's perspective over the war insider's, focuses on how experiences of horror and loss do not obligate the witness to truth telling. Urquhart states in her interview with Wyile that "I'm more interested in how people forget or why people forget... than whether or not we should or shouldn't."[35] Both *The Underpainter* and *The Stone Carvers* imagine ways that war insiders might find the means to forget safely, and this focus on the process of forgetting reflects an attitude toward the past concerned primarily with how the living make use of it to forge a sense of community. Thus, both authors explicitly participate in a uniquely Canadian mythologizing of the First World War as a site where the collective remembrance of war can simultaneously denounce the horrors of war and celebrate its productive effects.

Feeding the Man: Alan Cumyn's Representation of the Soldier-Artist in *The Sojourn* and *The Famished Lover*

Cumyn, perhaps more so than any other writer examined in this study, emphasizes tropes commonly associated with contemporary British reimaginings of the war, those that Sharon Ouditt enumerates as associated with "the theme of subaltern disillusion," as well as such familiar images as "northern France, trenches, gas, rats, lice, moldering corpses, incompetent generals... and the all-devouring mud."[36] In particular, Cumyn's two novels resonate with the acclaimed *Regeneration* series written by Pat Barker, not only because—as with Barker's portrayal of Dr. W.H.R. Rivers and Billy Prior—Cumyn chooses to revisit the character Ramsay Crome in more than one novel, but also because both Barker's works and Cumyn's explore the chasm between soldiers and those on the home front, the relationship between war and the erotic, and the way hallucinations and nightmares become part of the soldier's experience. Also, whereas Barker uses the works of British soldier-poets Owen and Sassoon as important touchstones, Cumyn's Ramsay is a visual artist whose output is informed by his trench experience and thereby engages the tension between the modernist impulse toward what Samuel Hynes refers to as "ugliness ... [as] truth-telling"[37] and nationalist memorial.

In "Regenerating Wilfred Owen: Pat Barker's Revisions," Kaley Joyes examines the way Barker's *Regeneration* uses Owen's poems as intertexts, sometimes more and sometimes less explicitly: "while Barker clearly reworks Owen's 'The Dead-Beat' and 'Anthem for Doomed Youth' into narrative, she uses 'The Parable of the Old Man and the Young' and 'Disabled' without drawing attention to her intertextual actions."[38] Joyes argues that, by occasionally camouflaging her textual allusions, Barker "challenges the authorial privilege conferred by the aesthetic of direct experience,"[39] thus making Owen's protest of the war comprehensible and available to those who are not first-hand witnesses. In considering why so many contemporary British reimaginings of the First World War revisit familiar tropes, Ouditt notes: "It seems that Owen, Sassoon, Graves and others have told us how to remember [the war], and it seems disrespectful to betray them. Perhaps we do not want those myths to be shattered."[40] Both Joyes and Ouditt point out that, even in such a challenging series as Barker's *Regeneration* trilogy, the condemnation sounded during and immediately after the war by British soldier-poets is ultimately confirmed. Despite Barker's contemporary prism, the basic attitude toward the war remains stable.

As Danielle Schaub notes in "Caught Between Desire to Live and Sense of Duty: Traumatized Narrative in Alan Cumyn's *The Sojourn*," Cumyn's first First World War novel differs from Barker's *Regeneration* in terms of its focus on "just a few days of Canadian soldier Ramsay's war experiences."[41] Schaub's assessment of the way Cumyn's prose "calls on all senses and narrates action at the front as if at the moment of occurrence ... convey[ing] events in mechanical and deadened rhythms,"[42] highlights how Cumyn's writing of trench experience in *The Sojourn* (and, by extension, that of the prisoner of war's experience in *The Famished Lover*) echoes the formal techniques of combatant novels, such as those examined by Cobley. Cumyn's simulation of the way combatant novels, as Cobley argues, "resort to description as their primary explanatory principle,"[43] corresponds logically to the way his two novels rehearse many of the same grievances against the war that tend to be associated with British soldier-poetry and fiction. Both Ouditt and David Trotter, following the work of Bernard Bergonzi, Eric Leed, and Samuel Hynes, enumerate features of the "paradigmatic British war novel"[44] that are picked up on by Cumyn, including the ways in which such texts depict "the incapacitating effects of an education in disgust";[45] the incompetence of the officer class; the psychological trauma experienced by soldiers, and the fact that the war is not won, but simply "suffer[ed]"[46] or miraculously "survive[d]."[47] In the Canadian context, Charles Yale Harrison's *Generals Die in Bed*, published in England in 1930, fits very well into this paradigm, as is evidenced by Cobley's inclusion of it among her corpus of First World War combatant narratives. In *Death So Noble*, Vance compares the way Harrison's novel was "vilified" by Canadian readers for its coarseness and pessimism to the way Will Bird's *And We Go On*—also published in 1930—was admired for its representation of the Canadian soldier as "clean in a metaphorical sense. Despite the inescapable dirt surrounding their bodies, the souls and spirits of Bird's soldiers remain pure."[48]

In the furiously paced first section of *The Sojourn*, Cumyn emphasizes what are often for him the twinned paradigmatic features of the staggering, physical horrors of the subaltern's trench experience and the stupidity and arrogance of officers whose ill-advised wielding of authority is at least partly to blame for those horrors. Cumyn explores a motif that Cobley describes in her discussion of the way combatant narratives represent "the soldier's contradictory subject position... [whereby] the soldier assumes that officers are active agents in control not only of themselves but of the world of men under their command."[49] As Cobley explains, the representation of the officer as a type of enemy is associated with the way in which mechanized warfare undermines the soldier's ability to cast himself in heroic terms; thus, "disappointed in the war as a test of manhood, soldiers blamed officers for their sense of impotence by accusing them of being guilty of caprice, maliciousness, ignorance, and incompetence."[50] The novel's first scene depicts Ramsay, a mere private in his unit, trying to pull a fellow soldier, Johnson, out of the suffocating mud. Ramsay feigns to an interfering lieutenant, who has advised Ramsay that "if a man has fallen in he's to be left to his own devices,"[51] that the man sinking is a major and therefore worthy of saving. The lieutenant's toadying is made to seem all the more repulsive as it is juxtaposed with Johnson's near-death experience in the mud and the chaos of an artillery barrage, during which the narrator describes making his way through the disgusting detritus of war.

The thematic juxtaposition of the horrors of war with the incompetence of the officer class is repeated twice more in the next forty pages of text, before Ramsay's unit is given leave to return to billets. During a rare break from what is depicted as their back-breaking and mind-numbing work as trench builders, Ramsay and members of his unit take time to discuss the quarrel between General Edwin Alderson and Munitions Minister Sam

Hughes about the continued use of the oft-malfunctioning Ross rifle. This is the second time the problem of the Ross rifle emerges in *The Sojourn;* earlier, the narrator Ramsay had mused to himself about the rifle's deficiencies as a combat weapon, its tendency to "jam."[52] Snug, an older member of the unit, whom Ramsay thinks of "like a father,"[53] now opines during the general discussion that "if the minister of munitions could pull his head out of his arse for a moment he'd fix it so we'd have the right rifles and enough artillery to finish this work and all go home."[54] Reese, the unit's "clown," responds that "someone told me Hughes is trying to throw Alderson out for criticizing the Ross rifle."[55] Ramsay, despite his earlier contemplation of the Ross rifle, states that he has no real patience for such discussions:

> I try not to think about ministers and generals. It just gives me a headache... The truth is that Fritz won't back down until we've fed him enough iron. It's all the Germans believe in, and if we don't give it to them, they'll give it to us. I came to paint signs, but since I'm here I'll do what it takes. We'll win despite the generals and politicians.[56]

As Tim Cook notes, Alderson and Hughes did indeed engage in some high-profile wrangling about the Ross rifle; when Alderson "urged the War Office to have the Ross replaced with the Lee-Enfield... Hughes reacted with characteristic anger, deriding Alderson in a letter he sent to all commanding officers in the Canadian Corps, belittling the general's judgment."[57] Whether it is credible that infantrymen as low down in the military's hierarchy as the men in Ramsay's unit would have a sense of this power struggle is one point of interest. There are numerous instances in Cumyn's novels when this somewhat anachronistic sensibility emerges, such as when Ramsay meditates on newspaper reports about the mass deportation of Armenians from Turkey, a series of events that have only more recently become a well-established site of concern, or in the way Ramsay's father has access to classified and complex information about war profiteering. However, the marked focus on the Ross rifle is thematically significant in terms of the way it indicates Cumyn's desire to privilege the figure of the dogged, dutiful Canadian subaltern.[58] It is this abiding objective to celebrate the concept of duty that distinguishes Cumyn's novels, especially from the paradigmatic British subaltern-text. While Ramsay and members of his unit are certainly pounded, both physically and mentally, by the horrors of mechanized warfare, they are represented as doing more than merely suffering or surviving (or not surviving) the war; these Canadian soldiers "win despite the generals and politicians," even if just by maintaining a fierce sense of "do[ing] what it takes."

As discussed in Chapter 1, Guy Vanderhaeghe takes up a less customary perspective in *Dancock's Dance*, focusing on the officer's struggle to come to terms with his own leadership; here, a comparison of Vanderhaeghe's portrayal of the officer with Cumyn's is illuminating. Cumyn's depiction of Lieutenant Lentworth in *The Sojourn*, in a scene almost immediately following the discussion mentioned above, is a familiar rendition of the incompetent officer whose orders directly contribute to the death of infantrymen. Ramsay reports to Lentworth, who is described as "a new man with the unit... soft-looking, as if he'd be hard-pressed to accomplish a push-up or shoulder his own pack,"[59] that a German sniper is in position behind their dugout. Lentworth rebuffs Ramsay's suggestion that the men launch bombs at the structure in which the sniper is probably hiding, and instead sends Ramsay and two other men on what is essentially a suicide mission; when Ramsay tries to explain this to Lentworth, the officer threatens to have Ramsay "shot for either insubordination or cowardice."[60] Not surprisingly, given the novel's clear adherence to the motif of subaltern disillusion, both Snug and another soldier die as a result of following Lentworth's obviously ill-informed and possibly mean-spirited orders. In Vanderhaeghe's version of a similar military moment, Dancock is faced not with a difference of opinion but with a soldier's paralyzing fear; feeling that he must assert his authority, he shoots a soldier for insubordination when the soldier refuses to go over the top.[61] As I have argued, however, Vanderhaeghe's drama absolves Dancock of this killing because it is presented in the context of a man trying to come to terms with his "natural" role as a leader, and within the exploration of a kind of masculinity that depends on confirming stable codes of honour. In *The Sojourn*, the perspective of the plain soldier is clearly preferred: Cumyn explores a masculinity that seems different from the sort that concerns Vanderhaeghe, but that is probably the other side of the same coin. Both writers are interested in defending fairly traditional notions of masculine honour and duty: whereas *Dancock's Dance* examines what it means to lead, both of Cumyn's war novels focus on what it means to be part of a unit of men and how masculine identity requires absolute loyalty to that unit.

In her study of masculinity and the British experience of the First World War, Joanna Bourke examines how the war provided an important and potent context for male bonding, defined as the "intimate, emotional interaction between men in which the individual identifies himself as an integral part of an all-male group."[62] After examining how factors such as British military culture and history, the British public school tradition, and the physical conditions of the trench experience encouraged male bonding, Bourke argues that such bonds failed to be maintained in peacetime for two reasons. First, the deeply ingrained British consciousness of class distinctions could never be entirely transcended, for "the ideology of male comradeship in war was never intended to subvert military rank and its associations with socio-economic class."[63] Second, when British servicemen returned to England after the war, they were eager to rejoin the domestic fold: "there was a greater stress on domestic emotional ties as being necessary to the stability of a masculine personality—and male-to-male friendships were increasingly seen as undermining (rather than complimenting) adult masculinity."[64] Ouditt points out that sorting through the "burdens of manhood"[65] as they are associated with sexuality, class, and masculinity is a predominant focus for contemporary British writers, including Barker, Sebastian Faulks (*Birdsong*, 1993), and Kate Atkinson (*Behind the Scenes at the Museum*, 1995).

Cumyn's representation of male bonding and its relationship to notions of masculinity differs from the pattern Bourke and Ouditt identify in British literature and culture as he works to establish the distinct characteristics of the Canadian First World War experience. This objective further explains the author's highlighting of the Canadian soldier's fraught experience with the Ross rifle, which Cook refers to as "Canada's national arm."[66] The narrative of *The Sojourn* continually marks Ramsay as a Canadian soldier. For example, his Uncle Manfred rehearses the story of the poison gas attack on Allied soldiers during the Second Battle of Ypres (1915), when, "my God, those Canadian troops held firm";[67] and his cousin Margaret tries to defend her fiancé's relative unfitness for the physical demands of warfare by contending, "'But you've lived in the wilds of Canada,'... 'You haven't grown up breathing the filth of London air. You're strong and fit and you probably already knew how to shoot a rifle before you joined up.'"[68] Margaret's desperation in this scene reveals Cumyn's ironic use of the stereotype of the "rugged, masculine identity"[69] that Renée Hulan identifies as part of the myth of Canadian Nordic culture; however, Cumyn's attention to the way Ramsay's masculinity is marked as different from British masculinity suggests that he also depends on the myth Hulan delineates. Furthermore, when Uncle Manfred wants to know why Ramsay enlisted as a private, "especially at a time when sons from the leadership classes are required to take their rightful positions," Ramsay becomes indignant: "'I knew nothing about waging war,' I say, feeling the hair bristling on the back of my neck. 'And if there's one thing all of us soldiers have learned, it's that officers should have a decent idea of what they're doing. When I joined up I had no pretensions about being better than anyone else. I simply wanted to do my bit and then go home.'"[70] Thus, Ramsay makes it clear to his British family members that, as a Canadian, he disdains their notions of class distinctions.

The narrative trajectory of *The Sojourn* and *The Famished Lover* portrays Ramsay's continual chafing against domestic space, from his inability to get used to the comforts of home during his leave in London and his choice to spend much of that leave drinking with fellow soldiers to his increasing unhappiness being married to Lillian, as represented in Ramsay's second First World War novel. The series of civilian living spaces described in *The Famished Lover* reflect the way Ramsay's masculinity is threatened by domesticity: the cabin he and Lillian go to on their honeymoon—on the advice of Ramsay's much more financially successful younger brother Rufus—is a cold, filthy shack; their apartment in Montreal is damp, small, and depressing; Lillian's father's home is taken away by the bank, and the house Ramsay and Lillian build burns down. While Cumyn's focus in *The Famished Lover* on the difficulty of adjusting to civilian life is not unique, the plotting of this series of domestic calamities is somewhat odd in terms of the way such scenes are juxtaposed with scenes depicting Ramsay's experiences as a prisoner of war. On the one hand, Ramsay's near-starvation in the German barracks, his agonizing stretch spent in an outdoor pit during solitary confinement, and the pathos of his escaping the camp only to find out, when he is nearly dead of exhaustion, that "the war is over, has been for two days,"[71] are all meant to enlarge *The Sojourn*'s focus on the war's horrors. On the other hand, it is as a POW rather than as a civilian that Ramsay finds himself among a community he can identify and communicate with, as when he draws nude sketches of women for them so as to "*help them remember the lovelier world beyond the wire.*"[72] Back at home, Ramsay is poor, while Rufus, the brother who did not fight, is wealthy. When Rufus tries to offer his older brother money, the response is "'I've handled far worse than this,'"[73] indicating that it is in war that the text locates Ramsay's masculine identity. In his marital relations, he is increasingly unmanned, as when Lillian interrupts their lovemaking because they cannot afford to have another child; yet he has an affair with Dorothy, who is attracted to him precisely because his eyes have "seen things. They know what they want."[74] In the letters Ramsay writes to Margaret from the camp, he claims to yearn for the world "*beyond the wire,*" but he is consistently represented as less of a man once he reaches that destination.

Cumyn's novels can further be distinguished from contemporary British reimaginings of the war in terms of how they represent the relationship between Ramsay and his father. In *A War Imagined*, Samuel Hynes notes that "the theme of the Old Men—the conviction that the war had empowered the elderly to send the young to their deaths,"[75] persists in many wartime and postwar British forms of expression, from popular journalism to novels, poetry, and visual art. Hynes further notes that "in common

British usage...Old Men was and is a generation term. But it was a class term as well. Wartime and post-war explosions of wrath against the Old Men were not directed at Old Farmers or Old Postmen, after all."[76] In *The Sojourn*, the narrator broaches the issue of familial intergenerational conflict almost immediately, when Ramsay comments that Snug is "like a father. Like no father I ever had."[77] This enigmatic comment is made sense of as the novel progresses: Uncle Manfred and Aunt Harriet relay stories of the elder Crome's eccentric passion for a South American Aboriginal woman as well as his legendary unsociability, while Ramsay tells his cousins about the time when he was seventeen and his father took him by train from the West Coast to Montreal, gave him fifty dollars, and left him. As Ramsay explains to his incredulous family, "'He wanted me to stand on my own feet, to be a man,'"[78] having earlier mused that an important part of becoming a man was, in his father's mind, "get[ting Ramsay] out from under [his] mother's skirts."[79] Yet the representation of Ramsay's father does not culminate in a version of "the theme of the Old Men." On the contrary, when Ramsay meets up with his father while on leave in London, the narrative makes it clear that the Canadian version of being pushed to become "a man" diverges from the British paradigm.

Like his son, Ramsay's father declares his contempt for the British class system, founding his disapproval of Ramsay's clear affection for his British cousin Margaret on the grounds that "there's nothing here for the likes of us. It's too crowded with eldest sons sitting on their wealth."[80] After trying to convince Ramsay to accept a transfer away from the front lines by referring to scandals of war profiteering, the elder Crome pronounces, "if other men want to send their sons off to slaughter for dubious reasons, then so be it, but you and I don't have to be part of the generalized insanity."[81] The image of sending sons to slaughter is precisely the same biblical allusion to the story of Abraham's binding of Isaac that Owen, and later Barker, make use of to describe British generational conflict, while the narrative's reference to the war as "generalized insanity" echoes the common trope in British anti-war rhetoric that the war was simply madness. In an inversion of "the theme of Old Men," Ramsay argues with his father that it is his "duty" to return to the front, while later determining that, in fact, "this is not his [father's] war."[82] In his study *Northern Love: An Exploration of Canadian Masculinity*, Paul Nonnekes argues that in American culture and literature the male affirms his masculinity in terms of an Oedipal father figure, becoming the "frontier male, virile, uncontained, and proudly violent";[83] in contrast to this, Canadian assertions of masculinity develop in conjunction with the notion of the imaginary father figure. Nonnekes explains that "the imaginary father is a figure...that provides the mother's love but at a distance from the wrapping of the mother;"[84] thus, "northern males, at least northern males who can be said to be heroes, do not flee the domesticated mother to identify with a powerful, undomesticated father, but remain tied to the mother's love and from that base negotiate a relationship to the father and his love."[85] Nonnekes's argument helps illuminate both Cumyn's inversion of the British paradigm and his representation of Ramsay's masculinity in the following way: first, Ramsay's father's insistence that his son "be a man" is not predicated on an Oedipal structure, for manliness is linked with pragmatism and a sense of duty to the mother country rather than with expressions of outsize and independent virility; and second, Ramsay's father is clearly, even anachronistically, on the right side of history, having already rejected the untenable class structure that defines the crumbling Old World. Finally, Ramsay's unqualified sense of duty, his sense that this is "his war" to fight, reflects Cumyn's sense that Canadian soldiers—Canadian sons—did not merely suffer the war; they fought to win, doing so to exercise not a sense of heroism but rather a sense of duty.

Ramsay Crome's status as an artist offers a final point of comparison with British paradigms. In his discussion of the way British soldier-artists represented their war experiences, Hynes identifies two major elements that came to define an emerging approach that coincided with similar developments in soldier-poetry. First, British soldier-art, in particular the work of Paul Nash, C.R.W. Nevinson, and William Orpen, represented "the disfigurements of the earth,"[86] as the British tradition of landscape painting was entirely overturned by depictions of chaotic and ruined natural spaces. Second, artists associated the attempt to depict "ugliness" as a type of "truth telling"; thus, the visual art of the First World War reflected the idea that "war is the end of beauty—and the end of beauty's conventions; that was one of the truths that had to be told."[87] In *Art or Memorial? The Forgotten History of Canada's War Art*, Laura Brandon examines the history of the national war art collection, exploring the competing interests of those intent on preserving commemorative and nationalist art versus those, such as the Group of Seven painters, who "aimed to help create the myth of a new, modern, and national school of art."[88] Brandon argues that this "new" approach to art was in part associated with the Group's war experiences: "many of its subjects after 1920—particularly dead trees and devastated ground—owe much to the landscape of war."[89] Brandon goes on to note, though, that "only careful formal analysis of the paintings can illuminate one now-forgotten source of the Group's art—the detritus of war and empire. Establishing a consensual vision of nation required a 'forgetting' that hid past histories and influences that did not fit the emerging model."[90] In considering how certain kinds of Canadian war art have become canonical, Brandon argues that "the best known focuses on the figurative, the landscape, and, above all, the heroic act,"[91] suggesting that the history of Canada's official war collection has often been subject to state-informed, strategic forgetting. Such scholarship on First World War soldier-artists operates as a useful context for exploring the representation over two novels of Ramsay Crome as a soldier-artist figure, particularly in terms of the identifiable tension between the impetus towards the "truth telling" of depicted ruin and the nationalistic memorial.

Over the course of *The Sojourn* and *The Famished Lover*, Cumyn shows how Ramsay undertakes three different kinds of artistic work: war art, commercial art, and privately circulated erotic art. In the long section of *The Sojourn* describing Ramsay's leave in London, he is often called upon by his cousin Margaret to describe the trenches, which he refuses to do. When he returns to the front, however, he makes a sketch, "with hard lines and dark shading, of an empty-eyed, grinning skull, teeth smashed in on one side, a sorry cigarette poking out the other."[92] He then writes a letter to Margaret meant to accompany the sketch, finally able to communicate part of his "story" to her and trying to show her that "it's not a theory, or an exercise, or even something most of us can talk about rationally."[93] This representation of the soldier-artist as truth teller, as the seer who has both the unique capacity and the sacred obligation to expose the war for what it is, is briefly followed up in *The Famished Lover*. Ramsay continues to send sketches to Margaret, portraying for her the awfulness of the POW barracks, and tries (and fails) to sell some of his "grimmer work about the war" to a commercial gallery in Montreal.[94] The two novels, however, do not focus primarily on this truth-telling function of the soldier-artist, and *The Famished Lover* indicates Ramsay's increasing ambivalence about this role: after initially trying to save his canvases from the fire when he and Lillian's house burns down, in the end he decides to "let them burn."[95] When he later speaks to Margaret about his attempt to repaint some of these canvases, it is clear that he has decided to repaint more images of Margaret than of the war; he imagines her looking at one that depicts her "sitting in the water, the sunlight favouring her right breast."[96]

Though Cumyn's textual representations of the war depend heavily on immediate, often graphically violent description, his representation of the artist is ultimately more concerned with how the war insider retains the ability to recollect beauty privately rather than portray ugliness publicly. The sustained characterization of Ramsay as a commercial artist by trade, from his initial enlistment in the war effort for what he thinks will be a job as a sign painter, through his work for Justin Frame as a commercial artist, to his employment with Dorothy Dorsett at a pin-up agency, reveals further that for Ramsay the function of widely circulating art is mostly unrelated to the way he thinks about the war. In this way, the important meaning of private art is put into further relief. What Cumyn wishes to focus on is not how the work of the soldier-artist operates as a memorial of the war—whether nationalistically approving or damning, truthful or untruthful—but rather how the work of the soldier-artist reveals the soldier to be an individual, a singular man capable of passion.

Ramsay tells his cousin Emily, younger sister of his beloved Margaret, that he is interested in painting "faces"—what he calls "the human aspect"[97]—rather than landscapes. Though Emily's own "fussy" paintings of "blurry hedgerow[s]" and "cows in a pasture"[98] are clearly representative of the style of landscape painting that Hynes argues was eradicated by the war, Cumyn does not present Ramsay as a follower of the Group of Seven (whose characteristic landscape paintings, Brandon suggests, "owe much to the landscape of war").[99] And though Ramsay tells Emily that he paints faces, Cumyn often depicts him drawing nude female bodies, from the sketch he gives to Emily just before returning to the front, through his drawings of Lillian, to the sketches he generates upon request for his fellow POWs. When he writes to Margaret about these sketches, he explains that "*in this weird and upside-down place an artist like me is suddenly wealthy. For men will trade with me all manner of things—their chocolate, even, their cakes from home, tinned meats, books, long underwear—for a scrap of paper with certain lines.*"[100]

The question of the value of Ramsay's artistic activity is raised in an early scene in *The Famished Lover*, when it is explained to him that he must be careful not to give his German captors the impression that his civilian job skills might "be useful to their war effort"; some of his fellow prisoners have told the Germans that they have such useless jobs as "lion tamer," "magician," and "bullfighter."[101] When Ramsay claims to be "an artist," the profession is meant to register as correspondingly worthless, though of course the inference is that art just might be more culturally productive than lion taming. Unlike Urquhart, whose representation of the non-combatant memorial artist is discussed below, Cumyn does not pursue this possibility. The nude drawings that Ramsay creates for the prisoners are a commodity he exchanges for food and other items. Those drawings are especially valuable to the captured men because they help sustain their humanity; the eroticized female bodies remind each individual man of his stolen vitality and virility. As Ramsay muses, the sketches make the men "animated," "full of fun," and given to "laugh[ing] like little boys." Furthermore, each man is "impatient to own the sketch as soon as I'm finished";[102] like Ramsay's collection of erotic paintings of Margaret, which he angrily tells Lillian are "mine and mine alone...not for you or the world,"[103] the point of this art is not to memorialize the war, but to feed the famished man. Just as with the regular references to Ramsay's modest aspiration to "do my bit and then go home," Cumyn's representation of the Canadian soldier-artist's work refuses to be subsumed into an allegorical tale whereby the soldier represents truth or sacrifice or the loss of innocence, or who has any particular gift as a cultural seer.

Cumyn's depiction of subaltern and POW war experience certainly makes use of formal techniques associated with the paradigmatic combatant novel. Yet in terms of attitude toward the war, his works may have more in common with Will Bird's *And We Go On* than with Charles Yale Harrison's *Generals Die in Bed*. In the final scenes of *The Famished Lover*, with the Second World War looming, Ramsay is called upon by Margaret to tell her son about his war experiences, if only to dissuade him from enlisting. Ramsay's tale for Margaret's son Alexander, and for the rest of Margaret's family and his own, operates very much as "an education in disgust,"[104] which David Trotter argues is an essential part of the British First World War novel. Ramsay relates an incident when, after he had been captured, he and fifty other POWs were given "sandstorm soup," which they all proceeded to eat out of helmets, out of boots, or off the ground;[105] at one point, he "heaved up the sandstorm soup...But I was so frightened I held it in my mouth. I swallowed it down again."[106] The image corresponds with an overarching theme of *The Famished Lover*, which considers how a man can be nourished in wartime and in civilian spaces that undermine his masculine identity. Still, like the soldiers portrayed by Bird, who "may gripe about their officers, their food, and the war in general,"[107] Ramsay remains devoted to the idea that he is part of a "brotherhood."[108] As Ramsay explains, "we were in defeat, but we were all fighters, you see...We fought, at times, for the pure pleasure of being young men and fighting."[109]

Vance argues that the initial backlash to Harrison's *Generals Die in Bed* can be understood as expressing the notion that "if the war had been as negative as the protest literature suggested, neither the survivors nor the grieving families had anything to be proud of."[110] At first glance, both of Cumyn's novels seem like protest literature, especially in terms of how the depiction of Ramsay's war experience echoes the formal techniques identified by Cobley as associated with early combatant narratives, and how the focus on officer incompetence, bureaucratic dishonesty, and the brutality of the subaltern experience resonates with contemporary British representations of the First World War that do protest the war. Yet the anti-war message that Margaret hopes Ramsay might communicate to her son is not straightforward. Though the sandstorm soup story is meant to convey just "a little part" of the war's horrors, Ramsay follows up the tale with a justification for why an individual might want to go to war: "Not for your country, not for your God, not for somebody's idea of empire, not for democracy or any other ideal, or worse yet, some kind of thrill or adventure. Risk your life only for those you love."[111] Thus, though Cumyn willingly rejects the rhetoric of national or ideological sacrifice, he leaves a space for a type of warfare than a man can still be proud of. Cumyn's remembrance of the war is, paradoxically, predicated on nostalgically locating in that historical moment something that transcends history: the ideal that men can be of service to a caring, dutiful, and honourable community. Whereas the historiographic metafiction is predicated on the pursuit of the gaps in history, Cumyn's novels look back to the past to recover a sense of wholeness.

The Artist and the Witness: Jane Urquhart's *The Underpainter* and *The Stone Carvers*

The crucial difference between the use of historical data in postmodern pastiche and Urquhart's use of history as "inspiration" for two fundamentally realistic novels is in the site of ambivalence. The transparent and often playful juxtaposition of fact and fiction in postmodern pastiche both signals authorial hesitancy and invites readerly skepticism regarding the stability of the historical record. Rather than presuming that facts can speak for themselves, postmodern writers call attention to their ambivalence about such a notion through instances of self-conscious fictionality. In highlighting the control he or she has over historical material, however, the postmodern writer will simultaneously announce that such an exercise of control is essentially meaningless because of the pains taken to make the procedure highly visible and therefore unfixed. That is to say, by emphasizing the re-creation process and, more importantly, the fact that this process is always subject to further playful modification, postmodern fiction absolves itself from the potentially damaging effects of deploying historical data to any particular purpose.

In contrast, the narrator of *The Underpainter*, Austin Fraser, both focalizes the stories of others and uses those stories in his paintings; Urquhart's version of Allward in *The Stone Carvers* is similarly concerned with how to deploy art so as to transcend historical specificity. Fraser and Allward thus replicate the artistic liberty that Urquhart admits to in her acknowledgements, her procedure of controlling history through fiction, and fact through art. Urquhart is unconvinced that experiential distance—especially as it is signalled by the self-conscious literariness in postmodern fiction—necessarily gives rise to a more stable ideological position or a more disinterested depiction of the horrors of war. Both of her First World War novels examine the grounds and functions of outsider renderings, questioning both the authority often granted to artistic reconstructions of experience over experience itself and the ambivalent role of the artist as a commemorator and exploiter of war. Furthermore, the novels interrogate what the operation of commemoration through art does to the witness, especially the witness who may want to forget what he or she has seen. Urquhart, then, is ambivalent not about the idea of the stable record but about the very re-creation process on which historiographic metafiction depends. In *The Underpainter* and *The Stone Carvers*, she turns her attention to the artist whose work derives from the experiences of others; both novels confront the pitfalls of such an artistic approach by employing a realistic mode that eschews the playful use of the historical document in favour of a more generalized historical setting. Urquhart seeks to challenge the superiority granted by Cobley, Kuester, and Colavincenzo to the reconstruction that is fundamental to artistic rendering, especially renderings alluding to circumstances about which the artist has no first-hand knowledge.

Unlike Cumyn, Urquhart avoids representing the subaltern experience. As an American, Austin Fraser—protagonist of *The Underpainter*—has no link to the war except through two Canadians: George Kearns, a china painter he befriends during his visits to Davenport, Ontario, in the summers of 1913 and 1914, and who worked as a pigeon dispatcher during the war; and George's lover, Augusta Moffatt, who comes to live with George in the China Hall after having served as a nurse in France. In *The Stone Carvers*, Eamon's war experience ends when he "vanishe[s],"[112] presumably in an airplane, though the details of his service are never made clear. As for Urquhart's representation of Tilman and Recouvrir, who bear the effects of war on their bodies, it is also the case that their experiences in battle are not depicted. Urquhart, in contrast to Cumyn, is not interested in sorting through how to make sense of the subaltern experience; rather, she is focused on how to make sense of the war insider's scars. Furthermore, Urquhart more so than Cumyn concerns herself with the process of public commemoration and how the effort of remembrance differs radically for the war outsider and the war insider.

Austin's first stays in Davenport are the result of his father's financial stake in a Canadian mine; his subsequent visits to Davenport and other towns on the North Shore of Lake Superior are motivated by his interest in painting. Via the words of his painting teacher Robert Henri that "art is a kind of mining," Austin makes the connection between his father's type of invasion and his own: "How right Robert H. was. About art. About success, ambition. The greed. The exploitation at the expense of nature and humanity. And, in the end, sometimes the beauty."[113] In particular, Part Two of *The Underpainter* dwells on the process whereby Augusta's experiences in Étaples, as well as her experience of recounting what she has witnessed, are mined by Austin for his painting *Night in the China Hall*, a painting he admits is "one of my least satisfactory canvases."[114] Austin's disappointment in the painting stems from his sense that he cannot comprehensively depict all the details of Augusta's story in an aesthetically pleasing manner, and that art can never be comprehensive in representation. The artist's disappointment, however, is set in tension with what the witness undergoes during the portrayal of experience: during her own recounting, Augusta exhausts herself so utterly that she cannot survive the process. Art here does not simply supplement the witness's account but manages, in the operation, to annihilate the witness.

At the beginning of this part of *The Underpainter*, titled "Night in the China Hall," Austin explains that for his most famous series of paintings, known as *The Erasures*, the artist's act of disassembling is crucial. These are works where fragmented images of a particular scene or story are painted with detailed realism and then painted over with several layers until the images are obscured. Austin initially claims that he has not "recomposed" Augusta,[115] and that it is her full story, ostensibly related to Austin on a single winter night in 1937, that has been treated in painting and will be narrated again. However, the formal features of this section and its revelations about Austin's character and behaviour undermine this avowal. First, Augusta's story is focalized for the reader by Austin so that her description of experience is shown at once to be shaped by him and to give his own story shape. For the first part of Augusta's tale, an extended section that concerns her childhood, Austin functions almost like an external narrator who has access to all of Augusta's thoughts and desires; yet even here, Urquhart continually indicates that the story has already been "said" to Austin. For all Cumyn's attention to the soldier-artist figure, Ramsay's process of creation is never particularly at issue; for Urquhart, in contrast, the artist's process is the primary concern.[116] Thus, attention is diverted from Augusta's story—her witness's account of war experience—to how that account functions as a new context for understanding the painter.

The first major interruption into Augusta's story follows directly on her first mention of the war; after this, the episodes of "Night in the China Hall" become truncated, their interest quite various, and chronology forsaken. More and more, Augusta's story is juxtaposed with either descriptions of how Austin has proceeded with a particular painting or with the aged Austin's reflections on his past behaviour. The memory of the war insider, the witness, is thus made to struggle for attention against a narrative focus on the work of the commemorator, to the point where the witness herself is almost entirely "erased" under the layers of the artist's memory and output. The most distressing aspects of Augusta's term at the hospital—her attempts to alleviate the pain of badly hurt soldiers; the exhaustion that leads to her use of morphine; the overdose of the drug she mercifully gives her best friend Maggie, who has been horribly injured in a bombing of the hospital—are unhinged from their original sites of meaning. These experiences become metaphors for Austin about the relationship between representation and anaesthetic that he tries to reveal in his *Erasure* paintings.

The literal and metaphorical use Urquhart makes of morphine signals her interest in distinguishing between the function of memory for the witness and for the artist, a difference that the process of recontextualizing threatens to obscure. The novel's first mention of morphine occurs during a description of Augusta's recovery from a tonsillectomy in a hospital in Davenport, the same hospital she had spent time in years before as a shell shock patient. Morphine is referred to as "Maggie's remembered gift,"[117] and the narrative later discloses that in France, occasionally, when very tired "the girls shared a needle."[118] The tonsillectomy scenes make it clear that, for Augusta, the addiction to morphine is also an addiction to forgetting; the drug benumbs its user to violent dreams and disturbing memories associated with the war. Like Ramsay Crome, both George and Augusta avoid talking to outsiders about the war, though in Ramsay's case this is because he simply distrusts listeners who have not shared his experience. His unwillingness to communicate represents a kind of loyalty to the brotherhood of soldiers, a brotherhood that forms the best context for his masculine identity. In the case of Urquhart's characters, the war insider is not trying to hold on to the past but rather is desperately hoping to move beyond it. When Augusta tells her story to Austin, it is an act of remembering that becomes too much for her. After telling Austin "there is no place at all for unhappiness such as mine in a world as beautiful as this,"[119] she goes to her room and kills herself with an overdose. Her statement indicates that, while the artist may control beauty, the witness both controls and is controlled by unhappiness, and that it is risky to transform one into the other; something (or someone) may be lost in the process.

Urquhart contrasts Augusta's necessary cautiousness regarding her own memories with the recklessness with which Austin uses the memories of others for his own art and whims; he refers to himself as "an accumulator, a hoarder. I trespassed everywhere and thieved constantly."[120] The disconsolation that Austin's meddling will produce in Augusta on the winter night in 1937 is foreshadowed by a scene describing his unwillingness to alleviate the shame of his long-time lover and model Sara, whom he has been two days late in meeting. Having failed to keep an appointment he capriciously made to meet her at a miner's hotel, Austin has forced Sara to endure two days of piteous looks from a strange group of men; after finally showing up, he will not join her in the breakfast room to publicly justify her waiting. He remarks that he wants to be able to "draw [shame] in her face and body, [...to] add pain to the composition." Austin believes he can visualize the miners' memories of lone Sara and asks the reader, "What [...] is more intimate than this: total recollection of a scene I had never witnessed, but one over which I nonetheless had perfect control?"[121] On the night of Augusta's storytelling and suicide, Austin once again meddles with memory by bringing George's pre-war lover Vivian—who left him the day after their elopement—back to the china shop for an impromptu reunion that proves horribly painful to all involved.

The point Urquhart makes here is that though Austin has initiated events, he has not considered himself to be involved. His pursuit of art, the "high art" against which he ridicules George's affinity for the decorative art of china painting, has turned Austin into a ruthless capitalist of loss and sorrow. After finding the bodies of Augusta and George, who has killed himself upon losing Augusta, Austin admits that what has transpired was a result, not of his "cruelty," but of his "carelessness."[122] What is important to note here is that in exploring Austin's belated cognizance of his own part in provoking a double suicide, Urquhart criticizes the artist's detachment from the living source of his art. Significantly, the concluding emphasis on Austin's self-indictment eradicates any sense that Urquhart is concerned with parsing the witness's story for its relative truthfulness or with exploring how the voice of the witness might produce a rethinking of the "official" record, as per the concerns of the historiographic metafiction. The veracity of Augusta's memories is never at issue in the novel. Rather, the narrative suggests that any steps the war insider may take to come to terms with personal trauma, even steps toward forgetting, are justifiable and perhaps necessary.

Though Urquhart's *The Stone Carvers* is likewise taken up with the paradoxical combination of control and detachment that defines an artist's relationship to his or her work, the novel culminates with a very different notion of caprice than the assorted descriptions of Austin's "carelessness." The narrator's declaration that "the impossible happens as a result of whims that turn into obsessions"[123] variously refers to Father Gstir's vision of the stone church in Shoneval, to the wild schemes of King Ludwig, and to the Vimy memorial and the political resolutions that have necessitated its erection. The matter of political "whim," of a nation's part in rendering massacre necessary, even mundane, is suggested repeatedly. Joseph Becker laments the work of the Canadian sawmills, in which he "witnessed the massacre of a tree trunk large enough for a beautiful sculpture of God the Father himself," and that reduce glorious, living trees to "the terrible ordinariness of planking."[124] This image of the destruction of the Canadian forests, felled to serve "an island referred to as the Motherland,"[125] acts as a metaphor for the deaths of soldiers who entered the First World War because of Canada's unquestioning support for England. The novel's framing of this national stance as a type of "carelessness" is clarified by the portrayal of Tilman's work and residence in the artificial limb factory after he returns to Canada as a war veteran:

> An otherwise dull and unpromising civil servant made a name for himself by suggesting that as most of the boys were still on crutches…some of them at least might be gainfully employed making wooden legs for themselves and others like themselves…After a day filled with the problems of construction geometry, bad meals served in the adjacent cafeteria, and struggles with inadequately maintained machinery, the young men, Tilman included, would clump painfully up the stairs to the dormitory. Here at night Tilman's dreams…would be interrupted by the shouts of nightmare-ridden men who had not even begun to recover from the trauma of the war.[126]

Like the trees Joseph grieves for, the young men, now physically and psychically wounded, are regarded only for their potential use-value. Unlike the forests, however, they appear to be non-renewable national resources. Once the need for artificial limbs has been exhausted, "the same government that had called these young men so earnestly to arms now cast them unceremoniously into the streets."[127]

Like Cumyn's *The Famished Lover*, *The Stone Carvers* explicitly critiques the returned soldiers' civilian experience, particularly in terms of how government policies undermined the returned soldiers' efforts to be productive in postwar Canada, simply in terms of finding gainful employment and/or working toward financial and domestic stability. As with Jack Hodgins's *Broken Ground*, the representation in Cumyn's and Urquhart's novels of the Canadian government's failure to take care of its returning soldiers reflects an interest in something other than the idea of the "value" of a soldier's military work. Vance argues that postwar Canadians strove to find ways to frame the war in terms of its "utility: those four years had to have been of some use";[128] for contemporary writers, the idea of "utility" is as important (and perhaps equally metaphorical). While Vance focuses on the way postwar Canadians sought to mythologize the war in terms of its potential to unite a country of uncomplaining, self-sacrificing, and ennobled citizens, Cumyn's writing of the war highlights the way such experience clarifies what it means to be a productive man, while Urquhart considers how the war teaches us about the difference between private forgetting and public efforts of remembrance. Thus, perhaps inconsistently, the utility of remembering the war is that, despite the failure of government to establish a creditable justification for Canada's participation in an "Old World" war and to deal adequately with the war's physical and emotional toll, and even despite a generalized sense that, as a military exercise, the war was a colossal and horrifying waste, contemporary writers often work to consider how the remembrance of the war has produced a shared sense among non-witnesses of how to behave as part of an idealized, active, national community.

Urquhart's use of the term "unceremonious" in her description of the way Tilman and men like him are treated by government is thus set in an ironic tension with the material context of commemoration, in particular the almost fanatical undertakings of the Canadian government to commemorate those who fought and fell in the war. As historian Alan R. Young asserts, in the 1920s and 1930s Canadian war memorials were erected "in almost every city, small town, and village throughout the nation."[129] Most of these memorials communicate "in a spirit of condolence a mythology [... in which the] dead are presented as warriors or knights who have fallen on the field of honour or lie sleeping after sacrificing themselves in defence of some great and good cause."[130] In *The Stone Carvers*, even the artist engaged in "high art" is associated with the forces of a somewhat thoughtless yet overbearing bureaucracy. Initially, Allward's work as a sculptor causes him to disregard the war, "his preoccupation with casting larger and larger objects blocking his view of the carnage in the papers."[131] The narrator frames his awakening to the war as an anticipation of the obligatory official response to horror. Allward's desire to memorialize the war is a desire for a grand gesture, for something that cannot be ignored, for something "perfect enough that it would seem to have been built by a vanished race of brilliant giants."[132] Thus, the problem of war art that Urquhart presents in this novel is similar to the matter of Austin, a war outsider, who engages in exploitation and erasure: the artist here is guilty of erasing horror by transforming the particular into the allegorical. Austin's longing for his work to be exhaustive is linked with Allward's resolve that the stone figures in his memorial stand for everyone.

Allward's whim turned obsession hinges on his aspirations toward perfect agelessness and ahistoricity: the stone he wants "must carry within it no previous history of organic life."[133] His indifference to the models he employs, who seem "too specifically human to be fully interesting," switches to a "huge compassion" for the sculpted figures who are "perfection[s] of plaster."[134] Allward's interview with Giorgio Vigamonti, a Canadian war veteran skilled at carving names, demonstrates the artist's insensitivity to the very group he is ostensibly seeking to honour. He responds to Giorgio's pained admission that he was promoted to corporal simply because, unlike his fellow soldiers, he "was neither missing nor dead" by branding the soldier unheroic and applauding him for it. In this scene, Allward even appears to forget why, as he puts it, "the whole vicinity still stank of death." Giorgio can "remember" the war, the cause of the smell.[135] Allward is like Cobley's privileged war outsider, unburdened by "an emotional reaction to the war";[136] he can choose to focus his attention on the stone, which has "nothing putrid about it."[137]

Giorgio's acknowledgement that he remembers the war, along with his desire to work on a monument to his memories, operates in tension with the novel's extensive investigation of both denial and disappearance, which are in this novel the forms of erasure that threaten to replace the experiences of the war insider. Urquhart's focus on the construction of the Vimy memorial is, in large part, a meditation on what it means to memorialize those who have "gone missing," and on what the value of so many carved names and so much attention to beauty might be in the face of a terrifying, mass vanishing. The narrator suggests that the disappearance of men is to be expected: "The young [men] were bred to run away, to flee toward that which was not easily known," whereby even daily work, the so-called "resumption of duty was an act of escape."[138] The novel warns of two effects of this sort of deliberate disappearance. For Tilman, apparently born with "wanderlust," the desire to eschew the intimacy he is somehow embarrassed by, to simply roam unfettered by any obligation toward another human, is ultimately recognized as a liability. His encounters with Phoebe, the vagrant-child whose grief for her dead baby alienates her both from her lover and from a secure sense of herself, and with Refuto, whose habit of refusing everything derives from his fear of being refused by those he thinks he has injured, serve as warnings for Tilman about "the burden of denial."[139] After the war, Tilman is encumbered by memories that no one, not even his sister, wants to hear about. His first real attempt at offering memory is met with a type of refusal; Recouvrir "understood very little of what the English-Canadian said."[140] Yet it is in this moment of attempted communication, in which Tilman abandons his former habit of isolation, that his first intimate bond is forged. Soon after, Tilman and Recouvrir become lovers and make "each other fresh and beautiful and whole again."[141] That the name Recouvrir means both "to recover" and "to cover up" in French, however, suggests that even here Urquhart is hesitant about what Tilman's act of bearing witness signifies. On the one hand, Tilman does manage to heal a part of himself and to become a source of healing for another; on the other, the intimacy between Tilman and Recouvrir functions to subdue and anaesthetize rather than to articulate their shared pain.

While it is male soldiers, such as Klara's lover Eamon, who go "missing in action" that Canada's Ministry of Defence tries to account for via the memorial, Urquhart is also interested in how the war triggers types of denial and/or disappearance in female war participants. In this way, Urquhart's novels diverge in focus from Cumyn's, which unfailingly figure the female as a muse for the male soldier. Even Margaret's pacifist activities, which as testified by Amy J. Shaw's recent study, *Crisis of Conscience: Conscientious Objection in Canada during the First World War*, constituted serious and difficult political work, are consistently represented as frivolous. Ramsay's response to Margaret's pacifist position on the war is usually some version of the phrase "'You haven't seen what I've seen.'"[142] In *The Underpainter*, Urquhart explores the link between Augusta's addiction to forgetting and her experience as a nurse in France; in *The Stone Carvers*, the category of the war participant is widened further to consider those—particularly women—who have been left behind to battle with the pain of remembering. Much more so than in *The Underpainter*, the issue of what constitutes appropriate work for men and women is also explored. Klara's skill in carving, tailoring, and farming—for "men's work," as the nuns deem it[143]—marks her as an odd sort of woman even more than the fact that she is unmarried. Moreover, her talent as a carver, which even Allward recognizes, develops in spite of the fact that her grandfather directs his instruction to her brother, only "reluctantly hand[ing] her some wood and a knife."[144]

The work of grieving for the vanished, however, is thought to be the province of women. As the carver Juliani explains to Giorgio, women instinctively know how to grieve and how to remember in an appropriately patriotic manner, as if they understand and prize their chief role in the war. The narrator suggests, though, that "no matter how much it is cherished, an absent face that is a fixed reference becomes tyrannical, and tyranny eventually demands revolt, escape."[145] Several of the novel's grieving women end up engaging in their own kinds of deliberate disappearances, which are as dangerous as those of the young men who go off to war. As in *The Underpainter*, Urquhart considers the possibility that certain forms of remembering may prove to be unsafe and that the capacity to forget may be essential to any war participant. Even before the narrator describes Phoebe's form of desertion, Helga, mother to Tilman and Klara, is portrayed as withdrawing into her own anger over "the total dematerialization of her son."[146] Though she believes that her mother's cancer was cultivated in this angry void, Klara is foolish enough to engage in a similar sort of retreating in the face of Eamon's departure. Klara's determination to "train herself in the art of stoic apartness"[147] eventually leads her to feel such rupture between herself and others that she cannot conceive of herself as existing in the present. It is only after her work on the memorial and her forgiveness of Eamon for vanishing that she, like her brother, can again participate in life, and in love. As with Tilman's intimate revelations to Recouvrir, Klara finds a means to heal herself by bearing witness, though, as with her brother's experience, this healing is bound up with forgetting; she must let Eamon go in order to pursue her love affair with Giorgio. In addition, Urquhart describes both scenes of Klara's rendering—her carving of Eamon's face and of his name—in terms of the artist's response to them: it is Allward's ratification of Klara's carving that ultimately gives her rendering meaning. Just as Austin's paintings provide the framing, communicative context for Augusta's experiences, Allward's memorial is described as the "huge urn he had designed to hold grief." The grief expressed by war insiders Klara and Giorgio in their carving the name of a vanished man becomes, in the end, a means for the artist to communicate publicly; the witness, in the meantime, must be permitted to forget private loss.

Urquhart's misgivings about the artist's reproduction of what the witness undergoes are set in tension with her own course of controlling the experiences of First World War insiders. To a large extent, Klara's achievement in *The Stone Carvers* reads as a fantasy of an author struggling with her own desire for balance in the re-creation of horrific circumstances. The novel enacts an outsider's desire to ratify the work of war insiders who really just want to forget what they have experienced. *The Underpainter* and *The Stone Carvers* are, however, as invested in valuing acts of commemoration as they are in distinguishing between the claims of the witness and those of the artists (and my use of the word "claims" is meant here to suggest both "rights" and "assertions"). Though the form of her novels does not invite the sort of collaborative readerly participation as that of *The Wars* or other historiographic metafictions, Urquhart's descriptions of Austin's process of painting and Allward's process of designing allow her to investigate the double relationship that commemorative art has to its audience. Diana Brydon suggests that the photographs in Findley's novel reflect his "focus on making the reader see."[148] Urquhart's two war novels depend on notional ekphrasis, or the literary representation of imaginary visual art. In writing the visual, she explores the distance between witness and artist, and then the distance between art and its witness.

Austin's technique of painting involves a long process whereby an underpainting of realistic images is covered by layers of paint. Austin is bemused by the critical response to this technique, commenting that "there is nothing, you understand, like an obscured subject to give critics something to talk about. Even those who had been either indifferent or hostile to my work in the past wrote long, reflective essays about the hidden subject matter that, under the circumstances, they were forced mostly to imagine."[149] The identification of the reader in this passage reminds us that, unlike Austin's critics, we are not "forced to imagine"; we have "seen" the subject matter of Austin's paintings. Likewise, Klara's carving may be "read" by us differently than by the "fictional" tourists and mourners who read the memorial for its allegorical representations. Through this paradoxical arrangement, Urquhart attempts to describe the double bind of art (whether visual, literary, or otherwise) that reproduces horror or trauma. On the one hand, though we cannot "see" Austin's paintings, we do know more about the underpainting than the fictional viewer does by way of narrative description; though we may know the Vimy memorial from photographs or postcards, we now "imagine" it as more specific than it appears. The encounter with art—Urquhart's art—reveals something of horror that might otherwise have remained hidden, yet that is not a whole story or is only one story of many, and that is only a necessarily overdetermined attempt to express the inexpressible. On the other hand, Austin's role as a "trespasser" and "thief," and Allward's as a perfectionist and allegorist, have revealed how the artist's relationship to horror and to remembrance is radically different from that of the witness, and that the contemporary aspiration to remember at all costs is a privilege that comes with having nothing of immediate horror to forget. Ultimately, then, Urquhart does not deem it the witness's responsibility to help the war outsider make meaning out of the past by way of accurate, useful remembrance, or to defend the steps taken toward healing and forgetting. Her exploration of the creation of commemorative art, in fact, takes as its premise the notion that only those who have nothing to forget might possibly find comfort in this sort of public ritualization of "healing," but that engaging in such rituals becomes an important site of communal, and national, activity.

In *The Underpainter* and *The Stone Carvers*, Urquhart redefines her interest in the relationship between myth and history that imbues her earlier work. As Young has noted, the prevailing understanding of Canada's participation in the First World War is heavily indebted to a myth of "heroic sacrifice." This myth entails that the wartime sacrifices made by Canadians were "noble," that Canadians "showed themselves in the Great War to be a special people" and had thus earned "the status of a distinct and separate nation."[150] Urquhart approaches this national myth not as a sort of ahistorical repository of innate beliefs, but as a form of reproduction, or art, that is also potentially a form of erasure. What the myth has is its beauty, which even Augusta associates with "this world," and with life. In turning the historical moment into allegory, the myth communicates to a wider audience, as is the objective of the memorial at Vimy. The wholeness of myth provokes remembrance from those who are both temporally and experientially distant from the past event, and thus has the potential to create a sense of national community. On the one hand, Urquhart suggests, particularly in *The Stone Carvers*, which depicts Tilman, Klara, and Giorgio participating in the conversion of their experiences into art, that the construction of a mythic memorial may provide the insider with an avenue toward forgetting and toward a safer sort of anaesthetic. On the other hand, her portrayal of Austin and Allward as men who turn a nation's grief into art "like...scientist[s]"[151] reveals that, as the raw material of such myths is recontextualized, particular moments of loss and love are obscured. Even as myth allows the war outsider to remember that which he or she has not seen, in its transcendence of the historical moment, myth, especially the mythic memorial, has the potential to eliminate any need for the war insider's act of bearing witness, and, perhaps, any obligation the greater populace has to recall the precise origins of their site of grieving and remembrance. For Urquhart, the letting go of origins—of the archaeological approach to history favoured in historiographic metafiction—is a necessary stage in forging the national collective.

In turning their attention away from the figure of the archivist and toward the work of the artist, both Cumyn and Urquhart signal a disinterest in the problem of the "official" historical record that so tenaciously occupied writers and critics of historiographic metafiction. Rather, both authors are concerned with how an individual, especially one who has been through the trauma of war, on the battlefield or at home, is able to function in a world that cannot comprehend particular experiences. Both authors suggest that it is impossible to recover the witness's experience, either because the witness may want to protect the meaning of that experience from the outsider or because the witness may choose to forget. Thus, the remembrance (and reimagining) of Canada's participation in the First World War is necessarily a process of mythologizing. Although Cumyn's representation of the soldier-artist who circulates his work privately among peers differs from Urquhart's representation of the commemorative artist whose objective is to speak to a mass audience, both authors provide narratives that consider how making sense of war either as experience or as event requires the fashioning of an active community, as well as the selection of a usable narrative. The narrative that Cumyn seems most interested in is the one that affirms a sense of duty to "loved ones," a category that might include family but also might include comrades. For her part, Urquhart is also interested in a narrative suggesting that intimacy across cultural and experiential divides can emerge out of even something like war. However, both authors write the remembrance of the war in such a way as to make use of—rather than wrestle with—the space between then and now. The return to the past via fiction is borne out of a sense of the generative potential of that space, whereby because the particular events of war have retreated into myth, they can be put to use in order to consider which aspects of myth—for example, with regard to ideas such as duty, intimacy, and the sharing of grief—we currently aspire to, or find comfort in.

Furthermore, for all the declarations and intimations the novels of Cumyn and Urquhart make about the horrors of war, both authors contribute to a conservative conception of how civic activity manifests itself, in that both resort to the valorization of community stability. In Cumyn's work, the national "trait" of dutifulness is a point of honour for infantryman Ramsay Crome; his unpretentious sense of duty distinguishes him as a Canadian soldier refusing to partake in British conceptions of class privilege and imbues his sense of a male community. The series of masculine brotherhoods Ramsay becomes part of—his fighting unit, soldiers on leave in London, and those in the POW camp—are depicted both in terms of their homogeneity and in terms of the fact that service to these communities produces a stable and productive sense of masculinity. In this way, the manifestation of a working collective is extolled irrespective of deliberations about the goals or virtue of the war itself. Urquhart's work, too—for all of its impatience with a postmodern ethos that privileges skepticism—culminates in the reification of those myths about Canadian participation in the war that seek to celebrate the way the nation came together in grief. Her thematic interest in erasure, disappearance, and forgetting thus runs counter to the aims of historiographic metafictions seeking to unsettle the collective memory of the dead.

Chapter 4

Other Canadians: The Representation of Alternative Versions of the Canadian War in *Vimy, Unity (1918), Three Day Road,* and *A Secret Between Us*

"Us" versus "Them": Historians and the Idea of the Canadian Collective
The idea of a cohesive "us" that constitutes Canadian participation in the First World War is common to many critical responses that, at least provisionally, take a shorthand approach to the issue of "our" experience in the war. This focus on the collectivity of the Canadian experience in the First World War allows contemporary writers, critics, and historians a conduit for working through the paradox that what Canadians gained conceptually through their participation was somehow worth the catastrophic human cost associated with, as Sandra Gwyn puts it, "the most monumentally stupid of all wars, [which achieved] nothing more than to make certain another 'great war' would succeed it."[1] In short, Canada's participation in the First World War might be considered a success, simply because that participation brought the populace together as Canadians, even if the general Allied military experience is to be considered a failure. This chapter focuses on what the idea of being "brought together" means, and on how the idea of "Other Canadians"—those Canadians with a somehow complicated ethnic, cultural, or even regional status in the Canadian collective—is dealt with. The point here is not to collapse the particularities of experience of all those participants in the First World War who were not part of the Central Anglo-Canadian community; nor is it to claim, for example, that

First Nations communities had the same response to the war as Quebecers, or German-Canadians, or Newfoundlanders (who were not, at that point in history, Canadians at all); rather, the point is to examine how a number of texts explore the myth of the homogenizing Canadian collective, either to challenge or to uphold that myth, by analyzing the work that goes into representing that collective. The discursive work of imagining a common national cause pervades contemporary Canadian literature about the First World War, and largely accounts for some of the perhaps puzzling nostalgia among contemporary writers for a time when Canadians were involved in "the most monumentally stupid of all wars."

Vern Thiessen's play *Vimy*, published in 2007, is an ensemble piece set in a field hospital in which four soldiers and one nurse recall events from before the war that influenced their respective enlistment, as well as, in the case of the soldiers, their experiences training for and participating in the April 1917 Battle of Vimy Ridge. The characters in *Vimy*, who are all to a greater or lesser extent based on historical counterparts, include representatives from various cultural or regional groups in Canada, and the main action of the play explores each character's distinct response to the war in general and to the battle in particular. Kevin Kerr's *Unity (1918)*, published in 2002, is a play set on the home front, in a small prairie town, during the height of the so-called "Spanish flu" epidemic. The play juxtaposes the townspeople's response to word of the war—including their response to a recently returned soldier—to their reaction to the new enemy: illness. Joseph Boyden's 2005 novel, *Three Day Road*, focuses on Xavier Bird, a member of the Cree nation, who enlists and takes part in various battles alongside his childhood friend, Elijah Whiskeyjack, a soldier who seems to relish his wartime experience. The novel weaves together portrayals of Xavier and Elijah's military activities and descriptions of Xavier's journey back to his home community after he has returned from war, wounded, addicted to morphine, and traumatized by his experience. Finally, Daniel Poliquin's *A Secret Between Us*, published in French as *La Kermesse* in 2006 and translated into English by Donald Winkler in 2007, examines wartime and postwar francophone Ottawa from the point of view of Lusignan, former member of Princess Patricia's Light Infantry, who becomes infatuated with his fellow officer, Essiambre d'Argenteuil, a staunch federalist from Quebec who is eventually killed at Passchendaele. When Lusignan returns from the war, an unemployed alcoholic, he begins corresponding with a young woman, Amalia Driscoll, who had been a lover of d'Argenteuil.

Each of these works approaches the myth of the Canadian collective differently, some more optimistically than others. Thiessen's concern with diversity and tolerance culminates in a narrative that undermines cultural specificity by making all stories equivalent, mitigating complex political and historical tensions with the representation of a naturally cohesive fighting unit. In *Unity (1918)*, Kerr suggests that deaths that cannot be situated within a collective retrospective sacrificial narrative are not deemed significant; the play interrogates how conceptions of "unity" are discursively constructed, especially when a community feels itself under threat by something it cannot control physically. Boyden's *Three Day Road* is less cynical than Kerr's play, in that it explores how stories of a previously marginalized community—in this case a First Nations community—can be productively written into a living history. Poliquin's *A Secret Between Us* takes up the subject of "Other Canadians" as a bit of a trick; the ostensible story of francophone Canadian participation in the First World War turns out to be a query into whether historical remembrance serves any real political purpose.

The complex weighting manoeuvre surrounding the use-value of Canada's participation in the war often plays out in the work of Canadian historians. In Granatstein and Morton's introduction to their 1989 study, *Canada and the Two World Wars* (republished in 2003), they boldly assert that "the single biggest impact of the First World War on Canadians was our evolution from British colonials to citizens of a sovereign nation."[2] In their overview of the political events and popular response leading up to the war, through Canadian wartime activity (in training, on the battlefield, and on the home front), to the war's political and cultural aftermath, they provide a narrative of ironic progress. In the chapter "Doing Your Bit," they point out that "a national crusade is more natural if a nation is united"[3] and that Canadians were not necessarily so; for example, French Canadians had little interest in the war, and Canada's German community was alienated. Yet in Chapter 6 of their study, "A National Crusade," the narrative explains the "triumph" of Vimy Ridge: "Canadians then and later knew that they had done a great thing and that on such deeds nations are built."[4] Granatstein and Morton conclude the section on the First World War with the chapter "Counting the Costs," in which they draw attention to the consequences of the country's "broken dreams, broken bodies, and broken families,"[5] but also to Canada's autonomous status at the League of Nations. With regard to Quebec's sense of the war's cost, the historians assert that "there were no more illusions about a Bonne Entente between Quebec and Ontario, although, in 1926, an Ontario Conservative government discreetly buried Regulation 17."[6]

More recently, some historians have inquired further into the narrative that Granatstein and Morton present. Jeff Keshen, for example, has examined how messages from the front, whether in censored letters or in various kinds of wartime journalism, "tended to confirm romantic stereotypes,"[7] especially regarding the uniquely Canadian brand of rugged heroism. Though Keshen acknowledges up front that "the link between this conflict and the flowering of Canadian nationalism is undeniable,"[8] his analysis of wartime (and some postwar) popular discourse shows that it "continued to depict superior, courageous, and noble soldiers who were...portrayed as being motivated by the highest ideals...and, as such, romanticizes events and distorts the past."[9] Donald Avery points out that recent scholarship surrounding the "ethnic and class conflict in western Canada during the First World War"[10] highlights a range of experiences for immigrant groups, most of whom were treated with hostility by Anglo-Canadians in that period. In *Hometown Horizons: Local Responses to Canada's Great War*, Robert Rutherdale considers the various ways in which the war generated divisions rather than unity: "The separations created between civilians and soldiers, between civilian men and women, between enemy aliens and the host society, or between conscription's supporters and opponents made collective action possible, but only through exclusionary practices that engendered distinct roles, patterns of social interaction, and modes of signifying social differences that linked past identities with present engagements."[11] Rutherdale concludes his study, however, by acknowledging that as early as December 1918, discursive cultural work was being done to "displace the realities of the carnage overseas with the narratives of an ideal past, stories of the war as a great and noble sacrifice." He posits that as a consequence, even those distinctive social identities that had become articulated because of the war lost their meaning and "became eclipsed by the effects of cyclical production and consumption of [the] most persuasive symbols and usable commemorations."[12]

Rutherdale's notion of the "usable" is explored even more fully in Vance's *Death So Noble*, which seeks to explain the stakes involved in mythologizing the meaning of the nation's collective sacrifice. Vance considers not the events of the war but rather the way "contemporaries conceived of the war, how they represented it, and how they accommodated it into their collective consciousness in the 1920s and 1930s." He argues that "Canadians remembered their first world war in terms that sometimes bore little resemblance to its actualities."[13] Through his examination of cultural artifacts such as newspaper reports about and photographs of Armistice Day and Peace Day celebrations, First World War memorials, articles about the war in local newspapers (including Church publications), amateur poetry and fiction, and materials about the war circulated to schoolchildren, Vance develops his argument that the myth of the war was to be used to instill a unified, nationalist spirit among Canadians: "that memory could sweep across the country like the north wind, purifying the nation's life, clarifying its true goals, and uniting the people in a common cause."[14] As Vance asserts in his conclusion, this idealistic vision proved a failure in the decades following the war:

> The memory of the Great War never realized the high promise that its most vigorous proponents saw in it because it was so obviously assimilationist... the myth of the war was to become a substitute for cultural diversity. It would give ethnic minorities the opportunity to surrender their own identities in exchange for membership in an imagined community that was homogenous in belief and outlook. For too many Canadians of non-British stock, it was a bad bargain at best.[15]

Thus, the decades following the war included the entrenchment of divisions among cultural, social, and political communities.

In his preface to *Sounding the Iceberg*, one of the first sustained critical attempts to survey the field of Canadian historical fiction, Dennis Duffy distinguishes true historical novels from fiction that simply presents "historical aspects of present-day settings": "The historical novel... emphasizes overtly or implicitly the otherness of [the] past... The reader is somewhere different, stepping out of a time machine. The point of the novel may be to teach readers that what they thought was temporally distant is morally contiguous, but that message begins in remoteness."[16] Duffy goes on to argue that Canadian writers in the nineteenth through the early and mid-twentieth centuries put the criterion of the "remoteness" of the past to various uses. Remoteness can offer a distant yet highly constructed, almost allegorically conceived space in which to put forward a utopian ideal, an ideal often having to do with the forging of nation. Remoteness can be used to delineate with quotidian detail an ostensibly "neutral" background for moral testing, especially as such testing relates to questions of social reform or entrenchment. Finally, a sense of remoteness can initiate an inquiry into our relationship to the established historical record, often in service of political redress and/or ideologically charged revision. Duffy thus suggests that the remoteness of the past operates simultaneously as a bridge and as a barrier for the writer and reader of historical literature, both of whom must negotiate vacillations between continuity and discontinuity. A crucial, and complicating, feature of historical literature is that, no matter how meticulous the author's research, or apparently seamless the presentation of a coherent world, or sensitive and comprehensive the use of documentary material, it will never present a totalizing picture, and thus its gaps as much as its fortifications will constitute its comprehensibility.

In their introduction to a special issue on historical fiction titled "Past Matters/Chose du passe," the editors of *Studies in Canadian Literature* point out that, particularly in the twentieth (and now the twenty-first) century, Canadian writers of historical fiction have ever more explored "the darker corners of Canadian history...draw[ing] attention to the mechanics of historical representation."[17] Wyile further notes in *Speculative Fictions* that much contemporary Canadian historical fiction entails a shift toward different political goals from those emphasized in nineteenth-century historical literature, as Canadian writers increasingly work to recover "previously neglected or marginalized histories, underlining that what is historically significant has been narrowly defined and ideologically overdetermined," and that "rather than serving to reinforce nationalist myths...[such work] has been inclined to deconstruct those myths, revealing their excluding effects."[18] Editors Andrea Cabajsky and Brett Josef Grubisic note in their introduction to *National Plots: Historical Fiction and Changing Ideas of Canada* that several critical essays in the collection "explicitly respond to the notion that a pervasive Eurocentrism has shaped the writing and reception of Canadian historical fiction."[19] As Canadian historians, literary critics, and writers display increasing self-consciousness of the past's "darker corners," however, they may also express anxiety as to what we are supposed to *do* with the our past, especially if deconstructing the traditional historical record results in an inability to make the past meaningful, or of clear utility.

The texts explored in this chapter make use of the mythical idea of the Canadian collective to test the idea of constructing a usable past out of the gaps in the historical record. Interestingly, the failure of that myth to gain a foothold in immediate postwar social practice does not appear to have diminished its force as a defining mythical framework for the Canadian collective remembrance of the war. In Vern Thiessen's play *Vimy*, a privileging of the Canadian collective is necessary in order to celebrate Canada's past. Though Thiessen declares in his playwright's note and elsewhere that his goal is to generate knowledge, the myth of the collective enterprise he presents primarily seeks to provide comfort for the Anglo-Canadian regarding the war's cultural meaning. In Kevin Kerr's *Unity (1918)*, the matter of the "Other Canadian" is raised in terms of its emphasis on those who died during the influenza epidemic of 1918. Kerr, however, also seeks to challenge the myth of the Canadian collective response to the war by interrogating how ideals regarding cultural or national unity are communicated, and how the home front response to the combination of the war and the epidemic produces conflict between the cultural insider and the cultural Other. Like *Unity (1918)*, Joseph Boyden's *Three Day Road* focuses on the work of recovering lost histories, as the narrative follows the experiences of two Cree Canadians who participate in the war. Boyden's novel, though, reworks the deconstructive impulse of some recent Canadian historical fiction in order to imagine how First Nations communities can make productive use of a past that has been discursively marginalized. Conversely, Daniel Poliquin's *A Secret Between Us* undermines the ideal of widening the scope of the Canadian collective via the work of historical recovery. Though at first glance, Poliquin's novel seems to highlight the contribution of the francophone soldier to the Canadian First World War effort, the novel's depiction of Lusignan, one-time member of Princess Patricia's Light Infantry, as well as its allusions to the historical figure of Talbot Papineau, the notable francophone Canadian nationalist, prove to be a ruse. Poliquin's novel ultimately skewers almost every sacred myth associated with the Canadian First World War experience, doing so in order to question how such myths become a matter of mere narrative convention. Together what these texts seem to suggest is that even though the national collective is an illusion, it is still—for better or worse—an ideal, as only via an enlarged, superficially heterogeneous conception of the collective can acts of citizenship be realized. This idealization is borne out of a contemporary anxiety about finding appropriate ways to articulate and activate civic service, which in turn produces—in some texts—an oddly nostalgic portrait of war activity as uncomplicated, meaningful service to a stable national collective.

The Myth of the Unified Experience: Vern Thiessen's *Vimy*

Vern Thiessen's play, *Vimy*, premiered at the Citadel Theatre in Edmonton in 2007. In much of the press surrounding the opening, the focus of discussion among journalists and those interviewed (including the playwright, the director of the Citadel production, James MacDonald, and individual actors) is the tension between the play's concern with public events on the one hand and with private matters on the other. The author's stated impetus for writing the play is the sheer scope of Canada's involvement in the battle at Vimy: as Thiessen notes, "there were 100,000 people involved in that battle, 100,000 Canadians. That's bigger than the population of Vancouver at the time."[20] In describing his own attachment to the project, MacDonald says, "I love it because of the idea that the battles and history might make the audience say, 'Wow, I didn't know that.' I hope they run home and look it up...We should be telling our own stories, know our history."[21] At the same time, however, those involved with the play are equally keen to point out that, though the play refers to Canadian history and should ideally make its audience aware of that history, the thematic focus of the drama is the individual's response to memory and how that response relates to the operation of collective remembrance. Thiessen explains in interviews that "I'm curious how memory operates in our lives. Does it heal us? Does it give us nightmares?"[22] Furthermore, in much of the press and in the playwright's note included in the published version of the play, Thiessen asserts that the play is not about war, but rather about how particular events come to be mythologized as part of a nation's collective memory. He asks: "Is there a gap between our memory as a country and our recollection as individuals? What is the no-man's-land between reality and memory, truth and dream, history and mythology?"[23] Thus, those involved in the production of *Vimy* are faced with a typical logical incompatibility. In order to make a case for the status of a historical event like the Battle of Vimy, it is necessary to show how that event has broad, enduring, and conspicuous significance. At the same time, in order to retain some kind of emotional and thematically resonant core to the imaginative depiction of historical events, it is usually necessary to tighten one's focus and, often, to dwell on individual responses to an event that have no bearing on that event's historical significance. This is what it means to write a fiction that depends to a greater or lesser extent on the events of a particular military event for its setting and for many of its story elements and still continue to declare: "This is not a work about war."

Thiessen's dramaturgical decision to write his play so that he could better highlight theme rather than historical event is not in any way unusual; in fact, it is probably inescapable, as should be clear by now in this study of the various ways authors have tried to negotiate the problem of producing historical literature. *Vimy*, though, is interesting in terms of the way the tension between public and private matters relates to an ethical issue raised (though quickly quelled) in the playwright's note: while Thiessen asserts that his play "does not ask whether a battle like the one fought at Vimy Ridge is worth the tremendous commitment and profound sacrifices made by the men and women involved,"[24] the very phrasing of this assertion provides an implicit response, one that operates as a tacit framework for the ensuing drama. The playwright's reference to "tremendous commitment and profound sacrifices" reveals that Thiessen has already decided that Canadian military activity is "worth" something. As discussed in Chapter 1 of this study, the narrative of meaningful sacrifice is always conceived retrospectively, and in Thiessen's play, this narrative is not even provisionally challenged. Unlike in plays such as *Dancock's Death* and *Unity (1918)*, the question of what constitutes productive military sacrifice is rarely raised in *Vimy*, except as it pertains to the issue that lies at the core of this play, which is the issue of national unity. In other words, Thiessen's play does not ask: was the horrendous human toll associated with the Battle of Vimy worth the gaining of particular military objectives or even the expression of a righteous cause, such as the promotion of codes of honour or duty or fortitude? Rather, *Vimy* is concerned with whether or not the horrendous human toll associated with the battle was worth its function as a catalyst for unifying the disparate ethnic and regional communities of a young nation. And, to an overwhelming extent, the play asserts that, yes, it was worth it.

As a text that is primarily concerned with the issue of national unity among Canadians, *Vimy* engages with a familiar paradox noted by various Canadian literary critics: in order to celebrate the particularly Canadian brand of unity, a Canadian literary text must concurrently celebrate cultural difference. In his 1989 essay "Disunity as Unity: A Canadian Strategy," Robert Kroetsch asserts that "Canadians cannot agree on what their metanarrative is... [and], in some perverse way, this very falling-apart of our story is what holds our story together."[25] Kroetsch further declares that the multiplicity of Canadian stories emerges from "the energy of the local, in the abundance that is diversity and difference."[26] More recently, and more cynically, Len Findlay has argued that Canadian literature is "construed from above as profoundly but sedatively social, in the sense of harmoniously socializing citizens, activating commonalities, and 'permitting' or 'respecting' differences."[27] Or, as Kit Dobson argues in reference to the implications for Canadian writers of the 1988 Multiculturalism Act, "difference need no longer be a disruptor of the national project—quite the reverse, in fact: the celebration of difference has become a part of Canadian nationalism... By articulating different bodies that seek recognition, writers assert their place within Canada and are frequently approved of for seeking inclusion (reform) rather than radical disruption (revolution)."[28] In the case of Thiessen's play, the unambiguous concern with the ethnic and regional diversity of those who participated at Vimy, to say nothing of gender difference—as *Vimy*'s inclusion of a female nurse among its ensemble reflects a wish to show women's involvement in military activity—is dramaturgically connected with the playwright's stated interest in focusing on individual responses to the war, and his concern with exploring how distinct individuals might still celebrate their commonality.

In his acknowledgements, Thiessen notes his research into the lives of such men and woman as Sid Unwin (1882–1917), who worked as a Canadian Rockies guide before entering the war; the Quebecer Jean Brilliant (1890–1918); Mike Mountain-Horse (1888–1964), a member of the Blood tribe; and Nova Scotia native Clare Gass, who served as a nurse in France during the war. The characters who make up the ensemble cast include Sid, "a construction worker from Winnipeg, Manitoba"; Jean-Paul, "a butcher from Montreal, Quebec"; Mike, "a Blood Indian from Standoff, Alberta," and Clare, a nurse from Nova Scotia. Rounding out the main cast are Will, "a canoe maker from Renfrew, Ontario," and Laurie, a mining engineer originally from Nova Scotia. These characters seem to have emerged from Thiessen's research into the lives of William Alexander and Laurence Gass but are less clearly connected to historical counterparts.[29] Thus, Thiessen appears to have built his play as a kind of "tapestry," to use the term Sandra Gwyn adopts for her own *Tapestry of War: A Private View of Canadians in the Great War*, a book that "recounts the Great War experiences of ten Canadians...of what they were doing and what they were thinking and feeling *at the time*."[30] *Vimy* includes various flashback scenes to reveal what motivated each character to join the Canadian war effort and what each character experiences leading up to and during the Battle of Vimy Ridge.

As much as every character in *Vimy* is an individual, more or less based on a historical personage, so too is he or she a type. Thiessen appears dedicated to include a representative from each of the "diverse" communities that made up early-twentieth-century Canada: we are met with a Westerner, an Ontarian, a Quebecer, a First Nations representative, a Maritimer, and a woman. Thiessen even goes so far as to include a scene in which Sid reaches out to Will in a moment charged with homoeroticism. Each representative figure, in particular those who are typically marked as Other (that is, the Quebecer and the First Nations representative), acts in a very representative way. The first act includes flashback scenes in which Jean-Paul argues the merits of joining the war effort with his friend Claude:

> J.P.: You wanna wait 'til the Huns come sailing down the St. Lawrence?
> CLAUDE: This is an Anglo war. Everyone knows that. You know what they're doin' in Ontario? French: banned in schools. You wanna fight for that, Jean-Paul?
> J.P.: No, I wanna fight *against* it, If we don't fight now, we're all gonna be talking *German*, never mind English.[31]

In Act II, Jean-Paul is ordered to take part in a firing squad charged with executing a man tried and convicted of cowardice and missing battle. The man turns out to be Claude, who prays in French before being shot, while Jean-Paul begs, "Ah, Claude...pardonne-moi."[32] By collapsing the cowardly-soldier-shot-for-insubordination plot into his dramatization of the ambivalence of the Quebec francophone response to the war, Thiessen oversimplifies the political, demographic, and cultural contexts of that ambivalence. Furthermore, though Jean-Paul expresses remorse for taking part in the execution of his friend and worries about how he is going to explain what transpired when he goes home, he, not Claude, is ultimately portrayed as the true Canadian soldier, craving the taste of a Labatt's and a bowl of saskatoons along with Will and Mike.

Mike's backstory also commences in Act I, in a scene where he and his brother, Bert, wait for a sacred vision; when they see the Northern Lights, they interpret them as a fire with a message:

> BERT: Flames licking the top of Chief Mountain. It's like they're saying:
> MIKE: "Go to the fire, boys."
> BERT: "Go fight under a sky of fire."
> MIKE: "Be warriors."
> BERT: Then that's what we're gonna do. We're gonna be brave. You and me. Right?
> MIKE: You and me.[33]

While the first scene between Jean-Paul and Claude depicts their argument about joining a Canadian military expedition, the two First Nations characters show no hesitation, a dramatization in keeping with a point Thiessen makes in his Historical Notes: "One in three Native men (Aboriginal, First Nations, Métis) volunteered to serve in the Great War. In total, approximately four thousand Native men served overseas."[34] Furthermore, Mike's story as it is presented in *Vimy* coheres very closely in terms of facts to what Mike Mountain-Horse relates in *My People, the Bloods*, picking up on such elements from Mountain-Horse's autobiography as the death of his older brother, who also fought in the war and died of tuberculosis on his way home from the front, and that he was awarded a Distinguished Conduct Medal.

Vimy's structure, however, undermines the distinctiveness of Mountain-Horse's history. Act I presents a succession of flashbacks to introduce the backstory of each main character within the ensemble, and in each case, the backstory revolves around a main character and his or her relationship with another. In Act II, each backstory is successively revisited, this time to portray the effect of the war on the relationship that has been introduced in Act I. This structure, together with the play's cast of representative figures from various Canadian "communities," makes each particular story an equivalent to every other story presented in the play, diminishing the sense that such stories should resonate as real or even particularly diverse, except in the most superficial way. Jean-Paul's struggle with his allegiance to English Canada and the guilt he feels for executing a fellow francophone who has questioned this allegiance is made structurally equivalent to Mike's story of his pact with his brother and the disillusionment he feels when his romantic concept of First Nations bravery is destroyed, as well as equivalent to Clare's story of her love affair with Laurie and Will's story of his homoerotic connection with Sid. The potential anxiety produced by difference, which the play ostensibly deals with, is structurally contained because each story is "harmoniously...permit[ted]"[35] and tends toward the desire for "inclusion."[36]

The ultimate effect of making individual stories structurally equivalent is to expose the focus on individual stories as a false front for a play that privileges the collective experience and the myth of the war's role in unifying the country. Such privileging is further revealed by the repetition of a section of dialogue that becomes a type of refrain for the characters in Act I. In the first moments of the play, Will and Mike have the following exchange:

> WILL: Who you with?
> MIKE: 10th Battalion.
> WILL: 1st Division?
> MIKE: Yeah.
> WILL: How you fare?
>   *Pause.*
> MIKE: Don' know.
>   *Pause.*
> WILL: What happened?
>   *Pause.*
> MIKE: Not sure. Can't remember.[37]

Mike and Will go on to repeat this piece of dialogue, this time with Mike initiating the questions, and later Jean-Paul and Sid repeat it as well. Significantly, in each version of the exchange, the character initiating the dialogue is able to confirm the particular division the other character belongs to, which suggests a sense of commonality among the various Canadian military units. In the last scenes of Act I, the characters describe the three months of training Canadian units went through to prepare for the attack on Vimy Ridge, for as Tim Cook points out, the offensive "would include all four of the [Canadian] divisions attacking together for the first time."[38] As both the backstory scenes of Act I and the revisitation scenes of Act II show, however, every character is entirely clear on "what happened." The memories of each character might be upsetting, but no one seems to have trouble accessing them. Thus, the "plot" of *Vimy* hinges less on the problem of the shell-shocked soldier who is unable to remember and come to terms with his experience, so much as it concerns how individual soldiers become part of a collective offensive, a collective that succeeds even if the individuals involved in it feel as if they have failed. In the final scene of the play, the actor playing Laurie gives voice to a letter he wrote to Clare before being killed in the battle, thereby putting on a prosopopoeiac mask similar to the one adopted by the character Charlie in *Mary's Wedding*. Laurie announces to Clare, "when I come back, I'm gonna have some story to tell...I'm gonna tell you the story of Vimy over and over and over."[39] Though the moment itself has a dramatic irony to it owing to Laurie's death, the overriding aim of the prosopopoeiac mask has in fact been met: "the story of Vimy" intrudes into the potential for an individual elegiac narrative. The play does not ultimately present a tapestry of stories but rather "*the* story" of that mythic collective enterprise.

The question then becomes: Does the myth of a meaningful collective enterprise emerge from an actual collective? In other words, once the individuals *Vimy* presents are recognized as types whose function is to represent the various regional, ethnic, and gendered groups implicated in a single story, does the story itself still manage to reflect diverse perspectives? Despite the ensemble cast of diverse types, the perspective that *Vimy* articulates is fairly unitary because the implied audience member for the play is singular. Just as Jean-Paul forms a pact with Claude, and Mike forms a pact with his brother Bert, so too does the play form a pact with its implied audience member, who is implicated as Anglo-Canadian. The audience member Thiessen writes to will ideally be only temporarily destabilized by the periodic use of French and Mi'kmaq, as is indicated by the fact that only the first three lines of the backstory scene between Jean-Paul and Claude are in French; after this, they converse in "character" English, as in "You know what they're doin' in Ontario? French: banned in schools. You wanna fight for that, Jean-Paul?"[40] Clare's few lines to Mike in Mi'kmaq are similarly staged to denote the audience as the unmarked not-Other, an Anglo-Canadian who is comfortable with his own twenty-first-century sense of tolerance for unproblematic difference.

The representations of difference in *Vimy* make such straightforward tolerance easy; the implied audience member is confronted with a socially adept Indian, a guilt-ridden francophone, the vaguest hint of a homoerotic relationship, and a multilingual, charismatic, hard-working woman who clearly deserves the right to vote. The political, historical, and cultural tensions among the various "communities" are expressed mainly in a scene in which an argument among Clare, Jean-Paul, Will, and Mike over who invented hockey devolves into an exchange of ethnic insults. Furthermore, this scene precedes the staging of the way all four Canadian divisions train to become a cohesive fighting unit. The military enemy, by contrast, is portrayed as an unproblematic "them"; Thiessen makes liberal use of such tags as "Hun" and "Fritz" throughout the play. Will's experience during the battle includes his stabbing a German soldier, who dies before his eyes, yet the play does not seriously engage with the theme of the commonality among all First World War soldiers. To do so would undermine *Vimy*'s mythologizing of the war's function as a unifying experience for Canadians. The Germans have to remain a "them," so as to set a cohesive "us" in greater relief.

Canadian participation in the First World War, and particularly in the iconic Battle of Vimy Ridge, must be figured in terms that heighten the war's importance in an origin story of building a functional national identity. The fantasy Thiessen offers to the implied audience member is that superficial ethnic differences can be transcended given a suitable unifying opportunity to participate as a collective, and thus can be viewed as mostly irrelevant whinging: as Clare remarks to Jean-Paul and Mike—whose argument about whether the francophone or the Blood Indian is braver has devolved into a fist fight—"You think you're the only ones want to do good?... You think you're the only ones who gave up something? Well you're not. I see dozens of ya every single day."[41] Furthermore, even before Clare has a chance to scold Jean-Paul and Mike, each representative of a community whose differences must be tolerated by the implied purveyor of the unmarked Canadian identity is portrayed in the act of fighting over who has best shown himself to be committed to national service. Thus, Thiessen's note that "*Vimy* is not a play about war" is sincere; rather, his text is about an ideal—that Canadians of all backgrounds long to prove their national allegiances, if only the present moment could offer a straightforward opportunity for activating citizenship.

Unity (1918): "Oh Canada! Oh Canada! Oh—"

Like Guy Vanderhaeghe's *Dancock's Dance*, Kevin Kerr's *Unity (1918)* is set during the final months of the war, when the "Spanish flu" was sweeping parts of the globe. Eventually, the pandemic would claim 50,000 Canadian lives. Also like *Dancock's Dance*, Kerr's play is set in a small town in Saskatchewan, though not because Kerr wants to draw attention to a particular historical event, as in Vanderheaghe's play; rather, he sets his play in Unity, Saskatchewan, in order to provoke a sense of irony. The play focuses on various citizens of Unity as they grapple with the way the town's epidemic both unites and divides them. Those citizens include the sisters Bea and Sissy and their friend Mary, each of whom also worries a lot about love; Sunna, who takes over as the town's mortician after her uncle Thorson dies (of drink, goes the rumour); Stan, a farmer whose wife has recently died giving birth; and Michael, a young farmhand born in a nearby town with whom Sissy is in love and who becomes Unity's first victim of the pandemic. The ensemble cast also includes Hart, a blinded returned soldier who arrives in the town to stay with Thorson, his father, not having heard that Thorson is dead; Hart remains an outsider in the town of Unity throughout the play.

In his Note on Events that prefaces the published version of the play, Kerr asserts that

> largely forgotten now, this was the deadliest outbreak of infectious virus in recorded history.[42] Although it is uncertain exactly how many people died, estimates range from twenty to fifty million people worldwide. The flu reached every corner of the globe and was aided by the movement of troops at the tail end of World War I. It was an especially unusual strain of this otherwise common sickness, as victims were mainly young adults...In Canada, where per capita war causalities were particularly severe, more people died in four weeks of the flu than did in four years of fighting.[43]

Vanderhaeghe in his play makes use of the influenza epidemic as historical background so that he can explore the plot of the damaged First World War officer who must learn to celebrate his inherent honorability and heroism, despite having been traumatized by his struggle to lead his men in the trenches. The patients in the North Battleford asylum become a proxy military unit that officer Dancock can lead to victory over the disease. Conversely, Kerr's note suggests that his subject is not primarily the war but rather the epidemic. Vanderhaeghe periodically dramatizes a trench setting via Dancock's hallucinations and memories, whereas Kerr's setting is decidedly the home front; his characters deal with receiving news of casualties from the front, with putting together care packages, with trying to reintegrate returning soldiers Hart and Glen back into the community, and with celebrating the armistice amidst the flu epidemic. It is only via a single speech of Hart's that the overseas experience is described directly. The point of his speech is to disparage the "stupid stor[ies]"[44] of extraordinary Canadian heroism, such as those encouraged by the office of Canada's official press representative, William Maxwell Aitken, and to contrast them with a short account of trench warfare that sounds many familiar notes, describing the mud, the corpses, and the infantryman's fear. Hart's speech draws attention to the disconnect between what is communicated and what is true, and in fact the issue of how things (mail, news, germs, social expectations) are "communicated" is the play's central concern.

Kerr's Note on Events rehearses an idea that has become another trope associated with the pandemic: that it was returning soldiers who brought the flu home to Canada. In "The Horror at Home: The Canadian Military and the 'Great' Influenza Epidemic of 1918," historian Mark Humphries notes that "Canadian historians generally agree that the disease had a European origin and was brought to Canada by soldiers returning from the First World War."[45] But he then argues that this idea is "inconsistent with the evidence,"[46] pointing out, first, that not enough soldiers travelled from Europe to Canada in the summer of 1918 to connect the spread of the disease with returning soldiers, and second, that statistics relating to the number of influenza cases in Canada indicate that the Canadian pandemic followed the American one, not the European one. In other words, "while the disease and the military had a significant relationship, it was different than is often thought. At Niagara-on-the-lake, St. Jean, and Sydney, influenza had arrived in Canada with American military recruits on their way to support the allied offensive in Europe."[47]

I am not suggesting that Kerr's Note on Events reflects a lack of thorough research: as it happens, Kerr's play was published three years before Humphries's article came out in the *Journal of the Canadian Historical Association*. What is interesting about Humphries's research as it relates to Kerr's play is that, like the many Canadian historians who were influenced by Dickin McGinnis's 1977 paper, "The Impact of Epidemic Influenza: Canada, 1918–1919," which Humphries calls the "most important source on the origins of the pandemic in Canada,"[48] Kerr is consumed by an almost mythic idea that Humphries articulates: "The pandemic is thus seen as a consequence of the war's end where the evils of war were brought home to the civilian population by soldiers returning from the front. The innocent civilian population was therefore 'contaminated' by the returning soldiers not only with disease but also with the horror of the trenches."[49] At several points in *Unity (1918)*, this idea of "contamination" is explored. When Hart arrives unexpectedly in Unity, Bea comments: "We all wanted from him something we had been waiting so long for—contact with that other world. A story. A war story. But instead he just talked about how everyone in Halifax had the flu."[50] Thus, the flu first enters the town through the blind soldier's talk. As Bea later articulates: "Word of the flu is spreading quickly. Like the flu itself."[51]

Kerr further explores the notion that influenza is a "communicable" disease in Act I, Scene 12, titled "Contagion," which represents Rose and Doris, the town's telephone operators, engaged in conversations, the first about the importance of reporting on cases of the disease and the second explaining why a fine has been imposed on spitting in public. The two conversations take place simultaneously, although the audience only hears one half of each conversation, for Rose and Doris are speaking on telephones. This staging highlights Kerr's interest in the interrelations among stories, rumours, and facts, as well as the problem Bea refers to in her desire to hear a story from "that other world," which is the problem of dialogue that seems to flow in only one direction. At one point, Rose insists to Gerald, the man on the other end of the line, that "you can't catch the flu over the phone," and tries to prove her point by blowing into the telephone and asking him, "Feel this wind?"[52] Though Rose is exasperated by Gerald's insistence that, indeed, he can feel her blowing into the telephone, her response to a telegraph reporting three more dead in a nearby town is that "the wind is blowing in from the east."[53] Kerr is not suggesting that mere talk causes disease, but rather that mere talk can become as powerful in social effect as disease.

Kerr's interest in the social effects of talk is observable in two of the play's objectives. In the first place, Kerr wants *Unity (1918)* to operate as a kind of memorial for the 50,000 (Other) Canadians who died in 1918, but whose deaths have been "largely forgotten now" because they were not directly associated with the war. In the first scene of Act I, while preparing her uncle's corpse for viewing, Sunna ruminates on the idea that one can never experience one's own death: "Someone might witness my death, but I never die."[54] The conditional phrase "someone might" makes clear the play's concern with how acts of collective remembrance are selective and discursively constructed: talking about the flu and its casualties is precisely what gives them meaning as historical occurrences. After Mary learns that Richard, her sweetheart who had been fighting overseas, has died of flu, she decides to hold a "burial" service for him, even though all such activity has been banned in the town. Speaking over an imitation grave, Mary declares: "We are gathered here today to pay respect to a brave soldier, a devoted son, and a dear friend who gave his life to protect us from the tyrant… Richard died fighting for his country—the greatest sacrifice, the greatest love after the love of God."[55] The irony of Mary's speech is noted by Bea, who suggests to herself that such a speech is only possible because Richard died "far enough away to imagine him carrying a flag as he coughed and sneezed his way across enemy lines."[56] Richard's own words are literally turned to ashes; his last letter home is accidentally burned when Rose and Doris try to disinfect it in an oven. Also significant is that the town, led by Stan, becomes increasingly hostile toward Hart, whom they blame for bringing the flu to Unity, even though Hart, in Bea's words, is a hero with a medal to prove it. Hart, however, refuses to talk about his war experiences, downplaying the fact that he has a medal by telling Bea, "they were just tossing these things out like jelly drops at a parade,"[57] and cutting short Bea's attempts to engage him on the subject by giving her a brief description of the trenches.

Kerr's point is to make visible the process by which a community will place death within a sacrificial narrative—that is, how the narrative of dying for one's country helps the citizens of Unity make sense of their own problematic responses to the epidemic. The townspeople take up the rhetoric of battle as they impose a quarantine, asserting that "Unity will not be victim to this disease," as well as the importance of "[k]now[ing] the enemy."[58] When Michael falls ill with the flu, he is quickly transformed from a town favourite, a young farmhand whose laughter and charm are called "contagious,"[59] to the "enemy...in our midst," struck down because, according the Stan, "he wasn't local."[60] Michael is packed onto a train and sent home, but then sent back to Unity because his family in Yorkton has all died. He rides back and forth on the train until he dies, after which his body is dropped off, "rolled in a gray blanket and dead."[61] Later in the play, it becomes clear that Stan has infected Hart with the flu, thus inverting the paradigm that Humphries refers to. Like the Michael-plot, this inversion suggests that the binary between "us" and "them" providing the framework for conceptions of "unity" is discursively constructed solely to fulfill social functions. As Kerr suggests, the citizens of Unity are able to rationalize death in the context of war, but not disease, because the war dead can be retrospectively defined within a narrative of meaningful collective sacrifice, a narrative that relies on a clear distinction between "us" and "them."

Thus, *Unity (1918)* explores the relationship between discourse and social effect by examining how the use of war rhetoric among the townspeople of Unity allows them to privilege the homogeneous community. Hart and Michael are explicitly marked as outsiders when the town begins to fear contagion and seek reasons for untimely deaths. The young mortician Sunna is also marked as an outsider, because her job is considered distasteful and also because of her immigrant status. In the play's Prologue, Bea and Mary gossip about how "strange" it is that a fifteen-year-old woman would take up the work of the town mortician, and Sunna's detached sensibility toward her work is strategically marked throughout the play. In one scene, Sunna arrives at the mortuary with a young man's body in a blanket and *"a makeshift satchel slung around her shoulder"*; when asked by Bea, "What's in there?", Sunna answers, "That's his head."[62] Thus, it is not simply that Kerr wants to show the way the town accuses Sunna of being strange; he also deliberately *constructs* her as strange. Rose's accusation that Sunna is a type of "flu-profiteer" is clearly unfair, revealing Rose as a xenophobe who dislikes Sunna because she is an outsider, "just like her uncle was."[63] Yet Kerr does represent Sunna as concerned with making as much money as she can so that she can leave Canada. Sunna also instructs Bea to realize the value of the work women must often do, work that need not be rationalized within a narrative of collective sacrifice:

SUNNA: You're the only nurse in town.
BEA: I'm not a nurse.
SUNNA: But it's what you're doing.
BEA: I'm trying to help win the war. What are you trying to do? You help the enemy.
SUNNA: War?
BEA: The war against the flu.
SUNNA: I don't have a war. Or an enemy. But this is my work. And it's all I have. It's what I can do.[64]

On the one hand, this scene articulates a theme that runs throughout the play: that the response to widespread social calamity—like the war and like the flu—is the purview not only of heroic male soldiers, but also of typically unsung women, whose work on the home front must be recognized. On the other, this scene reveals Sunna's rejection of the war rhetoric that has defined Unity's response to the flu, for to accept such rhetoric would also require her to accept her part as enemy outsider.

Sunna herself is acutely aware of the way the town's "talk" functions to define difference. She is the one who points out to Hart that he will likely be blamed for bringing the flu into Unity because "people need excuses."[65] However, like Jean-Paul and Mike in *Vimy*, Sunna must be constructed as Other in order for Kerr to articulate his critique of the town's fear of difference. In Act I, Scene 10, titled "Family," Sunna is introduced to Hart:

STAN: It's your cousin.
HART: My cousin?
STAN: Yes, it's...well tell him your name girl.
SUNNA: Sunna Gudmundsdóttir.
HART: From Iceland?[66]

Sunna's foreignness is emphasized not only because Stan cannot pronounce her last name, but simply because she announces it. Though some of the other full names are mentioned in the play—for example, Richard Stone and Beatrice Wilde—only Sunna introduces herself in this way. Kerr's "othering" of Sunna continues when she tells Hart her emigration story and when she admits to him that, though she arrived in Unity "a long time ago,"[67] she does not really know anyone in town. It is also significant that Stan takes Sunna as a wife, as Kerr explores the way hostility toward difference can manifest itself as sexual desire. Stan makes it clear in a conversation he has with Mary that he is on the lookout for some woman, any woman really, to help him take care of his house and his new baby, grumbling, "Don't know what's the matter with girls these days"[68] at the realization that Mary has turned him down. Stan, however, is also extremely vocal about his distrust of anyone who is not local, and his passionate embrace of Sunna at the gravesite of his baby makes this conflict within Stan clear; he kisses Sunna over the top of her mask. In Act II, Scene 7, titled "Anatomy," Stan groans under Sunna's touch, while Sunna deliberates on the patterns to be found in every body. The stage directions point out that Stan "*does not hear her speak*,"[69] further revealing the way Sunna functions as an incomprehensible body.

Kerr's goal in marking Sunna as Other is similar to Thiessen's goal in constructing Jean-Paul and Mike as representatives of particular communities: the presence of these characters allows each playwright to signal his interest in exploring the myth of the collective experience as it relates to Canada's participation in the First World War. Whereas Thiessen's play ultimately wishes to affirm the myth, Kerr's play wants to challenge it, the representation of Sunna notwithstanding. The final scene in the play consists of a song that ostensibly celebrates the nation's "day of reckoning" and "coming of age," defining that progressive narrative in relation to the way the First World War has become "everybody's fight...everybody's victory...everybody's misery."[70] The kind of self-conscious theatricality Kerr makes use of with this inclusion of a song is consistent with his overall attempt to echo many of the dramaturgical techniques developed by Caryl Churchill in the late 1970s and throughout the 1980s, techniques that include the use of overlapping dialogue; very short, sometimes lyrical episodic scenes; and non-realistic characters and scenarios (such as the dream sequences in Act I, Scenes 4 and 13). Such echoes in Churchillian dramaturgical technique highlight *Unity (1918)*'s function as a political play that, like Churchill's *Light Shining in Buckinghamshire* and *Mad Forest*, examines critically, often satirically, the mechanisms of political energy. Thus, when the cast of *Unity (1918)* sings "A hundred years of progress / A Century for us / Oh, Canada! / Oh, Canada! / Oh —," the cutting short of the final apostrophe to the nation reinforces the song's irony: the play's representation of the cultural outsider has undermined any simplistic notion of just who constitutes "everybody."

In Act II, Scene 16, titled "Hart and Bea," however, Kerr provides a somewhat hopeful metaphor for the act of confronting difference. As Bea nurses Hart, he tells her the story of an encounter he had overseas with a French prostitute, divulging his belief that he lost his sight after looking at the prostitute's vagina and seeing a flood of light. As he explains to Bea, "I saw through to the other side,"[71] by which he means that he was able to produce a moment of authentic self-recognition for himself and recognition of the woman via their erotic encounter, an encounter that opposes Stan's sexualizing of Sunna's difference. Bea, who has before this conversation primarily tried to see and conduct herself according to the terms set by the homogenous community, decides to take off her mask and kiss Hart, thus inviting in contagion; the stage directions, which call for a *"very bright light,"*[72] indicate that this act allows Bea to "[see] through to the other side." The potential for political optimism implicit in this image, however, is countered by the fact that Bea dies of the flu, leaving behind a diary that speaks only of her personal experience as opposed to what that experience might suggest about the way the people of Unity have responded to calamity. Kerr leaves it to his audience to listen to the words of the final song and see through it to the other side, a side that remains skeptical of a national narrative that can uncritically reiterate the myth of "everybody's fight." Yet by announcing his skepticism, Kerr also signals his belief in the ideal of a tolerant and civically minded collective—of real unity—and of the type of cataclysmic moment, such as a battle, when difference is transcended via the opportunity to act as one.

Three Day Road: Widening the Scope of Participants

More than three quarters of the way through *Three Day Road*, a novel portraying the fictional experiences of two Cree men fighting for Canada during the First World War, the historical figure Francis Pegahmagabow, an Ojibwe soldier known for his success as a First World War sniper, finally makes an appearance. Rumours of Pegahmagabow's feats have reached Boyden's protagonist, Xavier Bird, and his best friend, Elijah Whiskeyjack; Elijah in particular is keen to compare exploits with "Peggy," especially to weigh his own kills against those of the now famous "Indian," rumoured to be "the best hunter of us all."[73] An important objective of this encounter between fictional and historical figures is to emphasize an extratextual function of *Three Day Road* that recalls both Thiessen's and Kerr's author's notes, in terms of framing the function of the text as a vehicle to recall lost histories. In Boyden's own acknowledgements, he states: "I wish to honour the Native soldiers who fought in the Great War, and in all wars in which they so overwhelmingly volunteered. Your bravery and skill do not go unnoticed."[74] Boyden's use here of a helping verb phrase of negation—"do not"—draws special attention to the main part of the predicate "go unnoticed," and thus reveals the irony of his claim: the scene featuring Peggy proposes that First Nations soldiers were not at all "honoured" for their service in the First World War, and that this service went quite aggressively "unnoticed." As Boyden himself admits in an interview with Herb Wyile: "I think my acknowledgements were more wishful thinking than anything."[75] Peggy frankly asserts: "You know that the *wemistikoshiw* [the white men] do not care to believe us when they hear about our kills in the field... We do the nasty work for them and if we return home we will be treated liked pieces of shit once more."[76] Xavier and Elijah are repeatedly treated as second-class citizens: before they enlist for service they are, for example, made to sit in a separate train car for "Indians"; on the field of battle, their superiors are at once dismissive of traditional Cree beliefs and practices and pettily resentful of how bush hunting skills translate into military success.

Boyden's representation of such treatment itself serves "notice," proposing the novel's case for retroactive "honouring." The term "honour" is usefully flexible so as to suggest both the act of conferring high public regard and the act of acknowledging and paying a debt. Boyden creates what Laura Groening might call a "healing aesthetic," in which attention to "remote" cultural myths and the historical record transforms into a narrative that also looks forward and that is constructive. As Boyden asserts in his interview, "there's no question this is a war novel, but just as importantly this is a novel about the healing power and love of family and how that can save you."[77] Groening points out that, in defiance of cultural critics, especially non–First Nations critics, who expect fiction by First Nations writers to wallow in bitterness or primarily engage in "social and political analysis,"[78] writers such as Daniel David Moses and Basil Johnston have endorsed the writing of healing texts that transcend portrayals of First Nations characters as victims, and that depict "a culture alive and well."[79] Boyden's text seeks to recover a marginalized history, but not simply to point out the need to redress an iniquitous historical record, or the fact that, as Peggy asserts, "we do the nasty work for them and if we return home we will be treated liked pieces of shit once more."[80] *Three Day Road* is, paradoxically, a celebratory novel, whereby First Nations contributions to Canada's First World War effort are commemorated and given constructive meaning as part of a living community's narrative. Boyden's defamiliarizing of tropes associated with the First World War and assaults on First Nations culture operate in the context of his insistence on a genealogical plot that suggests familial continuity beyond the historical frame of the novel. Thus, his historical fiction is established on an ethic of constructive deconstruction and a forward-looking inclination toward healing and hope. His goal of reclaiming a marginalized history, however, is predicated on accepting the myth that the First World War operated as a series of events to define the distinctively Canadian collective.

After giving his assessment of *wemistikoshiw* prejudice, Peggy instructs Elijah—who doggedly seeks both official recognition for his many kills as well as legendary status among the men—to "think of me as your conscience... And you can be mine."[81] At the end of this chapter, Elijah admits to having contemplated murdering Peggy during their late night encounter, demonstrating his reluctance to be guided by conscience. Earlier in the chapter, Elijah points out to Xavier that the circumstances of war afford them a "freedom... [that] will not present itself again... this freedom to kill."[82] Xavier's choice to disavow Elijah's idea of freedom, even while fulfilling his duty as a soldier, indicates that the term conscience denotes the double consciousness that is necessary to maintain the ethical framework of the bush in a world almost entirely suffused with detached violence, as well as the negotiation between "yours" and "mine" that an ethics of conscience demands. Conscience further describes the ethical prerogative that Boyden's historical fictionalizing follows, in that his freedom as the author of contemporary historical fiction to emphasize the retroactive claims of redress and "kill" the established record is circumscribed by his duty to the symbolic meaning of the First World War that has been negotiated by Canadians, and by his decision to commemorate that meaning.

Three Day Road is filled with structural and figurative doublings that reiterate the complex idea of conscience, as Boyden explores how the First World War's status as a war of attrition becomes a rich site of oppositional comparison for a narrative of cultural genocide. The doubling of the term "medicine," for example, is clearly meant to set the dangerously addictive effects of morphine against the power of the traditional *matatosowin*, or sweating tent; whereas morphine merely numbs its user to physical pain and fear, the *matatosowin* encourages the natural excretion of bodily toxins and, more importantly, offers the opportunity to confront and move beyond barriers that impede psychic healing. Boyden's depiction of the healing *matatosowin* is charged, signalling the novel's partial objective to deconstruct cultural myth; Xavier and his aunt Niska's ceremonial measures do not result in a neo-romantic revelation of self customary in non-First Nations representations of First Nations spiritual rites, in which First Nations culture "is simply a stereotype against [which] the white man can assert the values of his own culture."[83] Rather, Xavier's lengthy and painful sweat coincides with an agonizing course of detoxification; the ceremony is more a physical necessity than a subject-oriented choice, as is demonstrated by its focalization by Niska rather than Xavier. Furthermore, the climactic realization that Xavier and Niska experience in the *matatosowin* is of Elijah's presence; notably, Boyden shifts the scene's emphasis from Xavier's healing to include the complicated mourning of his childhood friend, whom he still "cannot forgive,"[84] but whose death he must confront.

An even more convoluted deconstructing double emerges in Boyden's descriptions of hunting, on the one hand for game in the bush, and on the other hand for the enemy on the field of battle. During the war, Elijah constructs a "rabbit run," in which he snares a single German soldier by the neck with a piece of thin wire stretched across a trench opening, in part simply to be amused by the sight of the confusion produced by the "floating" dead soldier among his comrades.[85] This scene is a perverse doubling of the prologue's description of the snaring of a marten for its meat and fur. Elijah is convinced that both incidents show him to be a "great hunter,"[86] though, as the war continues, his hunting ability and his procedure of scalping his victims are shown to indicate a sort of bloodlust reminiscent of that of the *windigo*, the creature whose consumption of human flesh has triggered a descent into bloodthirsty madness. When Niska meditates on the tragedy of the human-turned-*windigo*, her conclusions are equally pertinent to the novel's representation of Elijah as a soldier gripped by the violence that surrounds him: "to know...that you have done something so damning out of a greed for life that you have been exiled from your people forever is a hard meal to swallow."[87] While this doubled representation of bloodlust appears at first glance to confirm the opposition of bush and battlefield, it jars against the novel's reputed commemorative function. At the very point in the novel when mounting evidence indicating that Elijah has turned *windigo* seems conclusive, Boyden disrupts such a reductive response to his character by having Elijah himself lucidly assess the commonplace paradox of military heroism: "I'm not crazy...What's mad is them putting us in trenches to begin with. The madness is to tell us to kill and to award those of us who do it well."[88] Elijah's success as a killer is, in fact, officially recognized: he is awarded a Military Medal. Significantly, Francis Pegahmagabow is known as the most decorated First Nations soldier, having been awarded two Military Medals.

Boyden's concurrent representation of Elijah as both a cruel, morphine-addled killer and a brave, decorated tribute to his people indicates a desire to construct structural and figurative doubles that are not merely oppositional, privileging bush over battlefield, but also dialectical, whereby doubled terms must be reconciled within an ethical paradigm, a framework of healing and conscience that makes constructive meaning out of First Nations' experience in history. Furthermore, his interest in exploring the differences between Elijah and Xavier undermines any sense of a simplistic binary narrative that seeks solely to add to what Wyile calls the "proliferation of revisionist historical fiction."[89] Boyden's desire to honour manifests itself not simply as a form of commemoration or even a call for redress for Other Canadians, but also as a provocative expression of cultural recuperation. By exploring First Nations participation in this mythologized narrative of national birth and the forging of a collective, Boyden interrupts what Groening refers to as "the most dangerous trope in Canadian literature: the

Indian as the member of a dead and dying people."[90] The double paradox of Elijah's death is that because it occurs on a French battlefield, it accrues the public currency of progress via noble sacrifice, as opposed to the taint of assimilation. Yet at the same time, because the death occurs at the hands of a tribal fellow, it does not constitute a sign of cultural subjugation. Here and elsewhere, via structural and figurative doubles, Boyden makes visible the mythmaking process that romanticizes both Canada's participation in the First World War and stereotypical representations of First Nations representatives that reduce the Other to a type.

As one side of the novel's oppositional representation of time's movement, historical time is clearly meant to operate as a negative term. Though the novel's structure deviates wildly from a chronological ordering of story events, Boyden identifies by name each battle that Xavier and Elijah's company, the fictional Southern Ontario Rifles, participates in so that their military experience might be followed in sequence.[91] The battle scenes are portrayed as Xavier's memories, recalled in a morphine haze over the course of his three-day canoe trek back into the bush with Niska, whose own memories from even further in the past are retold to Xavier as a healing story; the two sets of memories are juxtaposed in a double, echoing narrative. However, Boyden's use of time and location identifiers for the battle scenes, such as "We spend our first months in and near Saint-Eloi,"[92] "Now that the spring fighting along and around Saint-Eloi has died down, the men talk of being shipped to another place where a great summer battle is building,"[93] "Late in June our battalion is moved near a place called White Horse Cellars [near Ypres],"[94] and so on, as well as his inclusion of such well-known First World War occurrences as the use of chlorine gas and flame-throwers by the German army, ultimately mark the progression of the war as a crucial structuring principle of the novel. Significantly, Boyden draws attention to well-documented instances of specifically Canadian military strategy, fiasco, and success in the war—for example, the invention of the "creeping barrage" at Flers-Courcelette in the Somme and the apparent waste of subsequent months of attritional fighting, as well as the major victory at Vimy Ridge. In the chapter following the description of the taking of Vimy Ridge, Xavier assesses the implications of this success; in doing so, he parrots the same conventional mythology about Canada's birth in the trenches of the war that inspires Thiessen's play *Vimy*: "We've taken the place where hundreds of thousands of Frenchmen and Englishmen died in their attempt to do the same these last years. We are an army to be reckoned with suddenly, no longer the colonials, as the Englishmen call us."[95] Boyden, however, ironically undercuts the myth by following Xavier's almost publicly voiced assessment of Canadian heroics with a description of an injury sustained by a Canadian soldier referred to as Fat, which is either self-inflicted or simply the result of his own clumsiness.

Even more than it confronts national mythology, the historically informed, ostensibly progressive time structure of *Three Day Road* ironically traces a series of regressions. Juxtaposed with chapters describing a succession of battles are retroversions describing the deterioration of Niska and Xavier's community. First Niska's father and then her sister, Xavier's mother, fall victim to *wemistikoshiw* encroachment and law, and Niska's way of life in the bush becomes increasingly unsustainable. The historical battle scenes are the context for the decimation of Elijah and Xavier's original unit, as well as the background for Elijah's personal degeneration and Xavier's loss of faith in his friendships and himself. By the time Xavier awakens in an English hospital to find that the war is over and that his leg has been amputated, he has even lost his name: the identity tags he pulled from Elijah during their final encounter are taken to be his. Xavier fails to rectify the mistake, thinking "there is something calming in the idea that I am Elijah. There is something appealing in being the hero, the one who always does the right thing, says the funny thing."[96] Xavier's willingness to assume the identity of the decorated First Nations soldier, a model of historical progress, reveals Boyden's suspicions about this time structure, as it is a discursive construct.

In confronting and toying with the nationalist myth of Canada's special role in the First World War, especially as it is associated with the way the forging of national community involves the decimation/assimilation of a marginalized cultural group, Boyden participates in deconstructing the notion of an objective history. His deconstruction, however, must proceed with a difference if it is to function simultaneously within the framework of commemorative honouring. Boyden's project of illuminating First Nations contribution to national events necessitates that his writing of progression, though structurally convoluted, not be wholly destabilizing. *Three Day Road* insists on challenging an absolute reliance on a progressive time structure that can only explicate an inevitable regression of First Nations culture. The project of protest requires that historically grounded instances of cultural devastation be marked; at the same time, the project of cultural commemoration and recuperation forces Boyden to remain wary of simply participating in another sort of "othering," which may be the representation of a progressive (regressive) unfolding of the dying people trope. His wish to "honour" First Nations participation in the First World War must therefore promote a progressive and—to some extent—homogenizing ideal.

Xavier's provisional adopting of Elijah's name is a culmination of the novel's thematizing of the way names are associated with a sacred time structure, a structure that seeks to mitigate, but not do away with, the problematic paradigms associated with historical time. Xavier and Elijah are introduced as such in the prologue, and are referred to by these names by Niska in the opening chapter, though this scene of Niska's meeting with her nephew at the train station upon his return from the English hospital initiates the mystery of how and why the two young men's identities have criss-crossed. Niska assumes that she will be meeting Elijah, having heard official word that Xavier was killed in action; Xavier too is surprised, having had word from a family friend that his aunt was dead. This initial scene of resurrection, occasioned by a series of miscommunications, sets the stage for several scenes that deal with the process of sacred renewal, and how that process depends on the assuming of one's true name. The various names assumed by or assigned to Xavier and Elijah signify to what extent their identities transcend or fall victim to categories imposed by the progressions marked by historical time and the conception of a homogenous national community.

Elijah, perhaps because of his relative comfort and success with *wemistkoshiw* language and culture, has forgotten that the name assigned to him, Elijah Whiskeyjack, is a mispronunciation of his Cree name Weesageechak. He begins to inhabit an assigned identity, misconstruing in the process the appropriate path for his own sacred renewal. Weesageechak, Xavier's narration reports, "is the trickster, the one who takes different forms at will,"[97] and Elijah as the Weesageechak is indeed seemingly able to transcend the burden of historical progression, as well as its twin, cultural regression. He adapts well to trench life, using an English accent to mark his protective transformation and, as becomes clear quite late in the novel, has with humour and charm tried to distance himself from the sexual abuse he sustained as a child at the hands of a nun in a residential school. When Elijah jokes to Xavier about eating the flesh of a German, the narrative draws attention to "the gleam of the trickster [that] is in his eyes."[98] The Weesageechak here makes fun of Xavier's great fear of turning *windigo* and mocks his friend's attempts to make sense of seeming madness.[99]

But even the powerful trickster cannot experience a sacred renewal once he begins to behave in keeping with the name assigned to him in the context of historical progression. Elijah Whiskeyjack starts to believe that he is a type of bird, a chattering whiskeyjack jay bird, who is talkative, bold, and, most importantly, meant to fly. Elijah's fervent wish to fly in an airplane, "like a bird,"[100] proves a costly embracing of an assigned identity, as he realizes after his one flight that he "lost something up there."[101] More significantly, his addiction to morphine is represented in terms of his wanting "to leave my body and see what [is] around me."[102] The use of morphine makes

Elijah Whiskeyjack the perfect soldier, fearless and deadly, but his dependence on it to give him an "osprey's vision to spot the enemy"[103] undermines his opportunity to experience sacred renewal. Elijah's imposed identity—as the Whiskeyjack bird—operates as a version of the non–First Nations representative who superficially exploits First Nations myth to his own cultural ends. Over the course of his battlefield experiences, Elijah increasingly revels in the idea, expressed by his military comrades, superiors, and allies, that it is his "Indianness" that gives him "the charm" for military activity;[104] that, as even the despised Lieutenant Breech asserts, Elijah's success is a consequence of "our Indian blood, that our blood is closer to that of an animal than that of a man."[105] Elijah Whiskeyjack, in spite of (or perhaps because of) his success on the battlefield, is the kind of First Nations Other whose behaviour can be rationalized via a patronizing tolerance and inclusion of difference. Problematically, the Military Medal that Elijah receives posthumously allies him with the historical personage Francis Pegahmagabow, as if to suggest that such inclusion warrants honouring, even in a context that reaffirms First World War mythology.

The distinction Boyden wants to make between sacred and assigned names is made evident in Xavier's name story, which is plotted in such a way as to highlight a sacred name's function. The name Xavier, used in the prologue and the first chapter, is promptly supplemented by the name "Nephew," which Niska begins to use once the first resurrection has been enacted, once her relative is again "home."[106] The significance of Niska's use of the name "Nephew" is clarified several chapters later during a scene in which Niska recalls Elijah questioning his friend about her use of the name "Nephew":

> "Why does she call you Nephew and not your real name?" he asked.
> "Nephew is my real name," you answered. "I am her nephew."
> "Does she ever call you by your Christian name?" he asked.
> You shook your head, looked at me nervously. "My name is Nephew."
> "Your name is Xavier," your friend answered.[107]

The juxtaposition of Niska's notion of a name with Elijah's reveals Boyden's contention that names do shift according to perspective and that the bearer of those shifting names must carefully negotiate between ones that offer the opportunity for sacred renewal—as does the name "Nephew" in its capacity of marking a loving familial connection—and ones that produce an externally motivated, potentially exploitable, sense of identity.

The name "Xavier Bird," in fact, serves to reconcile this character's most false and most sacred names, and in another ironic doubling, each of these names is assigned during the celebration that follows a display of individual prowess. The almost ceremonial assigning of what will constitute Xavier Bird's most false name occurs following a marksmanship contest that takes place during combat training in Toronto: Xavier is the only soldier able to light a match placed twenty paces away with a shot from his rifle. The sergeant in charge of Xavier's winning company pronounces: "From now on you will no longer be called Xavier. You have a new name now. Your new name is simply X."[108] Though this name is meant to function not only as a well-meant honour but also as a marker of Xavier's absorption into a new community (a community he will, as the war progresses, come to think of in familial terms), it also constitutes a radical effacement, one that the narrative ironically makes note of. Xavier reflects in the moment that his new name ensures that "none of these who are here today can call me a useless bush Indian ever again. They might not say it out loud, but they know now that I have something special."[109] The ensuing narrative, however, proves his assessment problematic on two counts: first, his status as a bush Indian is repeatedly deemed a hindrance by commanding Lieutenant Breech, and second, his more sacred and special bush identity, gestured toward in the surname Bird, is obliterated by his newly found eagerness to inhabit the name "X." Much later in the novel, in the chapter immediately preceding the description of the identity tag swap, Niska recalls the ceremony during which her nephew received his sacred bush name, "Little Bird Dancer," given to celebrate Xavier's first solo hunt, as well as his witnessing of the rarely seen circle dance of the grouse. That this scene, redolent with life and laughter, occurs so late in the narrative demonstrates that the sacred name functions to invoke a circular sense of time as well a viable sense of identity; Niska's retrospective account is a critical though painful part of sacred healing, and the near-death state her nephew falls into after hearing the account marks the resumption of the sacred name as prerequisite to renewal.

What is potentially problematic, however, about a wholesale privileging of sacred time over historical time is the way such a paradigm appears to dispense with the systemic cultural recuperation that must occur in "real" time; the mythologizing of the sacred name is its own kind of empty "respecting" of difference that Len Findlay derides. Ultimately, what Boyden fashions may be likened to what Groening refers to as a "healing aesthetic," an aesthetic that neither exclusively calls attention to stories of "victimhood"[110] nor provides comfortingly symbolic applications of "the red man's myths [as] important to all Canadians in search of 'home.'"[111] Boyden does not, therefore, allow portrayals of historical time and sacred time to culminate in opposition; rather, he offers a genealogical sense of time as the scheme via which healing may occur. Contemporary recourses to tracing genealogy in literature often depend on locating a sense of familial continuity even when strict linear succession has been disrupted. Boyden's genealogical plot differs somewhat from Frances Itani's conservative deployment; in her plot, the crisis of genealogy is temporary. In *Three Day Road*, Boyden engages the contemporary sense of genealogical time in several significant ways, all of which operate, in the first place, to trouble the progressive–regressive time structure that links national progression with the dying First Nations culture, and in the second place, to indicate how sacred renewal is not a spiritually discrete, non-threatening process that occurs "out of time" but rather is associated with tangible cultural recuperation, as well as with the ideal of the functioning collective.

Early on in her narrative, Niska declares that she is "the second to last in a long line of *windigo* killers. There is still one more."[112] Niska's father was a *windigo* killer who was arrested by white lawmakers for killing a Cree woman, along with her child, who had thrice broken with the community: first, in wasting a piece of meat from a sacred bear feast; second, in leaving the starving tribe along with her husband to search for their own sustenance; and third, having failed to find game, for feeding on her husband's corpse and developing an incurable taste for human flesh. Boyden thus represents the *windigo* killer as a custodian of tribal values and collectivity, rather than as the purveyor of a particular bloodline or consecration, and it is acknowledged that the expression of such values, as well as the circumstances defining collectivity, will change over time. The role of *windigo* killer is taken on because it fulfills a community need, and in the case of both Niska and her nephew, Xavier, it is taken on rather inadvertently and somewhat reluctantly. Niska's explanation to Xavier that "sometimes one must be sacrificed if we all are to survive"[113] seems to refer to both the *windigo* and his or her killer, as first Niska's father, then Niska, and finally Xavier are removed from the physical and psychic borders of their community in order to fulfill the task of protecting the tribe from the "sadness...at the heart of the *windigo*;"[114] from the place, as Xavier tells Elijah, from where "there is no coming back."[115] Though Niska's original sense only refers to herself and "one more" *windigo* killer, the adaptability of this unfortunate role holds promise for the difficult yet necessarily ongoing process of guarding the developing community.

Boyden further relies on the more open and adaptable sense of familial continuity that is in keeping with the contemporary genealogical plot in his decision not to render birth scenes, which might invigorate a sense of bloodline importance and discrete succession, and in his rendering of the brotherhood that exists between Xavier and Elijah, who are not actually related by blood, as well as in Niska's adopting of her nephew and his friend as her own. In the final chapter of the novel, which depicts the painful process of Xavier's physical and psychic detoxification in the *matatosowin*, Boyden offers a culminating scene that suggests cultural continuity that does not depend on discrete familial succession, and in which the dialectic of historical time and sacred time is resolved. The final vision that Niska receives in the *matatosowin* is, as she asserts, a "good vision": "Children... They are two boys, naked, their brown backs to me as they throw little stones into the water. Their hair is long in the old way and is braided with strips of red cloth. But this isn't the past. It is what's still to come. They look to be brothers. Someone else besides me watches them. I sense that he watches to keep them from danger."[116] Though Niska deduces that this vision depicts her great-nephews, Xavier's sons, its many allusions to the past relationship between Xavier and Elijah implicate a genealogical future that moves beyond the limiting time structures of commemoration and redress. The boys look forward to the circular patterns emerging from stones dropped into water, even as their naked "backs" come into focus; the braiding of hair with red cloth not only implies a return to tradition, but also suggests the way the colour red, signifying earlier blood and loss, interweaves with what "is still to come"; the boys "look to be brothers," demonstrating that bonds forged out of a sense of community, continuity, and conscience make sacred renewal possible. The custodian figure, who "watches to keep them from danger," is also there, signalling that the requirement for a *windigo* killer may yet resurface, and that an eye to the often painful process of cultural recuperation and growth remains.

Niska's good vision of genealogical continuity ensures the health of her relation—his ability to make peace with his anguished past, to progress through what remains of his as yet uncharted history and to enact a sacred return to his name, his role, his home. In adopting historical fiction to his own recuperative ends, Boyden has rendered a First Nations history that is not bounded by what Groening refers to as the "field of opposition that consistently renders those once savage people as dead and dying, a thing of the past."[117] Though the Cree community that *Three Day Road* depicts is often under physical and psychic attack by encroaching *wemistkoshiw* culture, the violence included in this narrative is not strictly oppositional; more important, it is not depicted in the elegiac terms of a "last stand." Boyden is surprisingly optimistic in that *Three Day Road* explores how the stories of a previously marginalized community—in this case, a First Nations community—can be productively written into history. To that purpose, however, Boyden must reaffirm not only the myth that the First World War produced the Canadian nation, but also the idea that tolerance of diversity within the collective depends on such reaffirmations.

A Secret Between Us: Impersonating History

As is the case with the other texts explored in this chapter, the acknowledgements in *A Secret Between Us* draw attention to an extratextual agenda that has, apparently, provided the author with the impetus for writing. Daniel Poliquin describes an objective similar to Thiessen's stated intention to explore "why ... we pass over some moments in our history yet mythologize others"; to Kerr's, which is to bring to light the 1918 influenza epidemic, which he claims is "largely forgotten now"; and to Boyden's, which is to "honour the Native soldiers who fought in the Great War." For his part, Poliquin asserts that *A Secret Between Us* "is the literary expression of a collective memory that is slipping away more than it is spreading around."[118] Here he is referring to the memory of Ottawa, particularly the neighbourhood known as the LeBreton Flats, during the early twentieth century. Like the authors of *Vimy*, *Unity (1918)*, and *Three Day Road*, Poliquin delineates his novel as at least partly devoted to the work of recovery, whereby the literary representation of historical events and/or personages and/or social patterns will renovate the reading public's sense of which particularities of history are worth acts of remembrance.

There are, however, differences between Poliquin's concern with this work of recovery as it manifests itself in his novel and the way such interest operates in the other texts. First, his atypical use of historical personages as anchors for the novel obfuscates the record instead of illuminating or enlarging it; as discussed below, no English-speaking reviewer of the novel seems even to have noticed exactly how the book makes use of historical research, and this obliviousness is likely not a matter of a lack of attention but rather a product of Poliquin's own reservations about the work of recovery. Second, in a move similar to Kerr's, Poliquin draws on the First World War context in order to explore something else. While Kerr makes use of both war rhetoric and the idea that it was soldiers returning from war who brought influenza germs to Canada to explore the way flu deaths might also be made socially meaningful, Poliquin's references to the war, exceptional in their flippancy, are juxtaposed with his descriptions of inhabitants of the Flats who have done nothing particularly memorable or historically meaningful. Poliquin's writing of the First World War is distinct from representations that are a means to the end of historical recovery work. His writing of the war is a trick; the book's use of tropes associated with the Canadian historical novel, including irreverent references to Canada's mythic war, demolishes the idea of sacralized collective remembrance, especially as such collective remembrance depends on an arbitrary elevation of the representative individual who is supposed to stand for his or her distinct, though tolerated, community.

Most reviewers of Donald Winkler's 2007 translation of Poliquin's novel (originally published in 2006 as *La Kermesse*) more or less explicitly affirm the novel's surprise nomination for the 2007 Giller Prize as the impetus for their attention. Reviews by Kathryn Kuitenbrouwer, writing for the *Globe and Mail*, T.F. Rigelhof, writing for *Books in Canada*, and Melora Koepke, writing for the *Vancouver Sun*, make note of the novel's "dark horse" status,[119] while commenting on the way Poliquin works to reinvent the historical novel. Kuitenbrouwer asserts that *A Secret Between Us* "plays broadly with the term 'historical novel'... [as] Poliquin is not interested in historical veracity,"[120] while Rigelhof praises the novel for being such a remarkable "sendup of the earnestness, the self-importance, the whining, the pretentiousness that passes for artistic seriousness and social responsibility among the generality of those who write historical novels in this country."[121] Indeed, notwithstanding Poliquin's stated claim regarding the passing away of collective memory, his novel makes no attempt to honour the lives and/or deaths of those whom the historical record may have marginalized or overdetermined, or whose story might be retrospectively incorporated into a narrative of sacrifice.

In the first chapters of *A Secret Between Us*, Poliquin's satiric tone becomes clear in his invocation of the Battle of Vimy Ridge and in his description of the life and death of Private Léon Tard, a subaltern who worked with the protagonist and narrator—Lusignan—as a gravedigger in France. Tard is introduced when Lusignan must explain to him the reason for his gloom during one of their digging sessions: Lusignan has heard word via telegram that his mother has died, the news coming "just before the battle of Vimy."[122] The narrator's mention of Vimy here, coupled with the news of his mother's death, might, in a different Canadian literary text revisiting the First World War, have crucial symbolic significance. One might argue that Lusignan's mother represents the mother country, an idea all the more problematic because of Lusignan's status as a francophone Ontarian, and that her death before the momentous battle signals a painful but necessary turning point in Canada's maturation. Conversely, Poliquin's narrative follows up the stark report of the death with Lusignan's account of how he "sought out my warrant officer, hoping that my loss might garner me a two-day leave that would free me to go and ask Nurse Flavie from the Vendée if she might one day love me." The warrant officer rejects the appeal because Lusignan has already used his mother's death as an excuse to be granted leave on four previous occasions, recommending he "should try doing in [his] father for a change."[123] Tard, however, is overcome with sadness at the news about Lusignan's mother and feels compelled to tell the story of his own mother's death and of his unhappy childhood, which the narrator describes in two short paragraphs that primarily relate the abuse Tard suffered at the hands of his uncle and aunt, who "accused him of taking up too much space and eating like a pig."[124] In the next chapter, after Lusignan has described the arranged marriage of his lunatic mother to his simpleton father, he relates the story of Tard's death: "The next day, while I was delivering a message to headquarters, a German mine blew up the bunker. All I saw when I got back, in the place of Tard's face smiling serenely at the thought of pancakes in a lukewarm bed, was a smoking hole. There was nothing to do. The lice had already deserted his corpse."[125] The irreverence with which Poliquin represents the First World War soldier's life and death in these early chapters is merely a hint at what is to come; the novel goes on to poke fun at several conventions governing the writing of the Canadian First World War novel, from the subaltern's progression from innocence to experience in the war, through the representation of the war's horrors and the bravery of individual soldiers at the front, to the representation of how difficult it is for returning soldiers to return to their lives at home.

Like Rigelhof, Koepke is keen to emphasize the satire at the heart of *A Secret Between Us*, going so far as to point out how Poliquin's "detailing of the vices and negligible virtues of the First World War era" operate in contrast to "the vast library of earnest self-important historical novels about great Canadians and their important deeds."[126] The protagonist of *A Secret Between Us* is not a great Canadian, but a coward, a liar, a lecher, and a drunk. Furthermore, these vices are not in any way connected to his war experience—he is not, for example, a suffering postwar morphine addict like Xavier Bird or Augusta Moffat in *The Underpainter*—as he was blameworthy of all his vices well before he enlisted. As Lusignan explains to a young woman who has propositioned him and who wants him to "tell her about the war,"[127] he represents quite the opposite of what a heroic war insider is meant to be:

> Look, for example, I never killed anyone. The only men I killed were already dead. When we were alone, my friend Private Léon Tard and I, we discharged our guns into the corpses... Once, on our way back from our chores at the cemetery, we almost soiled ourselves when we came upon the cadavers of German soldiers raised from the mud by the last downpour of shells. They were erect there, eyes vitreous, skin green, and we rekilled them to the last man... When the Princess Pats arrived in France in 1915, I'd already been demoted to private, and I took no part in the first battles that killed off half our men. After two weeks I had to undergo a medical inspection because I was

feverish. The doctor discovered a virulent syphilis I'd caught from an Englishwoman whom I'd been too eager to sleep with, just because she was English.[128]

Lusignan's speech, which goes on in a similar vein for another full page, not only challenges the First World War's mythic status but also displays the extent to which the writing of these events from Canadian history has become entirely a matter of convention; his war stories are shocking only because excessively iterated stories of heroism and sacrifice, and of Canada's rejection of its status as a mere colony of Britain, have become all too familiar.

The war's link to discursive conventions is also made visible when the narrator explains his work writing official condolence letters to the families of soldiers who have been killed. Lusignan admits that writing such letters is no more than "a stylistic exercise" and that "to save time I copied some letters and sent them to several families, making sure they lived far enough away from one another that no one would doubt the sincerity of my sentiments."[129] Here, Poliquin's novel draws attention to the paradoxical relationship between convention, which depends on reiteration, and the discursive illusion of sincerity. As Cobley explains, part of the work of the war narrative is to create a frame for interpretation, so that the details of that narrative can ultimately be read symbolically.[130] Poliquin goes on to provide an example of one of Lusignan's "stylistic exercise[s]," a letter he writes to the family of Private Blondeau that waxes poetic about the soldier's heroism and nobility, in order to highlight further the degree to which our frame of interpretation for the war narrative depends on the ceaseless repetition of semiotic codes that are meant to signal "truth." And, in a final blow to the idea of the Canadian soldier's mythic status, the narrator concludes his mention of Blondeau with the flat assertion, "Private Blondeau was even more of a thief than my friend Tard, and he cheated at cards to boot. The third time he was recaptured after deserting, the non-commissioned officers quarrelled over who would command the firing squad. They played a little poker, and the winner had the honour of shouting 'fire.'"[131]

The parody of the official condolence letter is significant in *A Secret Between Us* not just because the form has been incorporated into other Canadian literary responses to the First World War, including *Broken Ground*, *Deafening*, *The Sojourn*, and *Unity (1918)*, but also because of the distinctive object of Poliquin's critique. While both Frances Itani and Alan Cumyn make use of the form without irony, whereby the rhetoric of duty to Empire is upheld so that the personal grief of the soldier's family can be emphasized, Hodgins and Kerr draw attention to condolence letters precisely to criticize the artificiality of that rhetoric. Poliquin, however, is less interested in the relative truthfulness or otherwise of military discourse than he is in challenging the very idea of the sacredness of truth. The description of Blondeau provided after Lusignan's overwrought condolence letter is not meant to register as a counteracting "realism" in the way that Itani's portrayal of Jim's experiences as a military medic or Hart's description of the front to Beatrice are meant to. The sheer hyperbole and profanity of Poliquin's depiction of Blondeau's actual death, which also lampoons the almost ubiquitous soldier-shot-for-cowardice plot, reflects the novel's absolute rejection of the idea that "truth" is ever anything but a discursive illusion, as well as its challenge to the idea that certain myths—for example, the myth of the dutiful First World War soldier—need to be respected.

Lusignan's brief stint as a letter writer also gestures toward a key plot of *A Secret Between Us*, which is Lusignan's intervention into the love affair between Essiambre d'Argenteuil, a military officer with whom he shared a single sexual encounter and whom he is infatuated with, and Amalia Driscoll, an Ottawa society woman who writes long, involved letters to d'Argenteuil after their own sexual interlude has ended. Lusignan steals Amalia's letters from d'Argenteuil, a theft that goes unnoticed as "Essiambre hated writing and never read his mail,"[132] and begins corresponding with her as d'Argenteuil. This act of impersonation is only one of many that Lusignan engages in, as he tries to live up to the "glorious ancestors"[133] whose name he bears by posing as others. After playing dress-up as a child and imitating a friend from school, he moves on to writing novels in a variety of styles, proving that he is "a master at toadying,"[134] and then pretending to be a series of literary critics responding favourably to the work. Poliquin also represents Lusignan's experiences as a returned soldier as a kind of impersonation; his wearing of the Princess Patricias' officer's uniform masks the fact that he was demoted from his position. Finally, the three central characters in *A Secret Between Us* are also impersonations: Poliquin's Lusignan, Essiambre d'Argenteuil, and Amalia Driscoll are more or less thinly veiled versions, respectively, of the Montreal journalist and novelist Rodolphe Girard, whose novel *Marie Calumet* (1904) was publicly condemned for its bawdy representation of Quebec society and the Church; Talbot Mercer Papineau, a lieutenant with the Princess Patricias from Quebec who argued against Henri Bourassa in favour of Quebec's involvement in the war; and Ethel Chadwick, a young woman who left a diary describing wartime Ottawa.

No English-language reviewer of *A Secret Between Us* seems to have detected the use the novel makes of Sandra Gwyn's *Tapestry of War*, despite Poliquin's citation of this work in his acknowledgements, which specifically mention Talbot Papineau and Ethel Chadwick.[135] In a few cases, this unawareness is made all too clear by specific references to the epistolary voice of Amalia Driscoll. In Michel Basilières's unfavourable review of *A Secret Between Us*, published in *Quill & Quire* before the announcement of the Giller Prize long list, he writes that Amalia's letters contain descriptions of "social graces, events, and attitudes bearing no relevance to us, Lusignan, or the plot [which] are detailed at length in Driscoll's pretentious and whining manner, making it easy to see why her fiancé would choose to leave her for the front."[136] Rigelhof takes Basilières to task for the sheer nastiness of his review, accusing him of "obtuseness" and "arrogance,"[137] yet he too remarks on a problem associated with Amalia's letters, asserting that "Poliquin is almost too good a mimic: the letters from Amalia to d'Argenteuil that interrupt Lusignan's reveries are seemingly so true to the underfed mind and straight circumstances of a gentlewoman of the era that it's all too easy to fall blindly into them and lose track of the larger sense of the novel" (10). Like Rigelhof, Koepke praises Poliquin for his rendition of Amalia's letters, calling "her lively epistolary voice…Poliquin's finest achievement in this book."[138]

But Amalia's letters are not exclusively Poliquin's achievement; he depends heavily on Gwyn's text in writing them. Like Chadwick, for example, Amalia is an upper-class immigrant from Ireland whose father works at McGill University, and who never quite recovers from the failure of the family fortune; also like Chadwick, Amalia makes use of her skating ability to garner attention from Ottawa's inner circle, in particular the Governor General, Prince Arthur. As much as Poliquin makes use of Gwyn's research and the style gleaned from Chadwick's diary, he is at the same time not particularly careful about remaining faithful to the historical record: while Amalia gains work as an advertising artist, "earn[ing] a real weekly salary, like a man,"[139] Ethel Chadwick "decorated lamp shades and tea trays in floral motifs to sell on consignment at local gift shops";[140] Chadwick lived out her life as a "provincial and circumscribed" spinster,[141] while Amalia takes lovers and becomes a painter of nudes. Poliquin's portrayal of Amalia is clearly not an attempt at historical veracity, but neither does it represent his own creative attempt to reconsider the role of the individual as he or she relates to the mythology of the collective. In her final letter to d'Argenteuil, Amalia admits to him that she no longer needs to write because she has taken up sex again, noting that "voluptuousness induces oblivion. The carnal act is the universal solvent of regret."[142] Yet while Amalia can give up her individual commitment to acts of witnessing and remembrance, it is supposed that the collective cannot because of its responsibility to keep the past from "slipping away."[143] Poliquin might reasonably have balked at the tone of Basilières's review; that said, his novel does seek to explore the problem of compulsive and compulsory remembrance of "events and attitudes bearing no relevance to us."[144] Ethel Chadwick's habit of writing a diary during the war years, even a diary devoid of "brilliance or wit,"[145] has afforded her a place in the historiographical record, whereas Poliquin's Amalia is juxtaposed with the character Concorde, who, despite having crossed paths with every figure in the novel who leaves some sort of historical trace and despite having risen in class, is destined to "[pass] her entire life unnoticed."[146]

Poliquin's play with history is thus distinct from Boyden's in that the point of *A Secret Between Us* is not to augment the scope of what is considered worthy of remembrance, but rather to consider whether the "spreading around" of history serves any useful purpose. Poliquin's d'Argenteuil is a version of Talbot Papineau, the francophone army captain who in 1916 famously tried to counter Henri Bourassa's anti-recruitment campaign in an open letter that queried "what mattered the why and wherefore of the war, whether we owed anything to England or not, and whether we were Imperialist or not, or whether we were French or English? The one simple commanding fact was that Canada was at war and Canada and Canadian liberties had to be protected."[147] Papineau's anchoring within the historical record connects to this public declaration of his Canadian nationalist perspective, as well as to the massive archive of letters to his mother and to an American woman, Beatrice Fox, that he left behind in which he described his wartime experiences. Though Gwyn cites Papineau's francophone background as the reason for referring to him as "the most unlikely Patricia of all,"[148] she is able to hone in on his voice as one of the distinctive and representative "prisms of history,"[149] mostly because of the extant material record. D'Argenteuil, in contrast, "hated writing and never read his mail."[150]

Poliquin's version of Papineau is directly associated with the historical record. He is a proud Canadian francophone with ancestral ties to eighteenth-century Quebec, a brilliant Ottawa lawyer, an inspiring military officer and noble soldier, and a figure "as authentic as a character in a novel"[151] in terms of the way he is popularly remembered. But Poliquin's d'Argenteuil is also a cad, a man who makes a habit of cementing the loyalty of his under-officers via sexual seduction and who ignores the letters from those who love him. Furthermore, at no point in *A Secret Between Us* does the issue of francophone loyalty to the Canadian nationalist enterprise come up, as it does, for example, in Thiessen's play, and this makes Poliquin's thinly veiled references to the famous Canadian nationalist francophone seem like a red herring. Poliquin's point here is to imagine the iconic historical figure as he is defined by fictional discourse, "as a character in a novel," rather than by the archival record; the implicit suggestion is that neither construction is any more trustworthy than the other, though one construction might have more mythical power. In other words, it is not just the historical record that Poliquin questions, but the narratives that emerge from it, including the one that would locate the source for current tensions between English and French Canada in the French-language laws of 1912 and the Conscription Crisis of 1917, thereby simplifying those tensions.

Poliquin's own relationship to francophone Canada is complex. Early in his career as a novelist and translator, this Franco-Ontarian was celebrated in Quebec; however, the 2001 publication of his *In the Name of the Father: An Essay on Quebec Nationalism*, a book that fiercely condemned Québécois nationalism as "the political embodiment of adolescence,"[152] set him at odds with Quebec nationalists.[153] However, Poliquin's refusal to write a healing narrative for francophone Canada (or perhaps for anglophone Canada) is not simply associated with his contempt for the viewpoint that Quebecers have been victimized by so-called English Canada and the "cartoonesque" notion that "Quebec's history is an endless darkness that lifts only when [the separatist intelligentsia] arrive[s] on the scene."[154] In taking on the issue of the competing Anglo- and Franco-nationalisms associated with the First World War in *A Secret Between Us,* Poliquin indicates his distrust of the very concept of redressing a necessarily reconstituted past via an increasingly convention-ridden set of narratives. This distrust is most apparent in his portrayal of the central character Lusignan. In a 2002 interview with François Ouellet, published in *Voix et Images*, Poliquin discusses his use of the historical figure Rodolphe Girard, focusing mostly on Girard's writing of "anti-imperialist novels,"[155] his work in the Senate, and, along with Jules Fournier and Olivar Asselin, his part as a "dissenter" who believed in the importance of Quebec nationalism.[156] In the novel, details about Girard's work as a novelist are reimagined in service of Poliquin's desire to call into question our sacred historical narratives and to rethink the practice of collective remembrance and its dependence on discourse.

In "Indigestible Stew and Holy Piss: The Politics of Food in Rodolphe Girard's *Marie Calumet*," Susan Kevra explains that Girard's novel, which "mocked rural Quebec society, with its harshest attacks levelled against the Catholic Church,"[157] was received with outrage; so harsh were the critical responses—which accused the writer of moral and aesthetic perversion—that Girard's career as a novelist was ruined. As Kevra describes, "he exiled himself to Ottawa, where he remained for the duration of his professional life, working primarily as a government translator."[158] During Lusignan's spree as a writer, he too writes a novel, titled *Franchonne,* that "instead of celebrating the French race and its sacred soil... [focuses] on mocking Father Lajoie, his servant... the churchwardens and the notary

Poitras," all figures from Lusignan's own rural Quebec upbringing.[159] Like Girard, Lusignan is faced with the material repercussions of critical disapproval: "All the critics who had praised me earlier recommended that the book be banned. My lucrative freelance work vanished, and I lost my job as a proofreader for *La Presse*."[160] What Poliquin adds to the tale of Girard's disgrace as a novelist is the playful description of the way Lusignan's own pseudonyms turn against him. Lusignan has invented Oscar Petit and Samuel Legris, reviewers who not only praise Lusignan's early novels, *The Knight of Malartic* and *The Fiancés of the Scaffold*, but who also argue with each other in print about whether or not Lusignan is meeting his potential as a writer. After *Franchonne* is published, "Oscar Petit said that he had never read such a piece of trash. Samuel Legris challenged me to a duel for defaming the Mother Church."[161] Lusignan admits that he "will doubtless never know who commandeered my bylines to turn them against me."[162] Poliquin's point here is to show how inherently pliable public writing is and to interrogate the absurdity of the idea that certain ideas are so dangerous that they should not be circulated.[163]

Arguably, the most profane idea circulating in *A Secret Between Us* is that Lusignan is a lousy soldier. Crucially, it is not because of the war's horrors that Lusignan loses his moral compass, his sense of honour, his work ethic, and so on; in fact, the novel has very little to say about the war's horrors, except in terms of the way descriptions of those horrors have become conventional. Describing the last impersonating letter he writes to Amalia, Lusignan notes that he "added three or four pages on the cold, the mud, the blood in the trenches, things of which I cannot speak but that I managed to write about with ease."[164] As Cobley notes, the descriptive detail of soldier narratives "is assumed to be the most objective window into phenomenal and experiential reality." While Cobley goes on to argue that the reliance on description makes first-hand accounts of the war "no less constructed, and hence open to distortion or ideological manipulation, than poetic and narrative strategies,"[165] Poliquin's narrative emphasizes the extent to which the descriptive list has become formulaic, a set of semiotic codes that contemporary authors can "write about with ease."

The upshot of Poliquin's refusal to consider the deficiencies of Lusignan's character in relation to the horrors of war is the startling implication that Lusignan is simply ignoble, lazy, and cowardly all on his own. That a Canadian First World War soldier can be presented in this way seems positively blasphemous, as it calls into question the most sacred of Canadian First World War myths: that, despite the repulsiveness of war, despite all of our fervent desires for peace, the Canadian soldier himself was honourable, and that his war work represented not only a necessary sacrifice but an enactment of all that is noble, pure, and good. As Vance points out, this myth of the Canadian soldier's transcendent virtue was not solely—or even primarily—a matter of considering the individual soldier's role in the war; it was mainly an outlet for defining the Canadian collective: "he was the nation's past, present, and future, and the embodiment of all its aspirations and potential."[166] The texts written by Thiessen, Kerr, and Boyden all attempt to add the stories of ever more individuals—individuals from increasingly diverse cultural communities—in such a way as to augment the idea of a collective, national enterprise; Poliquin, however, is unwilling to write the individual as anything more than a figment of imagination and passing records. In undermining the myth of Canadian First World War soldiers' noble sacrifice, Poliquin's novel challenges the notion that Canada's participation in the war operated as a testing ground to define particular national traits. The refusal to construct an emblematic figure—whose function is to represent dutifulness, earnestness, moral bravery, a rejection of Old World class systems, or the special inclusiveness of Canada's national collective—also culminates in a refusal to valorize an uncomplicated conception of civic participation or action. In this way, Poliquin signals his skepticism, not of official history, but rather of attempts to revisit history according to a particular political agenda, as doing so forces the same overdetermination and reiteration of myths as are ostensibly being written against.

Poliquin's narrative is startling because it seems to be the only contemporary Canadian First World War reimagining that does not culminate in a confirmation of the way in which remembering the war serves a useful purpose. *Vimy*, for example, tries to make the story of soldiers from diverse communities coming together for a single military objective communicate something to contemporary audiences about shared ideals among a tolerant, varied, but unified nation. Similarly, Boyden's *Three Day Road* attempts to widen the scope of participation in the war, not just to augment the historical record but to suggest that First Nations communities will continue to play a vibrant role within the collective known as Canada. Kerr's play, though perhaps more doubtful about how genuine expressions of tolerance are, especially when they only function to mark certain people as Other, places the story about "seeing through to the other side" in the mouth of a blinded returned soldier in a way that recalls the myth that Canadian First World War participants represented the best of Canada, in part because of the insight borne of experience.

What, then, can one say about *A Secret Between Us*? In the first place, Poliquin's skewering of the emblematic image of the noble, brave, and dutiful Canadian First World War soldier operates as a clear challenge to the homogenizing force of that image. Yet for all the satire and blasphemy in his novel, it should be noted that it is also a great deal of fun. The sheer exuberance of *A Secret Between Us* might be associated with Poliquin's admission that we need not be ashamed of attempts to hold on to our cultural myths, as long as we acknowledge that we do so because we need them. By drawing attention to the fact that the reiteration of cultural narratives is a matter of selection and choice, Poliquin signals an awareness of current anxieties about agency and citizenship. The mythology of the First World War—a set of narratives that so many writers have shown they can "write about with ease"—is proved to be amenable to the type of national self-fashioning required in an age when the very concept of the nation is in crisis. Thus, even in Poliquin's text, the return to the subject of Canada's participation in the First World War reflects an awareness of current nostalgia for a particular cultural code, one that equates Canadian nationalism with demonstrations of the tolerance of difference, with a confidence in the righteousness of collective action, with pride in dutiful service, and with a basic belief in cultural progress. Such expressions of "pride" in seemingly outdated conceptions of cultural heritage constitute an anxious attempt to "[shape] the future and [set] the terms of [a community's] encounters with the world."[167] In this sense, the idealization of cultural homogeneity that provides a stable foundation for the national collective—and even the satiric challenge to that idealization—reflects a climate in which restless citizens show their unease about having to confront their own powerlessness in confrontation with the faceless global imaginary. Thus, the nostalgia for myths associated with Canada's participation in the First World War, especially the myth of the working collective, emerges from a desire to re-entrench narratives that figure "everyday" citizens as meaningful contributors to the work of inventing the nation.

Conclusion: Representations of the First World War and Wishing

True story: in the summer of 2008, during which time I was in the thick of reading the novels and plays that make up the corpus for this study, I went to see a movie with some colleagues. In one of the trailers, images of muddy men shooting rifles and a wind-blown woman reading letters competed with voice-overs of a man saying things like, "I don't fight for glory or medals—I only fight for you," and a woman declaring, "I used to believe in things like sacrifice"; as the operatic music swelled, certain phrases appeared on the screen: "They fought for their country"; "Every war has its stories"; "This is our story." Before the trailer had ended, I nudged the person sitting beside me and made a guess: "This movie is going to be called *Vimy*." When the title *Passchendaele* appeared on the screen I grinned at my colleague, as if to say, "See? I was close!" My colleague, being an American, had very little idea what I was on about. Another story: sometime in late 2009, another colleague of mine offered to lend me her copy of the DVD of *Passchendaele*, as she thought I'd probably want to examine the film in the context of my research. I declined at the time, pronouncing (somewhat grumpily) that I just didn't have the energy for another portrayal of a plucky Canadian soldier who against all odds—which include both mud and the stupidity of officers—manages to do his duty and relate to those back home that war is hell, though somehow a necessary hell. My colleague responded: "Oh, so you have seen the movie." But I hadn't yet. For me, Paul Gross's big-budget film about the Great War from a Canadian serviceman's perspective marked my own sense that perhaps Robert Wiersema had been right in 2005: perhaps these historical events had been reimagined too many times in the space of ten or so years to produce anything more than a sense of déjà vu. As it happened, the release of *Passchendaele* coincided almost precisely with the end of the recent rush of Canadian First World War reimaginings.

The reviews for *Passchendaele* are fairly uniform: critics tend to praise the battle scenes for their gritty authenticity (which is considered all the more remarkable given the relatively meagre budget of $20 million), while panning the romance plot for being too clichéd and heavy-handed. As Jay Stone, writing for Canwest News Service, notes, "this is a romance—a conventional one at that—that happens to be set in 1917, and while it provides frighteningly authentic battle scenes, it slogs just as dangerously through knee-deep schmaltz."[1] Similarly, Cassandra Szklarski, writing for the *Telegraph-Journal*, praises the film for being "a valuable depiction of one of Canada's most important battles," after suggesting that "the courtship ultimately bogs down the first half of the film, also undermined by a stagey portrait of wartime Calgary that comes across too much like a televised heritage moment."[2] In press material put out before the film's major release, Gross, the film's writer, director, and lead actor, stated that he was more interested in the personal story than in the military one: "I've always been interested in the intimate casualties of war: What it does to families and communities. What it does to love, I suppose."[3] Gross's interest in love, community, and the space away from the war is comparable to the thematic concerns of most, if not all, of the texts examined in this study, which have often been praised for considering the way the military war is associated with other sorts of conflicts, objectives, fears, and losses.

On the home front, Sarah Mann, the female lead in *Passchendaele*, portrayed by Caroline Dhavarnas, loses her job as a nurse because she was born in Germany; her speech to Gross's character, Michael Dunne, about the way the war "tore [their] lives in half" recalls the discord felt by the German immigrant population portrayed in Urquhart's *The Stone Carvers*. The ethnic diversity of the platoon Michael reluctantly comes to lead just before the momentous battle at Passchendaele recalls the group Thiessen portrays in *Vimy*: it includes one First Nations representative ("Highway," played by Michael Greyeyes), who refers to himself as a "Skin"; one francophone Canadian ("Godin," played by Justin Michael Carriere); and various Anglo-Canadians, one of whom is clearly from a rural background as he can comfortably kill and pluck a chicken with his bare hands. Home front machinations depicted in the film concerning recruitment and war propaganda—including the continual rehearsal of the story of a Canadian NCO who was crucified against a barn door by German soldiers—as well as representations of cowardly, arrogant military superiors, personified in the character of Dobson-Hughes (played by Jim Mezon), correspond with similar disapproving explorations of political and military incompetence and callousness in Hodgins's *Broken Ground* and the war novels of Alan Cumyn. The film's explicit contrasting of the stunning Calgary landscape with the brutalized background of Flanders reflects the gulf in understanding between the war insider and the war outsider, a concern that prevails in such texts as Swan's *The Deep*, Itani's *Deafening*, and Kerr's *Unity (1918)*. Even the scene of Michael Dunne and Sarah Mann having sex in an unused tent on the night before the battle recalls representations of similarly desperate attempts to revel in sexual passion in a place of death in *Broken Ground*, *The Stone Carvers*, *The Sojourn*, and *Three Day Road*.

Yet none of these thematic explorations as they emerge in *Passchendaele* are deemed complex enough by film critics to mitigate the somehow misplaced love story that interrupts a gritty war movie. It may be that the contemporary war film—especially one that attempts to represent battle as realistically as possible (in the manner of *Saving Private Ryan*)—cannot abandon the conventions of its genre for a full seventy minutes without causing a sense of dislocation. Jay Winter has argued, however, that while film representations of historical events cannot sensibly be referred to as portraying "memories," the mediation of individual and group remembrances in film is "never mechanical...Film disturbs as many narratives as it confirms."[4] The questions then become these: What narrative was *Passchendaele* trying to tell, and why were so many critics ambivalent in their response to it? And is that ambivalence a signal that the narrative presented is disruptive, or simply all too confirming? What is interesting about Gross's film, and its reception, is the way the inclusion and subsequent popular rejection of a romance narrative reveals a refutation of the narrative of personal heroism and glorious sacrifice in war evident at the end of a decade of Canadian First World War reimaginings.

Stone argues that the plot of *Passchendaele* is grounded in the conventions of romance, though what he is referring to is the love story of Michael and Sarah rather than the quest narrative associated with the prose romance, the very sort of narrative that was popular with Canadian writers such as Ralph Conner and William Benjamin Basil King during the war years. Dagmar Novak asserts that the plots of Conner's and King's novels "follow a similar pattern; the hero descends into a lower world where he battles against evil, then re-emerges victorious in life or in death. They are replete with heroes and heroines who display fortitude and a capacity for courage and self-sacrifice that is truly extraordinary."[5] Michael Dunne is such a hero, though, as Gross writes and plays the character, he is also the epitome of Canadian unpretentiousness and no-nonsense dependability, not to mention just about the highest-functioning neurasthenic one could ever hope to meet in a First World War narrative. In a scene where he faces a kind of military tribunal to explain why he went AWOL—during which he is threatened with a charge of desertion and the punishment of execution—he has sufficient nerve to suggest that the story of the crucified Canadian soldier is a myth, that "a man in a trench—he's gonna see what he needs to see." He is unfazed by the news that Sarah's father fought for the German army and that she herself is suspected of being a saboteur, taking the time to punch one of her xenophobic neighbours in the nose. He refuses to parrot the patriotic line, even to military superiors, and tells Sarah's brother, David, that he isn't going to find "romance... in a trench." When David finally manages to sign up, Michael follows him to Flanders (using the name McCrae, an allusion that seems contrived, even for this film), and ends up saving him, single-handedly dragging David's near-crucified body back across no man's land, while Canadian and German soldiers alike stare in bewildered awe at Michael's valour. Significantly, there seems to be no self-reflexivity about the fact that, though Michael forcefully disputes the myth of the crucified Canadian soldier during his tribunal, Gross's film culminates in precisely this image. Michael gets David to safety just in time for Canadian relief soldiers to arrive and win the battle. And despite his forthright explanation to Dobson-Hughes that dry matches are the most important thing to a soldier, in case "you are in a barrage and you think a smoke might steady you up," and the recurrent emphasis on the image of the real soldier and his cigarettes, Paul Gross does not smoke.

The issue here is not simply the clash of two sets of generic conventions, but that there are two competing attitudes toward the war—one that Michael Dunne articulates in words, and another that he articulates in action. Szklarski notes that "Gross... manages to juggle smart, sober themes on the futility of war and heroic personal sacrifice without treading too heavily on the morality of armed conflict."[6] Sitting in a sopping trench with David, Michael gives a speech that relies on images and ideas culled from First World War mythology: "Look around you. You see any poets in this shit? We're all in a slaughter yard and there isn't a single guy here who knows why... It's something we do all the time because we're good at it. And we're good at it because we're used to it. And we're used to it because we do it all the time." The reference to the lack of "poets" in this speech, of course, is meant to bring to mind the work of British soldier-poets, while the neat tautological structure in Michael's simple meditation on why humans go to war reveals Gross's desire to align his film with that legacy. This is the attitude toward the war that critics of the film are eager to attend to, though the anti-war stance implicit in this attitude is not sustained. As Cobley might argue, the position that humans are simply doomed to be "good" at war is its own kind of complicity with such activity. Furthermore, the generic "we" that Michael uses in his speech transforms into a much more specific "we"—namely, the Canadian Corps, whose "taking" of Passchendaele is meant to register as heroic rather than ironic, of a piece with the "reluctant coming-of-age" narrative that Palmateer Pennee suggests has become all too gratifying.[7] Even with its inherent contradictions, however, the attitude to war expressed in this speech remains tolerable because it sidesteps the romance paradigm of the singular hero, the "extraordinary" man. When Michael takes up the cross bearing David's body, he oversteps the boundaries of acceptable myth. While a tacit approval of the idea that war is a necessary and perhaps unavoidable evil finds purchase, showy individual valour does not. Paradoxically, the scene in which Michael kills an unarmed German soldier by sticking a bayonet into his skull—an event based on a real-life incident that haunted Gross's grandfather—is deemed straightforwardly meaningful, while scenes that figure Michael as a hero–Christ figure produce only discomfort.

A look back over the texts examined in this study might offer an explanation for this discomfort. What becomes clear when we do so is that, in general, contemporary Canadian literature about the First World War subordinates the ideal of personal heroism to the ideals of community and duty toward that community. Works such as Thiessen's *Vimy* and the novels of Alan Cumyn focus explicitly on the distinctive bonds and shared sense of purpose felt by common infantrymen; and particularly in the case of the community represented in *Vimy*, that shared sense of purpose is meant to be a sign of the nation's potential for the glorious tolerance of diversity. It is also significant that many of these texts avoid the issue of personal military heroism by representing other kinds of war work, the kind of "soldiering" (to use Donna Coates's phrase) that privileges a commitment to duty over a commitment to fighting.[8] In Swan's *The Deep*, Thiessen's *Vimy*, and Urquhart's *The Underpainter*, the efforts of nursing sisters are highlighted; *The Underpainter* and Itani's *Deafening* additionally present men involved in military service that does not involve combat—George Kearns is responsible for carrier pigeons, and Jim Lloyd is a stretcher carrier and field medic. In Urquhart's second First World War novel, *The Stone Carvers*, both Tilman Becker and Giorgio Vigamonti refer to their status as former infantrymen, Tilman having taken part in the Battle of Vimy Ridge and Giorgio having been promoted to corporal only "because [he] was neither missing nor dead."[9] Urquhart, however, presents taking part in the massive communal undertaking of carving the Vimy Memorial as the most important war work done by Tilman, Giorgio, and also Klara Becker. Thus, the representation of both front line and home front activity is significant not because it confirms a plot of personal heroism or because an individual type of activity makes a statement one way or the other about the toll of war; rather, such activity operates as an articulation of citizenship.

As discussed in detail throughout this study, the figure of the officer—a figure generally associated with obtuseness and arrogance in British representations of the war—is given complex treatment in such works as Hodgins's *Broken Ground*, Poliquin's *A Secret Between Us*, and Vanderhaeghe's *Dancock's Dance*. Both Hodgins's Matt Pearson and Vanderhaeghe's John Carlyle Dancock are represented in terms of their struggle to find the sort of leadership qualities that will best serve their units, and it is significant that in both cases the motley group that ultimately comes together under such leadership is a non-military community. And, of course, Poliquin represents in Lusignan a Canadian officer who is totally lacking both bravery and a code of sacrifice, thus skewering at every turn the myth of personal heroism. Finally, in terms of other representations of soldiers who may, on the surface, be viewed as embodying the ideal of personal heroism so central to Paul Gross's character in *Passchendaele*, the depictions of military medal winners in Massicotte's *Mary's Wedding*, Kerr's *Unity (1918)*, and Hodgins's *Broken Ground* reveal only hesitancy about being so distinguished. In the context of Massicotte's dream space, the historical personage of Lieutenant Gordon Muriel Flowerdew, who was awarded a Victoria Cross for leading the charge at Moreuil Wood, is buried beneath the fictional mask of Charlie Edwards, a man who will not admit to being a hero and who can only say of the charge that "it wasn't...poetry."[10] Kerr's returned soldier Hart refuses to let Beatrice make much of his Victoria Cross, insisting "they were just tossing these things out like jelly drops at a parade."[11] Finally, and most complicated, is the case of Xavier Bird's Military Medal, which he receives only because he is mistaken for Elijah Whiskeyjack during his recovery from injury. Xavier's comment to himself that "there is something appealing in being the hero"[12] is fraught with complexity, both because Elijah's own "heroism" is represented as a kind of crazed bloodlust and because Xavier's comfort in being taken for a hero occurs at a point when he has lost, in literal and metaphorical terms, his claim to a personal and cultural identity. Thus, the version of the "best Canadian self" that is depicted in most contemporary Canadian reimaginings of the war is not a romance hero, but rather someone who does his or her duty, on and off the battlefield. Paul Gross's character, though also dutiful, does more than just "his bit," and for this reason oversteps the boundaries of the cultural narrative defining distinctively Canadian military activity.

The timing of *Passchendaele*'s release also seems a crucial factor in providing a context for discomfort. Much was made in the press surrounding the film's opening, as well as in the featurette titled "The Road to Passchendaele" included in the DVD, of the participation of the Canadian Armed Forces in the making of the film. Gross notes that "having real soldiers on the set gave the project a real sobriety, because in war people can [be] and are killed... There is a direct line between the soldiers of the Canadian Expeditionary Force who fought at Passchendaele in the First World War and the men and women who are fighting in the sands of Afghanistan right now."[13] In fact, Gross's willingness to construct a tale of personal heroism may be associated with his desire to explicitly mark war activity as more than simply duty. The idea of "the direct line," however, is problematic. As the character Michael Dunne himself asserts, "lines are tricky. They're so goddamn many of them... lines you don't even know about, lines you can't see 'til you cross them." Canada deployed its first troops to Afghanistan in 2002, participating significantly between 2003 and 2005 as part of the International Security Assistance Force (ISAF) in Kabul, but the role of those troops changed significantly in 2006 when Britain took charge of the mission and Canadian forces were placed in Kandahar as part of counter-insurgency activities.[14] This shift had two outcomes: first, Canada's involvement in the war began to register serious opposition in Parliament, and second, more and more Canadian soldiers began to die. Between 2002 and 2005 there were eight Canadian casualties of the war in Afghanistan—including four soldiers who died as a result of "friendly fire"—whereas between 2006 and 2011, there were one hundred fifty combat-related deaths.[15]

In her study of Findley's *The Wars* in a post-colonial context, Donna Palmateer Pennee explores the way Canada has variously defined itself in relation to the concept of war:

> The Vietnam War figured "Canada" as a pacifist haven in the period of anti-American cultural and economic nationalism in the 1970s. The Cold War similarly gave Canada a moral edge: during the Cold War, Canada rose to middle power status, building on the international recognition gained for its roles as ally and mediator during and after World War II... War continues to facilitate meanings or identifications of "Canada" in the early twenty-first century: think of the anger and judgment at (Canadian) soldiers' death by friendly (U.S.) fire... think of the left-liberal pride at Jean Chretien's refusal to join the U.S. and Britain in the war against Iraq because it was not sanctioned by the UN. But think, too, of how difficult it is to maintain a not-American identification after the shame of Rwanda or Khandahar.[16]

Palmateer Pennee asks, "How do we reconcile such repeated definitional moments for 'Canada' produced by complicities in the atrocities of war with decades of 'Canada's' signature as a peacekeeping, mediating nation in foreign affairs?"[17] A recent collection of essays titled *Afghanistan and Canada: Is There an Alternative to War?* positions itself as a call "to end Canada's military involvement in a wasteful and costly war,"[18] often citing Canada's status as a "middle-power country that as a peacekeeper, has always been highly respected on the international stage."[19] In the late 1990s and early twenty-first century it was still possible to locate a moral substance within the lessons learned in the First World War, and to celebrate the kinds of Canadian values that were forged on its various fronts—quiet, dignified fortitude, a sense of duty toward community, an ability to appreciate justice, and a recognition that even though Canadian fighters were a force to be reckoned with on a battlefield, war should mostly be avoided in favour of mediation. But by the time of *Passchendaele*'s release in late 2008 a straightforward identification with those cultural myths was no longer sustainable. While the reluctant father figure Matt Pearson, or the earnest and experienced field medic Jim Lloyd, or the fiercely loyal Ramsay Crome might have been acceptable purveyors of the national military spirit in the years leading up to Canada's increased participation in Afghanistan, by 2008 it was no longer possible to figure Michael Dunne as this sort of emblematic figure, because the so-called national spirit was no longer an illusion that could be so easily articulated or accepted.

As the end of Canada's participation in Afghanistan in 2011 is digested, various controversies have subjected Canada's war record to intense scrutiny. Those controversies include the detainee abuse scandal of 2007–9; the 2010 military trial of Captain Robert Semrau, accused of killing a wounded insurgent and found guilty of disgraceful conduct; the financial cost of the war, which far exceeded government estimations; and continuing complaints about the work of the Veterans Affairs Department. Furthermore, as Ian McKay and Jamie Swift point out in their biting critique of the "rebranding" of Canada as a "Warrior Nation," popular conceptions of Canada's military history have become a matter of intense political manoeuvring, as "the 'Canada' that shimmers in the imagination of right-wing politicians, militarists, and new warrior historians...is one based on blood and soil, sanctified by battle deaths and engaged in a perpetual war with the tyranny and terror championed by less-evolved peoples."[20] McKay and Swift, writing in 2012, lament:

> Not two decades ago, Remembrance Day, as it was generally observed in public schools, was in good measure about peace. Little children recited poems about the horrors of war; school assemblies mourned

the lives cut down by violent conflict—sometimes even Japanese and German lives. In the rebranded Canada as Warrior Nation, Remembrance Day is mainly about war, with proud homage paid to our valiant soldiers who, it is claimed, created Canada's freedom. In the cult of the soldier, all Canadians who died in the service of the Anglosphere...indiscriminately receive the "big hero" treatment.[21]

Though Gross's "big hero" representation of the Canadian First World War hero fell flat, with *Passchendaele* receiving mostly mixed to unenthusiastic reviews and ending up as a commercial failure, McKay and Swift's point about the way such rhetoric has moved into classroom discourse is important. As Noah Richler notes in his recent book, *What We Talk about When We Talk about War*, the Dominion Institute—renamed in 2009 the Institut Historica–Dominion Institute—published an education guide "as part of its 'Passchendaele in the Classroom' initiative for teachers using the film as an educational tool." Richler notes Gross's fervently patriotic tone as expressed in the guide, including his assertion that "'our notion of what it means to be Canadian was forged in the crucible of the Western Front.'"[22] Without a doubt, as the centenary of the First World War looms, literary representations of and popular discourse about Canada at war will be looked at with fresh eyes, as critics continue to interrogate—perhaps with increased political urgency—how remembrance of the "Great" war is discursively deployed.

Paul Ricoeur in *Memory, History, Forgetting* writes that "faithfulness to the past is not a given, but a wish. Like all wishes, it can be disappointed, even betrayed."[23] The texts explored in this study work to find productive meaning in the remembrance of the First World War, looking to the past with a mind to call attention to forgiveness, healing, the agency of citizens, a return to familial or community wholeness, and a sense of promise for a future that cherishes love. Such emphases ensue, however, on the grounds that the events of the First World War were so cataclysmic, so appalling in their capacity to produce chaos and loss, that efforts of remembrance—of faithfulness—are necessarily, almost conventionally, painful and complex, yet also culturally productive, like Xavier Bird's healing journey up the river to home. Writers are safely able to locate productive meaning in the First World War precisely because of their sense of assurance regarding the proper kinds of effort Canadians put into collective remembrance and also regarding the kinds of myths we have learned to reiterate, like Lusignan, writing the letter he knows is expected of a soldier who had been at Passchendaele: "I added three or four pages on the cold, the mud, the blood in the trenches, things...that I managed to write about with ease."[24] Richler suggests that, as both a "creation myth and a cautionary tale," the story of Canada's participation in the First World War has become too comforting, a reiterated wish that relies on the notion of our progress through the crucible of war to our "stronger, finer" selves.[25]

During the years between 1995 (the publication year of Major's *No Man's Land* and the production year of the first performance of *Dancock's Dance*) and 2007 (the publication year of the English translation of *A Secret Between Us* and the production year of the world premiere of *Vimy*), the prevailing notion concerning the First World War was that the series of events was behind us, and that our greatest worry might be sorting out how best to commemorate the imminent death of the last Canadian veteran of the war. In the past several years, however, "war" as a concept and as a daily set of political affairs and physical consequences is ever more complex than our remembrance of the First World War. Thus, to a great extent our response to Canada's participation in the First World War—that first mechanized war of the modern era, with all its associated horrors—is associated with nostalgia for a past that, amazingly, seems entirely comprehensible and that has not been betrayed. It is no surprise that a political campaign, such as the 2010 "How Will You Remember?" campaign organized by Veterans Affairs Canada, insists there is a "direct line" from Canada's First World War participants and Canadian UN peacekeepers to—as the descriptive transcript to the widely broadcast television vignette puts it—Canadians "who continue to serve our country today."[26] It is precisely because the myths we have reiterated about Canada's participation in the First World War, as a productive set of activities in the forging of Canadian values, have proven to constitute a fervent, collective wish, that such linkages are possible and pervasive.

In his conclusion to *Speculative Fictions*, Herb Wyile notes with enthusiasm that "the historical fiction keeps on coming," and mentions the publication of *Broken Ground* as an example of the continuing interest in the genre.[27] The recent publication of the essay collection *National Plots: Historical Fiction and Changing Ideas of Canada* in 2010 further establishes the way writing about Canada's past has captured the imaginations of authors and literary critics alike, arguably more than ever before. As I write this conclusion, however, I am more cautious about the probability that the outpouring of Canadian First World War narratives might continue; as I mention above, *Passchendaele* appears to have functioned as the finale to a decade-long phenomenon. This cautiousness is not solely, or even primarily, related to the problem of "premise fatigue"; rather, it is mainly associated with a sense that it has become more difficult for Canadian writers to make productive use of this part of our past, and to explore even the possibility of "promise, certainty, and goodness."[28] War is something real for Canadians again. It is not surprising that a novel such as David Bergen's

The Matter With Morris, nominated for the 2010 Giller Prize, focuses on the trauma associated with a Canadian soldier killed by "friendly fire" in Afghanistan or that Christie Blatchford's *Fifteen Days: Stories of Bravery, Friendship, Life, and Death from Inside the New Canadian Army*, winner of the 2008 Governor General's Award for non-fiction, captured the reading public's attention so intensely. Johanna Skibsrud's *The Sentimentalists* (which won the 2010 Giller) and Anne Michael's *The Winter Vault*, novels that feature war as a topic and the memory of war experience as a central issue, deal with more recent military events: the Vietnam War and the post–Second World War period, respectively. Jane Urquhart in her most recent novel, *Sanctuary Line*, returns once again to the topic of Canadian military activity, but has shifted her attention away from the First World War to consider Canada's participation in the war in Afghanistan. Attention has thus moved toward events that are part of "living history," especially for a post-boomer demographic, and away from something like the First World War, which can function only as what Halbwachs would call "historical memory." In the final moments of Kerr's *Unity (1918)*, the ensemble cast sings an ironic song about Canada's "hundred years of progress," a song that ends with an implicit call for further reflection on what our memory of the war might mean:

> Oh, Canada!
> Oh, Canada!
>   Oh –
> *Curtain*.[29]

Paradoxically, as the centenary of the First World War approaches, those events themselves may have become a closed book.

Notes

Notes to Introduction

1 Wiersema, "Four Cures for 'Premise Fatigue,'" D10.
2 In her entry on "Canada and the Great War," included in *The Cambridge History of Canadian Literature*, Susan Fisher lists almost all of these works, as well as making note of a number of children's books (241n78) and David Macfarlane's memoir, *The Danger Tree* (Fisher 241), published by Random House. There were also a number of self-published and/or genre fiction Canadian First World War novels that came out in this period, including Mel Bradshaw's mystery novel *Quarrel with the Foe* (2005), which reunites four soldiers who fought together at Flanders as they investigate the murder of a prominent Canadian industrialist and suspected war profiteer; Eric J. Brown's *The Promise* (2004), a novel that focuses on one soldier's experiences during the Battle of the Somme; David B. Clark's *Lucifer's Gate* (2002), which focuses on the Canadian army in 1917, in particular the activities occurring at the Menin Gate, the gateway to the Ypres Salient; and Michael J. Goodspeed's *Three to a Loaf* (2008), the story of a Canadian soldier of Anglo-German descent who becomes a spy for the British army. I have only considered English-Canadian works, with the exception of Donald Winkler's translation of Daniel Poliquin's *A Secret Between Us*, as the nomination of the English translation for the 2007 Giller Prize places it firmly within the cluster of texts I am interested in. Fisher's survey, which deftly weaves among English and French works, does not mention any French-language First World War texts written after the 1950s, suggesting that the substantial concern with remembering this series of events is felt more acutely in English than in French Canada.
3 McCrae, "In Flanders Fields," ll. 10–12.
4 Winter, *Remembering War*, 154.

5 Halbwachs, *The Collective Memory*, 24.
6 Becker, "Memory Gaps," 109.
7 Huyssen, *Twilight Memories*, 3.
8 Huyssen, *Twilight Memories*, 3.
9 Halbwachs, *The Collective Memory*, 50.
10 Halbwachs, *The Collective Memory*, 51.
11 Halbwachs, *The Collective Memory*, 56–57.
12 Halbwachs, *The Collective Memory*, 51.
13 Halbwachs, *The Collective Memory*, 59.
14 Winter, *Remembering War*, 3.
15 Winter, *Remembering War*, 185.
16 I have not dealt with any Canadian First World War poetry, simply because the lyric poetry generally associated with that war does not meet my basic concern with how the war is plotted. For those interested in the subject, Joel Baetz's recent anthology, *Canadian Poetry from World War I*, not only collects war poetry by such authors as Charles G.D. Roberts, Frank Prewett, and Helena Coleman, but also includes a critical introduction to the material, situating it as "a culturally informed archive of ideas...about an extraordinary range of topics, including strength, race, community, obligation, gender, vulnerability, truth, obscurity, trauma, and death" (Baetz 5). More recent Canadian poetry that revisits the First World War includes Ted Plantos's *Passchendaele* (1983), Marilyn Bowering's *Grandfather was a Soldier* (1987), and individual poems such as Alden Nolan's "Ypres: 1915" (1969) and poems by Raymond Souster.
17 In her introduction to the anthology *Canada and the Theatre of War*, vol. I, Sherrill Grace comments on the significance of the performance text: "I am convinced that these plays are at their best on smaller stages, in intimate venues where performers and audience members are in close proximity and a whisper is more effective than a rocket blast" (Grace vii).
18 Lukács, *The Historical Novel*, 106.
19 Lukács, *The Historical Novel*, 107–8.
20 Lukács, *The Historical Novel*, 109–10.
21 The national award given to *Little Man* and the general popularity of the Bartholomew Bandy comic novels has thus far not translated into critical interest, although the University of Calgary recently acquired Jack's papers. Susan Fisher also mentions Jean Simard's *Mon fils pourtant heureux* (published in 1956) in her survey of Canadian First World War fiction ("Canada and the Great War" 236); I have chosen in this survey to focus only on English-Canadian work, although Fisher's mention of certain Quebec novels, in particular her description of Louis Caron's *L'Emmitouflé* as a novel "published in the same year as *The Wars*, [but] reflect[ing] a very different memory of the war," ("Canada and the Great War" 237) raises many further sites of inquiry.
22 Fisher also mentions references to the First World War in such novels as Robertson Davies *Fifth Business* and Margaret Laurence's *A Bird in the House* and *The Diviners* (Fisher 236); more recently, Ann-Marie MacDonald's *Fall*

on Your Knees (1996), Dionne Brand's *At the Full and Change of the Moon* (1999), Michael Crummey's *The Wreckage* (2005), and Ami McKay's *The Birth House* (2007) also refer to events of the war.
23 Such is the organizing structure of Evelyn Cobley's *Representing War: Form and Ideology in First World War Narratives* (1993), Dagmar Novak's *Dubious Glory: The Two World Wars and the Canadian Novel* (1999), and two unpublished dissertations: M. Jeanne Yardley's *Writing the Great War: Language and Structures in English-Canadian Prose Narratives of World War I* (1989) and Peter Webb's *Occupants of Memory: War in Twentieth-Century Canadian Fiction* (2007). David Williams's *Media, Memory, and the First World War* (2009) reaches just beyond *The Wars* to also consider R.H. Thomson's *The Lost Boys*, while Fisher's section of *The Cambridge History of Canadian Literature*, titled "Rediscovering the Great War," is really the first survey to start accounting for work that has been published since *The Wars*.
24 See also Novak's *Dubious Glory*, which examines these same three works, and Cobley's *Representing War* and Vance's *Death So Noble,* which have, respectively, explored the structural devices and popular reception of Harrison's novel.
25 Thompson, "Canadian Fiction of the Great War," 84.
26 Thompson, "Canadian Fiction of the Great War," 85.
27 Thompson, "Canadian Fiction of the Great War," 94.
28 Thompson, "Canadian Fiction of the Great War," 95.
29 Harrison, quoted in Cobley, *Representing War*, 7.
30 Cobley, *Representing War*, 9.
31 Cobley, *Representing War*, 17.
32 Cobley, *Representing War*, 143.
33 The status of *Generals Die in Bed* as a Canadian novel is complicated by the fact that, though Harrison did indeed serve as a member of the Royal Montreal Regiment, he was American by birth and returned to the United States soon after the war ended.
34 Vance, *Death So Noble*, 187.
35 Fisher, "Canada and the Great War," 233.
36 Atwood, "Timothy Findley: *The Wars*," 290.
37 Atwood, "Timothy Findley: *The Wars*," 295.
38 Gwyn, "Putting a Human Face on the Tragedy of War," G13.
39 Rigelhof, "War Is Hell, Novel Is Brilliant," D6.
40 Cook, *Clio's Warriors*, 242.
41 Brydon, "'It Could Not be Told,'" 66.
42 Vauthier, "The Dubious Battle of Storytelling," 35.
43 Vauthier, "The Dubious Battle of Storytelling," 35.
44 Palmateer Pennee, *Moral Metafiction*, 18.
45 York, *Front Lines*, xviii.
46 See, for example, Peter Klovan's "'Bright and Good': Findley's *The Wars*" (1981); Bruce Pirie's "The Dragon in the Fog: 'Displaced Mythology in *The*

Wars" (1989); Shane Rhodes's "Buggering with History: Sexual Warfare and Historical Reconstruction in Timothy Findley's *The Wars*" (1989); Valdimir Tumanov's "De-Automatization in Timothy Findley's *The Wars*" (1991); and Peter Webb's "'At War With Nature': Animals in Timothy Findley's *The Wars*" (2007).

47 Hastings, "'Their Fathers Did It to Them': Findley's Appeal to the Great War Myth of a Generational Conflict in *The Wars*," 90–91.
48 See, for example, Elizabeth Epperly's "Chivalry and Romance: L.M. Montgomery's Re-Vision of the Great War in *Rainbow Valley*" (1993); Alan R. Young's "L.M. Montgomery's *Rilla of Ingleside:* Romance and the Experience of War" (1993); and Amy Tector's "A Righteous War?: L.M. Montgomery's Depiction of the First World War in *Rilla of Ingleside*" (2003).
49 Cobley, *Representing War*, 5.
50 Palmateer Pennee, "Imagined Innocence, Endlessly Mourned," 89.
51 Sherry, "Introduction," 5.
52 Ouditt, "Myths, Memories, and Monuments," 247.
53 Ouditt, "Myths, Memories, and Monuments," 259.
54 Lloyd, *Battlefield Tourism*, 182.
55 Lloyd, *Battlefield Tourism*, 182–83.
56 Zacharias, "'Some Great Crisis,'" 120.
57 Zacharias, "'Some Great Crisis,'" 128.
58 Zacharias, "'Some Great Crisis,'" 120.
59 Thiessen, *Vimy*, 72. In *Shock Troops: Canadians Fighting the Great War 1917–1918*, Tim Cook details the logistical preparation that went into the taking of Vimy Ridge, going into specifics that are absent from the popular memory.
60 Lloyd, *Battlefield Tourism*, 193.
61 Lloyd, *Battlefield Tourism*, 204.
62 Lloyd, *Battlefield Tourism*, 208–9.
63 Thomson, "The Anzac Legend," 74.
64 Otto, "Rereading David Malouf's *Fly Away Peter*," 39.
65 Coates, "The Digger on the Lofty Pedestal," 9.
66 Coates, "The Digger on the Lofty Pedestal," 13.
67 Williams, *Media, Memory, and the First World War*, 270.
68 Williams also considers the work of non-Canadian writers Wilfred Owen, Erich Maria Remarque, and Siegfried Sassoon.
69 Winter, *Remembering War*, 180.
70 Fisher, "Canada and the Great War," 237.
71 See Statistics Canada, Table: "Population by selected ethnic origins, by province and territory (2006 Census) (Canada)," (http://www40.statcan.ca/l01/cst01/demo26a-eng.htm). The figure of 36 percent results from dividing the total population in 2006 (31,241,030) by the total number reporting British Isles origin (11,098,610).
72 Cameron, *Multiculturalism and Immigration in Canada*, 398.
73 Fisher, "Canada and the Great War," 237.

74 Granatstein, *Who Killed the Canadian Military?*, 3. In their recently published *Warrior Nation: Rebranding Canada in an Age of Anxiety*, Ian McKay and Jamie Swift survey in detail the way that "Granatstein and others have since the 1990s been attempting, recently with Ottawa's active assistance ... to [attack] not just their professional rivals but those forces that they think their rivals represent—naïve romantic tendencies excessively wedded to the ideals of peacekeeping" (9).
75 Williams, *Media, Memory, and the First World War*, 270.
76 Williams, *Imagined Nations*, xii–xiii.
77 Williams, *Media, Memory, and the First World War*, 270.
78 Fisher, "Canada and the Great War," 238.
79 Fisher, "Canada and the Great War," 238.
80 Fisher, "Canada and the Great War," 239, emphasis added.
81 Vance, *Death So Noble*, 9.
82 Vance, *Death So Noble*, 9.
83 Vance, *Death So Noble*, 9.
84 Fisher, "Canada and the Great War," 239.
85 Morphine abuse is also represented in Urquhart's *The Underpainter* and Paul Gross's recent film, *Passchendaele*.
86 Wyile, *Speculative Fictions*, 264.
87 Francis, *National Dreams*, 176.
88 Vance, *Death So Noble*, 266.
89 Dobson, *Transnational Canadas*, xvii–xviii.
90 Brydon, "Metamorphoses of a Discipline," 14–15.
91 Boyden, *Three Day Road*, 224.
92 Boyden, *Three Day Road*, 353.
93 Sugars and Turcotte, "Canadian Literature and the Postcolonial Gothic," xiv.
94 Sugars and Turcotte, "Canadian Literature and the Postcolonial Gothic," xxi.
95 The range of literary texts examined in these works is broad, though the work of Margaret Atwood and Jane Urquhart is frequently discussed, as is work by such Aboriginal and First Nations authors as Maria Campbell, Tomson Highway, Eden Robinson, and Thomas King.
96 Goldman, *DisPossession*, 8.
97 A popular culture example of the strategy of synthesizing previously marginalized groups into a dominant narrative is visible in the 2012 "Remembrance Vignette," produced by Veterans Affairs Canada. The historical images include African Canadian soldiers, nursing sisters, and a First Nations soldier, all of whom become part of a homogenous legacy of service to one's nation (see http://www.veterans.gc.ca/eng/video-gallery/video/9044).
98 Brydon, "Metamorphoses of a Discipline," 2.
99 Brydon, "Metamorphoses of a Discipline," 14.
100 Palmateer Pennee, "Literary Citizenship: Culture (Un)Bounded, Culture (*Re*) Distributed," 76.
101 Palmateer Pennee, "Literary Citizenship," 81.

102 Palmateer Pennee, "Literary Citizenship," 77.
103 Brydon, "Metamorphoses of a Discipline," 11.
104 Brydon, "Negotiating Belonging in Global Times," 254. The series of events Brydon analyzes in this essay consist of the posting of a "code of conduct" for new immigrants on the town's website, and the Canadian media's response to this act.
105 Brydon, "Negotiating Belonging in Global Times," 254.
106 Brydon, "Negotiating Belonging in Global Times," 258.
107 Brydon, "Negotiating Belonging in Global Times," 266.
108 Ricoeur, *Memory, History, Forgetting*, 285, emphasis added.
109 Ricoeur, *Memory, History, Forgetting*, 410.

Notes to Chapter 1

1 McCrae, "In Flanders Fields."
2 Prescott, *In Flanders Fields*, 133, emphasis added.
3 Holmes, "In Flanders Fields," 11.
4 Clarkson, "Remembrance Day Message."
5 Peritz and Richter, "It Was Quite Different Than Years Before," A7.
6 McCrae's 1899 poem "Disarmament," for example, derides the "one" voice that speaks in favour of laying down arms in the face of the unified voice of "a million British graves" who maintain the moral imperative of carrying on the work of "might." Even after the bloody battles of Ypres that occasioned the writing of his famous poem, McCrae's pro-war attitude did not alter, as Prescott demonstrates in his quoting of fellow soldier C.L.C. Allinson's recollection of McCrae's frustrated response when he was transferred from the front line to the Canadian Army Medical Corps: "'Allinson, all the goddamn doctors in the world will not win this bloody war: what we need is more and more fighting men.'"
7 Holmes, "In Flanders Fields," 21.
8 Holmes, "In Flanders Fields," 22.
9 Holmes, "In Flanders Fields," 31.
10 de Man, "Autobiography as De-facement," 926.
11 de Man, "Autobiography as De-facement," 928, emphasis added.
12 de Man, "Autobiography as De-facement," 930.
13 Watkin, *On Mourning*, 7.
14 Kennedy, *Elegy*, 21.
15 Holmes, "In Flanders Fields," 29.
16 Holmes, "In Flanders Fields," 30.
17 Holmes, "In Flanders Fields," 30.
18 Holmes later admits the difficulty of dealing with historical war poetry, because it makes us "both sympathize and recoil" (26).
19 Keenan, *The Question of Sacrifice*, 10.
20 Keenan, *The Question of Sacrifice*, 27–28.

21 McKenna, *Violence and Difference*, 30.
22 Keenan, *The Question of Sacrifice*, 2.
23 Keenan, *The Question of Sacrifice*, 5.
24 Holmes, "In Flanders Fields," 26.
25 Wyile, *Speaking in the Past Tense*, 31–32.
26 Wyile, *Speaking in the Past Tense*, 26.
27 Though there is no criticism on Vanderhaeghe's use of history in *Dancock's Dance*, several scholars have taken up the issue as it plays out in *The Englishman's Boy*. See, for example, Herb Wyile's "Dances with Wolfers: Choreographing History in *The Englishman's Boy*"; Martin Kuester's "'A Mythic Act of Possession': Constructing the North American Frontiers(s) in Guy Vanderhaeghe's *The Englishman's Boy*"; and Daniela Janes, "Truth and History: Representing the Aura in *The Englishman's Boy*."
28 Wyile, *Speaking in the Past Tense*, 29.
29 Wyile, *Speaking in the Past Tense*, 40.
30 Wyile, *Speaking in the Past Tense*, 41.
31 Coleman, *White Civility*, 6–7.
32 Trotter, "The British Novel and the War," 43.
33 Vanderhaeghe, *Dancock's Dance*, 13.
34 Vance, *Death So Noble*, 193–96.
35 Thompson, "Canadian Fiction of the Great War," 87.
36 Thompson, "Canadian Fiction of the Great War," 88.
37 Cobley, *Representing War*, 144.
38 Cobley, *Representing War*, 144–45.
39 Wyile, *Speaking in the Past Tense*, 49.
40 Vanderhaeghe, *Dancock's Dance*, 18.
41 Vanderhaeghe, *Dancock's Dance*, 26.
42 Vanderhaeghe, *Dancock's Dance*, 35.
43 Vanderhaeghe, *Dancock's Dance*, 51.
44 As Granatstein and Morton note in *Canada and the Two World Wars*, despite the sizable and deeply entrenched German immigrant population in Canada in 1914, popular fear of and action against "enemy aliens" became all too common, as when mobs attacked German-owned businesses following the sinking of the *Lusitania*, when boycotts in Berlin, Ontario, forced the city to change its name to Kitchener, and when "German-born officials and civil servants were fired and university professors and teachers were driven from their jobs" (17–18). Gordon Bölling, in "Acts of (Re-)Construction," examines the way Jane Urquhart's *The Stone Carvers* is similarly concerned with examining the important role German immigrants played in settling Canada during the nineteenth century, as well as with challenging a simplistic collapsing of the German immigrant to Canada and the stereotype of the barbaric "Hun" (310).
45 Vanderhaeghe, *Dancock's Dance*, 18–19.
46 Coleman, *White Civility*, 39.

47 Vanderhaeghe, *Dancock's Dance*, 64–65.
48 Vanderhaeghe, *Dancock's Dance*, 66.
49 Vanderhaeghe, *Dancock's Dance*, 66.
50 Vanderhaeghe, *Dancock's Dance*, 51.
51 Vanderhaeghe, *Dancock's Dance*, 69.
52 Vanderhaeghe, *Dancock's Dance*, 67.
53 Vanderhaeghe, *Dancock's Dance*, 68.
54 Vanderhaeghe, *Dancock's Dance*, 68.
55 de Man, "Autobiography as De-Facement," 928.
56 Wyile, *Speaking in the Past Tense*, 50.
57 Massicotte, *Mary's Wedding*, vii.
58 Winter, *Sites of Memory*, 51.
59 Massicotte, *Mary's Wedding*, 63.
60 de Man, "Autobiography as De-Facement," 978.
61 Massicotte, *Mary's Wedding*, 3.
62 Massicotte, *Mary's Wedding*, 3
63 Winter, *Remembering War*, 12.
64 Fussell, *The Great War and Modern Memory*, 87.
65 Swan, *The Deep*, 75.
66 Massicotte, *Mary's Wedding*, 28.
67 Massicotte, *Mary's Wedding*, 32.
68 Cook, *At the Sharp End*, 178.
69 Cook, *At the Sharp End*, 180.
70 Cook, *At the Sharp End*, 213–14.
71 Massicotte, *Mary's Wedding*, 32.
72 Massicotte, *Mary's Wedding*, 33.
73 Massicotte, *Mary's Wedding*, 48.
74 Massicotte, *Mary's Wedding*, 26.
75 Massicotte, *Mary's Wedding*, 61. This sentiment is echoed in *Canada and the Two World Wars* and in Tim Cook's *Shock Troops: Canadians Fighting the Great War 1917–1918*. Cook's recounting of the battle makes specific reference to Flowerdew's part in it, including his reported cry, "It's a charge, boys, it's a charge." Cook ends his account with the assertion that "despite their losses, the Canadian Cavalry Brigade had stabilized the front and had, with their lives, purchased precious time for the retreating British forces to establish a new defensive line to the rear" (394).
76 Massicotte, *Mary's Wedding*, v.
77 Sugars and Turcotte, "Canadian Literature and the Postcolonial Gothic," xiii.
78 Swan, *The Deep*, 32.
79 Swan, *The Deep*, 20.
80 Winter, *Remembering War*, 11.
81 Winter, *Remembering War*, 278.
82 Swan, *The Deep*, 39.
83 Swan, *The Deep*, 55.

84 Swan, *The Deep*, 56.
85 Sugars and Turcotte, "Canadian Literature and the Postcolonial Gothic," xiv.
86 Swan, *The Deep*, 34–35.
87 Swan, *The Deep*, 40.
88 Swan, *The Deep*, 80.
89 Swan, *The Deep*, 93.
90 Swan, *The Deep*, 21.
91 Coates, "The Best Soldiers of All," 69.
92 Coates, "The Best Soldiers of All," 72.
93 Coates, "The Best Soldiers of All," 93.
94 Swan, *The Deep*, 65.
95 Swan, *The Deep*, 67.
96 Swan, *The Deep*, 24.
97 Swan, *The Deep*, 4.
98 In another work, *The Boys in the Trees*, Swan was "inspired by a sensational footnote in the history of Guelph, where Swan lives—she came across the story by chance when she was working in the reference department at the University of Guelph library in 2002… 'It was in 1888 or 1889,' she says. 'There was a man who killed his wife and daughters and then took off to Toronto trying to kill his son, who was living there, and [the father] was arrested and brought back and executed in Guelph'" (Dean, "Mary Swan").
99 Swan, *The Deep*, 14.
100 Swan, *The Deep*, 69.
101 Swan, *The Deep*, 44.
102 Swan, *The Deep*, 53.
103 Vance, "A Game of Ghosts," 131.
104 Swan, *The Deep*, 74.
105 Swan, *The Deep*, 74.
106 Swan, *The Deep*, 81.
107 Swan, *The Deep*, 74.
108 Swan, *The Deep*, 83.
109 Goldman, *DisPossession*, 8.
110 Swan, *The Deep*, 91.

Notes to Chapter 2

1 Williams, *Imagined Nations*, 5.
2 Williams, *Imagined Nations*, xii.
3 Williams, *Imagined Nations*, 7.
4 MacLennan, *Barometer Rising*, 37.
5 MacLennan, *Barometer Rising*, 218.
6 MacLennan, *Barometer Rising*, 217.
7 MacLennan, *Barometer Rising*, 218.
8 MacLennan, *Barometer Rising*, 219.

9 Williams, *Imagined Nations*, 19.
10 Kertzer, *Worrying the Nation*, 15.
11 Kertzer, *Worrying the Nation*, 6–7.
12 Kertzer, *Worrying the Nation*, 8.
13 Kertzer, *Worrying the Nation*, 9.
14 Brydon, "Metamorphoses of a Discipline," 6. See in particular, Smaro Kamboureli and Roy Miki, eds., *Trans.Can.Lit: Resituating the Study of Canadian Literature*; Kit Dobson, ed., *Transnational Canadas: Anglo-Canadian Literature and Globalization*; and Robert David Stacey's 'State of Shock': History and Crisis in Hugh MacLennan's *Barometer Rising*," in which Stacey argues that "the subject of [*Barometer Rising*] is not the nation per se, but what we might call the *nation-in-history*, a formulation that foregrounds the necessarily temporal dimension of the nation and national identity" (54).
15 In *Transnational Canadas*, Dobson queries Kertzer's line of inquiry regarding the inevitability of recourse to the idea of nation, especially in terms of thinking about "legitimizing" various cultural groups: "Indigenous and transnational debates about sovereignty and nationhood suggest that, at the very least, the nation is a variable construct, and that it might be possible to do politics differently" (154).
16 Francis, *National Dreams*, 176.
17 Goldman, *Rewriting Apocalypse in Canadian Fiction*, 7.
18 Many literary critics have examined Hodgins's literary output in the context of his challenge to inherited knowledge. See, for example, Susan Beckmann, "Canadian Burlesque: Jack Hodgins' *The Invention of the World*," Carol Langhelle, *The Counterfeit and the Real in Jack Hodgins' The Invention of the World*; and essays in J.R. Struthers, ed., *On the Coasts of Eternity: Jack Hodgins' Fictional Universe*.
19 Hodgins, *Broken Ground*, 256.
20 Goldman, *Rewriting Apocalypse in Canadian Fiction*, 4.
21 Reddish, *Apocalyptic Literature*, 21.
22 Hodgins, *Broken Ground*, 148.
23 Hodgins, *Broken Ground*, 9.
24 Hodgins, *Broken Ground*, 167.
25 Hodgins, *Broken Ground*, 180.
26 Hodgins, *Broken Ground*, 300.
27 Hodgins, *Broken Ground*, 328.
28 Wyile, *Speculative Fictions*, 166.
29 Wyile, *Speculative Fictions*, 172.
30 Hodgins, *Broken Ground*, 329–30.
31 Hodgins, *Broken Ground*, 44–45.
32 Hodgins, *Broken Ground*, 40–41.
33 Hodgins, *Broken Ground*, 41.
34 Hodgins, *Broken Ground*, 72.
35 Hodgins, *Broken Ground*, 57.

36 Hodgins, *Broken Ground*, 103.
37 Vance, *Death So Noble*, 11.
38 Hodgins, *Broken Ground*, 111.
39 Hodgins, *Broken Ground*, 116.
40 Hodgins, *Broken Ground*, 91.
41 Hodgins, *Broken Ground*, 218.
42 Hodgins, *Broken Ground*, 330.
43 Hodgins, *Broken Ground*, 281.
44 Hodgins, *Broken Ground*, 256.
45 Hodgins, *Broken Ground*, 255.
46 Hodgins, *Broken Ground*, 98.
47 Cook, *Shock Troops*, 306.
48 Cook, *Shock Troops*, 306.
49 Hodgins, *Broken Ground*, 98.
50 Hodgins, *Broken Ground*, 98.
51 Hodgins, *Broken Ground*, 100.
52 Cook, *Shock Troops*, 246.
53 Cook, *Shock Troops*, 251.
54 Hodgins, *Broken Ground*, 311.
55 Hodgins, *Broken Ground*, 94.
56 Hodgins, *Broken Ground*, 96.
57 Hodgins, *Broken Ground*, 97.
58 Hodgins, *Broken Ground*, 97.
59 The name of this character—Matthew Pearson—recalls that of former Prime Minister Lester B. "Mike" Pearson, generally considered one of the most influential Canadians of the twentieth century. Because he was awarded the Nobel Prize for Peace and later introduced universal health care in Canada, he is seen as representing the "best" in Canadian values.
60 Hodgins, *Broken Ground*, 273.
61 Hodgins, *Broken Ground*, 271.
62 Hodgins, *Broken Ground*, 309–10.
63 Hodgins, *Broken Ground*, 337–38.
64 Thiessen, *Vimy*, vi.
65 New, "Review: Ice Crystals," 569.
66 Hodgins, *Broken Ground*, 334.
67 Hodgins, *Broken Ground*, 333.
68 Hodgins, *Broken Ground*, 334.
69 Wyile, *Speculative Fictions*, 5.
70 Wyile, *Speculative Fictions*, 5.
71 Wyile, *Speculative Fictions*, 6.
72 Itani, *Deafening*, 30.
73 Itani, *Deafening*, 30.
74 "Fire Report," *Deseronto Tribune*. A fuller exploration of the significance of Itani's undocumented use of material from local newspapers was presented in

2009 at the annual ACCUTE conference in Ottawa, in a paper titled, "Copying Code: The Undocumented use of Historical Sources in Itani's *Deafening*." This paper was co-written with, and presented by, Alicia Robinette, doctoral candidate at the University of Western Ontario.

75   Itani, *Deafening*, 30.
76   Itani, *Deafening*, 33.
77   Itani, *Deafening*, 36.
78   Goldman, *Rewriting Apocalypse in Canadian Fiction*, 4.
79   Itani, *Deafening*, 35.
80   Itani, *Deafening*, 36.
81   The image of the man and his plate of potatoes is also taken directly from the *Deseronto Tribune*.
82   Itani, *Deafening*, 39.
83   Itani, *Deafening*, 40.
84   Itani, *Deafening*, 289.
85   Itani, *Deafening*, 292.
86   Itani, *Deafening*, 292.
87   Itani, *Deafening*, 267.
88   Itani, *Deafening*, 103.
89   Itani, *Deafening*, 113.
90   Itani, *Deafening*, 128.
91   Itani, *Deafening*, 128.
92   Itani, *Deafening*, 275.
93   Itani, *Deafening*, 33.
94   Itani, *Deafening*, 111.
95   Itani, *Deafening*, 216.
96   Itani, *Deafening*, 285.
97   Itani, *Deafening*, 345.
98   Of the list of texts I mention at the beginning of the introduction to this study, only Kevin Major's *No Man's Land* is set entirely on a battlefield.
99   Itani, *Deafening*, ii.
100 Cobley, *Representing War*, 74–75.
101 Itani, *Deafening*, 164.
102 Palmateer Pennee, "Imagined Innocence, Endlessly Mourned," 89.
103 Trotter, "The British Novel and the War," 36.
104 Trotter, "The British Novel and the War," 42.
105 Trotter, "The British Novel and the War," 52.
106 Ouditt, "Myths, Memories, and Monuments," 259.
107 Itani, *Deafening*, 177.
108 Cobley, *Representing War*, 76.
109 Cobley, *Representing War*, 76.
110 Cobley, *Representing War*, 129.
111 Itani, *Deafening*, 185.
112 Itani, *Deafening*, 109.

113 Itani, *Deafening*, 377.
114 Itani, *Deafening*, 378.
115 Itani, *Deafening*, 206.
116 Itani, *Deafening*, 377.
117 Itani, *Deafening*, 378.
118 Kertzer, *Worrying the Nation*, 164–65.
119 Kertzer, *Worrying the Nation*, 175.
120 Kertzer, *Worrying the Nation*, 174.

Notes to Chapter 3

1 Susan R. Fisher in her recent study *Boys and Girls in No Man's Land: English-Canadian Children and the First World War* notes that, despite scenes depicting war activity, "nothing in Connor's [work] would have cast doubt on the honour and integrity of the Canadian soldier, or on the rightness of the Empire's and Canada's cause" (23).
2 Novak, *Dubious Glory*, 132.
3 Thompson, "Canadian Fiction of the Great War," 92.
4 Cobley, *Representing War*, 109.
5 Cobley, *Representing War*, 108.
6 Cobley, *Representing War*, 107.
7 Cobley, *Representing War*, 137–38.
8 Cobley, *Representing War*, 107–8.
9 Cabajsky and Grubisic, "Historical Fiction and Changing Ideas of Canada," x.
10 Hutcheon, *The Canadian Postmodern*, 49–50.
11 See Brydon, "'It Could Not Be Told': Making Meaning in Timothy Findley's *The Wars*"; and Vauthier, "The Dubious Battle of Story-Telling: Narrative Strategies in Timothy Findley's *The Wars*."
12 Hutcheon, *The Canadian Postmodern*, 13–14, emphasis added.
13 Hutcheon, *The Canadian Postmodern*, 23, emphasis added.
14 Kuester, *Framing Truths*, 56.
15 Kuester, *Framing Truths*, 67.
16 Kuester, quoting Vauthier, *Framing Truths*, 68.
17 Colavincenzo, "Trading Magic for Fact," xxii.
18 Colavincenzo, "Trading Magic for Fact," 203.
19 Colavincenzo, "Trading Magic for Fact," 217.
20 Colavincenzo, "Trading Magic for Fact," 224.
21 Wyile, *Speculative Fictions*, 141.
22 Wyile, *Speculative Fictions*, 141.
23 Wyile, *Speculative Fictions*, 141–42.
24 Wyile *Speculative Fictions*, 263.
25 Cabajsky and Grubisic, "Historical Fiction and Changing Ideas of Canada," xiv.
26 Robert Henri (1865-1929) was a leader of the American Ashcan School of urban realist painting. Rockwell Kent (1882-1971) was one of Henri's students and went on to work as a graphic artist.

27 Urquhart, *The Underpainter*, 343.
28 Urquhart, *The Stone Carvers*, 391. In an interview with Wyile, collected in *Speaking in the Past Tense: Canadian Novelists on Writing Historical Fiction*, Urquhart readily admits, "I'm the kind of person who doesn't take notes when I'm doing research...the facts are points of embarkation for me rather than a final destination" (82).
29 Cumyn, *The Sojourn*, 314, and *The Famished Lover*, 340.
30 Cumyn, *The Sojourn*, 314, and *The Famished Lover*, 340.
31 In an interview included on the publisher's website for *The Sojourn*, Cumyn goes over these same points.
32 Wyile, *Speculative Fictions*, 264.
33 Cook, *Clio's Warriors*, 4.
34 Wyile, *Speaking in the Past Tense*, 86.
35 Wyile, *Speaking in the Past Tense*, 96.
36 Ouditt, "Myths, Memories, and Monuments," 245.
37 Hynes, *A War Imagined*, 201.
38 Joyes, "Regenerating Wilfred Owen," 170–71.
39 Joyes, "Regenerating Wilfred Owen," 171.
40 Ouditt, "Myths, Memories, and Monuments," 259.
41 Schaub, "Caught Between Desire to Live and Sense of Duty," 253.
42 Schaub, "Caught Between Desire to Live and Sense of Duty," 253–54.
43 Cobley, *Representing War*, 11.
44 Trotter, "The British Novel and the War," 35.
45 Trotter, "The British Novel and the War," 40.
46 Trotter, "The British Novel and the War," 42.
47 Ouditt, "Myths, Memories, and Monuments," 248.
48 Vance, *Death So Noble*, 195.
49 Cobley, *Representing War*, 139.
50 Cobley, *Representing War*, 140.
51 Cumyn, *The Sojourn*, 6.
52 Cumyn, *The Sojourn*, 19.
53 Cumyn, *The Sojourn*, 15.
54 Cumyn, *The Sojourn*, 35.
55 Cumyn, *The Sojourn*, 35.
56 Cumyn, *The Sojourn*, 36.
57 Cook, *At the Sharp End*, 313.
58 The problem of the Ross rifle is also, of course, alluded to in *The Wars*, in the naming of Findley's protagonist Robert Ross.
59 Cumyn, *The Sojourn*, 41.
60 Cumyn, *The Sojourn*, 42.
61 Vanderhaeghe, *Dancock's Dance*, 66.
62 Bourke, *Dismembering the Male*, 127.
63 Bourke, *Dismembering the Male*, 145.
64 Bourke, *Dismembering the Male*, 163.

65 Ouditt, "Myths, Memories, and Monuments," 250.
66 Cook, *At the Sharp End*, 313.
67 Cumyn, *The Sojourn*, 92.
68 Cumyn, *The Sojourn*, 160.
69 Hulan, *Northern Experience and the Myths of Canadian Culture*, 18–19.
70 Cumyn, *The Sojourn*, 105–6.
71 Cumyn, *The Famished Lover*, 215.
72 Cumyn, *The Famished Lover*, 125.
73 Cumyn, *The Famished Lover*, 115.
74 Cumyn, *The Famished Lover*, 221.
75 Hynes, *A War Imagined*, 246.
76 Hynes, *A War Imagined*, 248.
77 Cumyn, *The Sojourn*, 15.
78 Cumyn, *The Sojourn*, 99.
79 Cumyn, *The Sojourn*, 71.
80 Cumyn, *The Sojourn*, 211.
81 Cumyn, *The Sojourn*, 212–13.
82 Cumyn, *The Sojourn*, 280.
83 Nonnekes, *Northern Love*, 2.
84 Nonnekes, *Northern Love*, 9.
85 Nonnekes, *Northern Love*, 127.
86 Hynes, *A War Imagined*, 200.
87 Hynes, *A War Imagined*, 201.
88 Brandon, *Art or Memorial?*, 41.
89 Brandon, *Art or Memorial?*, 22.
90 Brandon, *Art or Memorial?*, 23.
91 Brandon, *Art or Memorial?*, 33.
92 Cumyn, *The Sojourn*, 281.
93 Cumyn, *The Sojourn*, 282.
94 Cumyn, *The Famished Lover*, 123.
95 Cumyn, *The Sojourn*, 167.
96 Cumyn, *The Sojourn*, 287.
97 Cumyn, *The Sojourn*, 110.
98 Cumyn, *The Sojourn*, 109.
99 Brandon, *Art or Memorial?*, 22.
100 Cumyn, *The Famished Lover*, 125.
101 Cumyn, *The Sojourn*, 54.
102 Cumyn, *The Sojourn*, 121.
103 Cumyn, *The Sojourn*, 45.
104 Trotter, "The British Novel and the War," 40.
105 Cumyn, *The Famished Lover*, 292.
106 Cumyn, *The Sojourn*, 293.
107 Vance, *Death So Noble*, 195.
108 Vance, *Death So Noble*, 196.

109 Cumyn, *The Famished Lover*, 292–93.
110 Vance, *Death So Noble*, 197.
111 Cumyn, *The Sojourn*, 293–94.
112 Urquhart, *The Stone Carvers*, 166.
113 Urquhart, *The Underpainter*, 84.
114 Urquhart, *The Underpainter*, 276.
115 Urquhart, *The Underpainter*, 108.
116 In "Intimate and Conditional: Artistic Gesture in Jane Urquhart's *False Shuffles, The Underpainter,* and *A Map of Glass*," I take up further the way Urquhart examines the artist's process, focusing on the ways in which her frequent representations of artist figures draw on notions of dialogism, as well as the aesthetic models employed by her husband, Tony Urquhart.
117 Urquhart, *The Underpainter*, 154.
118 Urquhart, *The Underpainter*, 235.
119 Urquhart, *The Underpainter*, 304.
120 Urquhart, *The Underpainter*, 33.
121 Urquhart, *The Underpainter*, 203.
122 Urquhart, *The Underpainter*, 312.
123 Urquhart, *The Stone Carvers*, 390.
124 Urquhart, *The Stone Carvers*, 17.
125 Urquhart, *The Stone Carvers*, 74.
126 Urquhart, *The Stone Carvers*, 232–33.
127 Urquhart, *The Stone Carvers*, 235.
128 Vance, *Death So Noble*, 9.
129 Young, "'We Throw the Torch,'" 5.
130 Young, "'We Throw the Torch,'" 13.
131 Urquhart, *The Stone Carvers*, 266.
132 Urquhart, *The Stone Carvers*, 269.
133 Urquhart, *The Stone Carvers*, 269.
134 Urquhart, *The Stone Carvers*, 350.
135 Urquhart, *The Stone Carvers*, 288.
136 Cobley, *Representing War*, 107.
137 Urquhart, *The Stone Carvers*, 289.
138 Urquhart, *The Stone Carvers*, 152.
139 Urquhart, *The Stone Carvers*, 209.
140 Urquhart, *The Stone Carvers*, 325.
141 Urquhart, *The Stone Carvers*, 330.
142 Cumyn, *The Sojourn*, 122.
143 Urquhart, *The Stone Carvers*, 10.
144 Urquhart, *The Stone Carvers*, 39.
145 Urquhart, *The Stone Carvers*, 332.
146 Urquhart, *The Stone Carvers*, 33.
147 Urquhart, *The Stone Carvers*, 31.
148 Brydon, "'It Could Not Be Told,'" 57.

149 Urquhart, *The Underpainter*, 183–84.
150 Young, "The Great War and National Mythology," 155.
151 Urquhart, *The Stone Carvers*, 350.

Notes to Chapter 4

1. Gwyn, *Tapestry of War*, xxv.
2. Granatstein and Morton, *Canada and the Two World Wars*, xiv.
3. Granatstein and Morton, *Canada and the Two World Wars*, 17.
4. Granatstein and Morton, *Canada and the Two World Wars*, 91.
5. Granatstein and Morton, *Canada and the Two World Wars*, 164.
6. Granatstein and Morton, *Canada and the Two World Wars*, 166. Regulation 17 was issued by the Ontario Ministry of Education in 1912, restricting the use of French-language instruction. This regulation is referred to by Claude in Thiessen's *Vimy*, when he points out to Jean-Paul that French has been banned in Ontario schools (11).
7. Keshen, "The Great War Soldier as Nation Builder," 5.
8. Keshen, "The Great War Soldier as Nation Builder," 3.
9. Keshen, "The Great War Soldier as Nation Builder," 20–21.
10. Avery, "Ethnic and Class Relations in Western Canada," 290.
11. Rutherdale, *Hometown Horizons*, 265.
12. Rutherdale, *Hometown Horizons*, 279.
13. Vance, *Death So Noble*, 4.
14. Vance, *Death So Noble*, 256.
15. Vance, *Death So Noble*, 260–61.
16. Duffy, *Sounding the Iceberg*, iv.
17. Andrews, ""Introduction: Past Matters / Chose du passe," 6.
18. Wyile, *Speculative Fictions*, 6.
19. Cabajsky and Grubisic, "Historical Fiction and Changing Ideas of Canada," xv.
20. "Edmonton Premieres Play about Crucible of Vimy Ridge."
21. Clarke, "Trench Mind."
22. "Edmonton Premieres Play about Crucible of Vimy Ridge."
23. Thiessen, *Vimy*, v. Thiessen's consistent refrain in interviews and in his playwright's note that "this is not a play about war" is likely connected with the play's first production date of fall 2007. In the year preceding, Canada's role in the invasion of Afghanistan was a source of much debate among politicians and pundits, as opposition parties began to demand that Canadian troops be pulled out of Afghanistan and as the scandal involving Canada's tacit acceptance of the torture of political prisoners by Afghan officials resulted in the demotion of Defence Minister Gordon O'Connor.
24. Thiessen, *Vimy*, v.
25. Kroetsch, "Disunity as Unity," 355.
26. Kroetsch, "Disunity as Unity," 357.
27. Findlay, "TransCanada Collectives," 174–75.

28 Dobson, *Transnational Canadas*, 73–74.
29 Thiessen, *Vimy*, 2.
30 Gwyn, *Tapestry of War*, xxii.
31 Thiessen, *Vimy*, 11.
32 Thiessen, *Vimy*, 69.
33 Thiessen, *Vimy*, 29.
34 Thiessen, *Vimy*, xii.
35 Findlay, "TransCanada Collectives," 174–75.
36 Dobson, *Transnational Canadas*, 74.
37 Thiessen, *Vimy*, 5.
38 Cook, *Shock Troops*, 74.
39 Thiessen, *Vimy*, 77.
40 Thiessen, *Vimy*, 11.
41 Thiessen, *Vimy*, 36.
42 Ironically, the past few years have seen fairly consistent dialogue about one potential pandemic or another—from Avian flu to SARS to H1N1 flu—which has made the 1918 influenza epidemic a current and popular topic of discussion once again.
43 Kerr, *Unity (1918)*, 8. Kerr exaggerates slightly here: according to Tim Cook, while it is true that "51,748 Canadian soldiers and nursing sisters were killed in action or died of their wounds," if one includes other types of death that occurred as a direct result of the war, "a total of 60,932 Canadians met their death during the course of the war, as well as 1,305 Newfoundlanders, who were killed while serving the British forces" (*Shock Troops* 612).
44 Kerr, *Unity (1918)*, 97.
45 Humphries, "The Horror at Home," 239.
46 Humphries, "The Horror at Home," 240.
47 Humphries, "The Horror at Home," 252.
48 Humphries, "The Horror at Home," 240.
49 Humphries, "The Horror at Home," 240.
50 Kerr, *Unity (1918)*, 37.
51 Kerr, *Unity (1918)*, 47.
52 Kerr, *Unity (1918)*, 53.
53 Kerr, *Unity (1918)*, 54.
54 Kerr, *Unity (1918)*, 15.
55 Kerr, *Unity (1918)*, 87.
56 Kerr, *Unity (1918)*, 88.
57 Kerr, *Unity (1918)*, 59. Hart does not explain to Bea which medal he has, and indeed, all Canadian soldiers received the British War Medal 1914–1920 and the Allied Victory Medal 1914–1919. However, as Tim Cook explains, "there were also gallantry awards for those who performed uncommon bravery and sacrifice" (*Shock Troops* 209). The stage directions indicate that Hart wears the Victoria Cross (Kerr 35), which was only awarded to 70 Canadians who

fought in the First World War (*Shock Troops* 210). Cook points out, though, that even Distinguished Service Order and Military Cross medals were sometimes treated with skepticism by soldiers (*Shock Troops* 213).
58 Kerr, *Unity (1918)*, 72–73.
59 Kerr, *Unity (1918)*, 23.
60 Kerr, *Unity (1918)*, 78.
61 Kerr, *Unity (1918)*, 78.
62 Kerr, *Unity (1918)*, 65.
63 Kerr, *Unity (1918)*, 103–4.
64 Kerr, *Unity (1918)*, 118.
65 Kerr, *Unity (1918)*, 65.
66 Kerr, *Unity (1918)*, 42.
67 Kerr, *Unity (1918)*, 44.
68 Kerr, *Unity (1918)*, 49.
69 Kerr, *Unity (1918)*, 93.
70 Kerr, *Unity (1918)*, 127.
71 Kerr, *Unity (1918)*, 123.
72 Kerr, *Unity (1918)*, 124.
73 Boyden, *Three Day Road*, 187. The military and postwar experiences of Francis Pegahmagabow have recently been written about in detail by historian-journalist Adrian Hayes in *Pegahmagabow: Legendary Warrior, Forgotten Hero*; Hayes notes that Pegahmagabow "remains the most decorated native soldier in Canadian history" (Hayes 8), while also documenting his numerous postwar clashes with the Canadian government, which repeatedly refused the loan applications he had made under the Soldier Settlement Act of 1919 (8–9). Boyden does not cite Hayes's book, but his representation of Pegahmagabow's cynicism demonstrates that his research into Pegahmagabow's life, like Hayes's, extends beyond accounts that "tell only the story of the young, idealistic soldier and nothing of the bitter veteran" (Hayes 9).
74 Boyden, *Three Day Road*, 353.
75 Wyile, *Speaking in the Past Tense*, 222.
76 Boyden, *Three Day Road*, 265.
77 Wyile, *Speaking in the Past Tense*, 238.
78 Groening, *Listening to Old Woman Speak*, 145.
79 Groening, *Listening to Old Woman Speak*, 151.
80 Boyden, *Three Day Road*, 265.
81 Boyden, *Three Day Road*, 266.
82 Boyden, *Three Day Road*, 262.
83 Monkman, *A Native Heritage*, 161.
84 Boyden, *Three Day Road*, 349.
85 Boyden, *Three Day Road*, 250.
86 Boyden, *Three Day Road*, 2.
87 Boyden, *Three Day Road*, 242.

88 Boyden, *Three Day Road*, 322.
89 Wyile, *Speculative Fictions*, 6.
90 Groening, *Listening to Old Woman Speak*, 21.
91 As Wyile notes in "Windigo Killing: Joseph Boyden's *Three Day Road*," the structure of the novel was "Originally written in chronological form…[but] was radically revised by Boyden to give the novel a circular, elliptical narrative structure and an oral narrative framework" (84).
92 Boyden, *Three Day Road*, 28.
93 Boyden, *Three Day Road*, 59.
94 Boyden, *Three Day Road*, 88.
95 Boyden, *Three Day Road*, 222.
96 Boyden, *Three Day Road*, 343.
97 Boyden, *Three Day Road*, 143.
98 Boyden, *Three Day Road*, 287.
99 See also Wyile, "Windigo Killing."
100 Boyden, *Three Day Road*, 27.
101 Boyden, *Three Day Road*, 322.
102 Boyden, *Three Day Road*, 118.
103 Boyden, *Three Day Road*, 195.
104 Boyden, *Three Day Road*, 73.
105 Boyden, *Three Day Road*, 92.
106 Boyden, *Three Day Road*, 6.
107 Boyden, *Three Day Road*, 248.
108 Boyden, *Three Day Road*, 100.
109 Boyden, *Three Day Road*, 100.
110 Groening, *Listening to Old Woman Speak*, 147.
111 Monkman, *A Native Heritage*, 127.
112 Boyden, *Three Day Road*, 44.
113 Boyden, *Three Day Road*, 245.
114 Boyden, *Three Day Road*, 242.
115 Boyden, *Three Day Road*, 340.
116 Boyden, *Three Day Road*, 350.
117 Groening, *Listening to Old Woman Speak*, 156.
118 Poliquin, *A Secret Between Us*, 293.
119 Kuitenbrouwer, "Lusignan on the loose," D16.
120 Kuitenbrouwer, "Lusignan on the loose," D16.
121 Rigelhof, "Subversion à la Günter Grass," 10.
122 Poliquin, *A Secret Between Us*, 2.
123 Poliquin, *A Secret Between Us*, 2–3.
124 Poliquin, *A Secret Between Us*, 4.
125 Poliquin, *A Secret Between Us*, 14.
126 Koepke, "Canadian History on a Skewer."
127 Poliquin, *A Secret Between Us*, 71.

128 Poliquin, *A Secret Between Us*, 72.
129 Poliquin, *A Secret Between Us*, 152.
130 Cobley, *Representing War*, 51–52.
131 Poliquin, *A Secret Between Us*, 153.
132 Poliquin, *A Secret Between Us*, 105.
133 Poliquin, *A Secret Between Us*, 28.
134 Poliquin, *A Secret Between Us*, 54.
135 Gwyn, *Tapestry of War*, 294.
136 Basilières, "A Secret Between Us."
137 Rigelhof, "Subversion à la Günter Grass," 11.
138 Koepke, "Canadian History on a Skewer."
139 Poliquin, *A Secret Between Us*, 211.
140 Gwyn, *Tapestry of War*, 177.
141 Gwyn, *Tapestry of War*, 178.
142 Poliquin, *A Secret Between Us*, 212.
143 Poliquin, *A Secret Between Us*, 293.
144 Basilières, "A Secret Between Us."
145 Gwyn, *Tapestry of War*, 178.
146 Poliquin, *A Secret Between Us*, 286.
147 Quoted in Gwyn, *Tapestry of War*, 286.
148 Gwyn, *Tapestry of War*, 77.
149 Gwyn, *Tapestry of War*, xxiv.
150 Poliquin, *A Secret Between Us*, 105.
151 Poliquin, *A Secret Between Us*, 77.
152 Poliquin, *In the Name of the Father*, 194.
153 Barber, "Daniel Poliquin, Canada's perpetual literary nominee."
154 Poliquin, *In the Name of the Father*, 90.
155 Ouellet, "Le roman de 'l'etre-ecrivant' entre l'amonymat et la reconnaissance," 417.
156 Ouellet, "Le roman de 'l'etre-ecrivant' entre l'amonymat et la reconnaissance," 417. Translation from the French by Cassandra Scavetta.
157 Kevra, "Indigestible Stew and Holy Piss," 111.
158 Kevra, "Indigestible Stew and Holy Piss," 111.
159 Poliquin, *A Secret Between Us*, 57–58.
160 Poliquin, *A Secret Between Us*, 58.
161 Poliquin, *A Secret Between Us*, 58.
162 Poliquin, *A Secret Between Us*, 58–59.
163 There is also, of course, a correlation between Lusignan's fate and Poliquin's after the publication of *In the Name of the Father*, which "created a storm in the French Quebec press when it first came out" (Arnopoulus).
164 Poliquin, *A Secret Between Us*, 181.
165 Cobley, *Representing War*, 33.
166 Vance, *Death So Noble*, 136.
167 Brydon, "Negotiating Belonging in Global Times," 254.

Notes to Conclusion

1. Stone, "Canadian War Epic Suffers from Sentimentality," D9.
2. Szklarski, "'Passchendaele' Grim but Realistic," D1.
3. Stone, "Paul Gross's War Epic," E2.
4. Winter, *Remembering War*, 185–86.
5. Novak, *Dubious Glory*, 29.
6. Szklarski, "'Passchendaele' Grim but Realistic," D1.
7. Palmateer Pennee, "Imagined Innocence, Endlessly Mourned," 89.
8. In Coates's article "The Best Soldiers of All: Unsung Heroines in Canadian Women's Great War Fictions," on the one hand, she discusses the way novels show women "in action" as they engage in political discourse and take on "heroic" roles, in particular as sacrificing mothers (89); and on the other, she asserts that "ultimately, Canadian women's novels are, in subtle ways, pleas for peace, instructions on how to avoid war" (93).
9. Urquhart, *The Stone Carvers*, 288.
10. Massicotte, *Mary's Wedding*, 59.
11. Kerr, *Unity (1918)*, 59.
12. Boyden, *Three Day Road*, 343.
13. Shore, "Canadian Soldiers Lend Authenticity to War Movie," D1.
14. Warnock, "What Is Canada Promoting in Afghanistan?", 38.
15. http://opencanada.org/features/blogs/roundtable/adding-up-kandahar/
16. Palmateer Pennee, "Imagined Innocence, Endlessly Mourned," 92–93.
17. Palmateer Pennee, "Imagined Innocence, Endlessly Mourned," 93.
18. Kowaluk and Staples, "Introduction," xi.
19. Kowaluk and Staples, "Introduction," xv–xvi.
20. McKay and Swift, *Warrior Nation*, 11.
21. McKay and Swift, *Warrior Nation*, 283–84.
22. Richler, *What We Talk about When We Talk about War*, 86.
23. Ricoeur, *Memory, History, Forgetting*, 494.
24. Polinquin, *A Secret Between Us*, 181.
25. Richler, *What We Talk about When We Talk about War*, 56.
26. Visit http://www.veterans.gc.ca/remembers/sub.cfm?source=feature/week2010/vignette.
27. Wyile, *Speculative Fictions*, 265.
28. Vance, *Death So Noble*, 266.
29. Kerr, *Unity (1918)*, 128.

Bibliography

Acland, Peregrine. *All Else Is Folly, a Tale of War and Passion*. Toronto: McClelland and Stewart, 1929.
Andrews, Jennifer, et al. "Introduction: Past Matters / Chose du passe." *Studies in Canadian Literature* 27, no. 1 (2002): 5–14.
Arnopoulos, Sheila. "Pilloried Intelligentsia Aplenty." Review of *In the Name of the Father* by Daniel Poliquin. *mRb*. AELAQ, 2001. Web. 28 March 2013.
Atwood, Margaret. "Timothy Findley: *The Wars*." In *Second Words: Selected Critical Prose*. Toronto: Anansi, 1982. 290–95.
Avery, Donald. "Ethnic and Class Relations in Western Canada during the First World War: A Case Study of European Immigrants and Anglo-Canadian Nativism." In *Canada and the First World War: Essays in Honour of Robert Craig Brown*. Ed. David MacKenzie. Toronto: University of Toronto Press, 2005. 272–99.
Baetz, Joel. "Introduction: Beyond Flanders Fields." *Canadian Poetry from World War I: An Anthology*. Ed. Joel Baetz. Toronto: Oxford University Press, 2009. 1–15.
Barber, John. "Daniel Poliquin, Canada's Perpetual Literary Nominee." *Globe and Mail,* 6 February 2010, F7.
Basilières, Michel. "A Secret Between Us." Review of *A Secret Between Us* by Daniel Poliquin. *Quill & Quire,* October 2007.
Becker, Annette. "Memory Gaps: Maurice Halbwachs, Memory, and the Great War." *Journal of European Studies* 35 (2005): 102–13.
Beckmann, Susan. "Canadian Burlesque: Jack Hodgins' *The Invention of the World*." *Essays on Canadian Writing* 20 (1980): 106–25.
Bergonzi, Bernard. *Heroes' Twilight: A Study of the Literature of the Great War*. London: Constable, 1965.
Bird, Will R. *And We Go On*. Toronto: Hunter-Rose Co, 1930.

Bölling, Gordon. "Acts of (Re-)Construction: Traces of Germany in Jane Urquhart's Novel *The Stone Carvers*." In *Refractions of Germany in Canadian Literature and Culture*. Ed. Heinz Antor, Sylvia Brown, John Considine, and Klaus Stierstorfer. Berlin: Walter de Gruyter, 2003. 295–317.

Bourke, Joanna. *Dismembering the Male: Men's Bodies, Britain, and the Great War*. Chicago: University of Chicago Press, 1996.

Boyden, Joseph. *Three Day Road*. Toronto: Viking Canada, 2005.

Bowering, Marilyn. *Grandfather Was a Soldier*. Victoria: Press Porcépic, 1987.

Bradshaw, Mel. *Quarrel with the Foe*. Toronto: RendezVous Press, 2005.

Brand, Dionne. *At the Full and Change of the Moon*. Toronto: Alfred A. Knopf, 1999.

Brandon, Laura. *Art or Memorial? The Forgotten History of Canada's War Art*. Calgary: University of Calgary Press, 2006.

Brown, Eric J. *The Promise*. Entwistle: Magnolia Press, 2004.

Brydon, Diana. "Negotiating Belonging in Global Times: The Hérouxville Debates." In *Crosstalk: Canadian and Global Imaginaries in Dialogue*. Ed. Diana Brydon and Marta Dvořák. Waterloo: Wilfrid Laurier University Press, 2012. 253–71.

———. "Metamorphoses of a Discipline." In *Trans.Can.Lit: Resituating the Study of Canadian Literature*. Ed. Smaro Kamboureli and Roy Miki. Waterloo: Wilfrid Laurier University Press, 2007. 1–16.

———. "'It Could Not Be Told': Making Meaning in Timothy Findley's *The Wars*." *Journal of Commonwealth Literature* 21, no. 1 (1986): 62–79.

Cabajsky, Andrea, and Brett Josef Grubisic. "Historical Fiction and Changing Ideas of Canada." In *National Plots: Historical Fiction and Changing Ideas of Canada*. Ed. Andrea Cabajsky and Brett Josef Grubisic. Waterloo: Wilfrid Laurier University Press, 2010. vii–xxiv.

Cameron, Elspeth, ed. *Multiculturalism and Immigration in Canada: An Introductory Reader*. Toronto: Canadian Scholars' Press, 2004.

Caron, Louis. *L'Emmitouflé*. Paris: R. Laffont, 1977.

Child, Philip. *God's Sparrows*. London: Butterworth, 1937.

Chislett, Anne. *Quiet in the Land*. Toronto: Coach House Press, 1983.

Clark, David B. *Lucifer's Gate*. Renfrew: General Store Press House, 2002.

Clarke, Eva Marie. "Trench Mind: Citadel's Vimy Gets Inside the Head of WWI Canadian Soldiers." *VUE Arts Weekly*, 24 October 2007. Web.

Clarkson, Adrienne. "Remembrance Day Message from Her Excellency the Right Honourable Adrienne Clarkson, Governor General and Commander-in-Chief of Canada." 7 November 2003.

Coates, Donna. "The Digger on the Lofty Pedestal: Australian Women's Fictions of the Great War." *Australian and New Zealand Studies in Canada* 10 (1993): 1–22.

———. "The Best Soldiers of All: Unsung Heroines in Canadian Women's Great War Fictions." *Canadian Literature* 151 (1996): 66–99.

Cobley, Evelyn. *Representing War: Form and Ideology in First World War Narratives*. Toronto: University of Toronto Press, 1993.

Colavincenzo, Marc. *"Trading Magic for Fact," Fact for Magic: Myth and Mythologizing in Postmodern Canadian Historical Fiction*. Amsterdam and New York: Rodopi, 2003.
Coleman, Daniel. *White Civility: The Literary Project of English Canada*. Toronto: University of Toronto Press, 2006.
Cook, Tim. *Shock Troops: Canadians Fighting the Great War 1917-1918*. Toronto: Viking Canada, 2008.
———. *At the Sharp End: Canadians Fighting the Great War 1914-1916*. Toronto: Viking Canada, 2007.
———. *Clio's Warriors: Canadian Historians and the Writing of the World Wars*. Vancouver: UBC Press, 2006.
Crummey, Michael. *The Wreckage: A Novel*. Toronto: Doubleday Canada, 2005.
Cumyn, Alan. "Author Interview." *McClelland.com*.
———. *The Famished Lover*. Fredericton: Goose Lane, 2006.
———. *The Sojourn*. Toronto: Emblem Editions, 2003.
Davies, Robertson. *Fifth Business: A Novel*. Toronto: Macmillan of Canada, 1970.
Dean, Flannery. "Mary Swan: Southern Ontario Gothic." *Quill & Quire*, March 2008. Web.
de Man, Paul. "Autobiography as De-facement." *MLN* 94, no. 5 (1979): 919-30.
Dobson, Kit. *Transnational Canadas: Anglo-Canadian Literature and Globalization*. Waterloo: Wilfrid Laurier University Press, 2009.
Duffy, Dennis. *Sounding the Iceberg: An Essay on Canadian Historical Novels*. Toronto: ECW Press, 1986.
"Edmonton Premieres Play about Crucible of Vimy Ridge." *CBCnews.ca*. 20 October 2007.
Edwards, Justin D. *Gothic Canada: Reading the Spectre of a National Literature*. Edmonton: University of Alberta Press, 2005.
Epperly, Elizabeth R. "Chivalry and Romance: L.M. Montgomery's Re-Vision of the Great War in *Rainbow Valley*." In *Myth and Milieu: Atlantic Literature and Culture 1918-1939*. Ed. Gwendolyn Davies and Carrie MacMillan. Fredericton: Acadiensis, 1993. 87-94.
Findlay, Len. "TransCanada Collectives: Social Imagination, the Cunning of Production, and the Multilateral Sublime." In *Trans.Can.Lit: Resituating the Study of Canadian Literature*. Ed. Smaro Kamboureli and Roy Miki. Waterloo: Wilfrid Laurier University Press, 2007. 173-86.
Findley, Timothy. *The Wars*. 1977. Toronto: Penguin Books Canada, 1996.
"Fire Report." *Deseronto Tribune*, 29 May 1896.
Fisher, Susan R. *Boys and Girls in No Man's Land: English-Canadian Children and the First World War*. University of Toronto Press, 2011.
———. "Canada and the Great War." In *The Cambridge History of Canadian Literature*, ed. Coral Ann Howells and Eva-Marie Kröller. Cambridge: Cambridge University Press, 2009. 224-43.
Francis, Daniel. *National Dreams: Myth, Memory, and Canadian History*. Vancouver: Arsenal Pulp Press, 1997.

French, David. *Soldier's Heart*. Toronto: Talonbooks, 2002.
Fussell, Paul. *The Great War and Modern Memory*. 2nd ed. New York: Oxford University Press, 1975.
Goldman, Marlene. *DisPossession: Haunting in Canadian Fiction*. Montreal and Kingston: McGill-Queen's University Press, 2012.
———. *Rewriting Apocalypse in Canadian Fiction*. Montreal and Kingston: McGill-Queen's University Press, 2005.
Goodspeed, Michael J. *Three to Loaf*. Toronto: Blue Butterfly, 2008.
Gordon, Neta. "Intimate and Conditional: Artistic Gesture in Jane Urquhart's *False Shuffles*, *The Underpainter*, and *A Map of Glass*." In *Resurgence in Jane Urquhart's Oeuvre*. Ed. Héliane Daziron-Ventura and Marta Dvořák. New York: Peter Lang, 2010. 159–74.
Grace, Sherrill. "Introduction: 'A Different Kind of Theatre.'" In *Canada and the Theatre of War*, vol. I. Ed. Donna Coates and Sherrill Grace. Toronto: Playwrights Canada Press, 2008. iii–ix.
Granatstein, J.L. *Who Killed the Canadian Military?* Toronto: HarperCollins, 2004.
Granatstein, J.L., and Desmond Morton. *Canada and the Two World Wars*. Toronto: Key Porter Books, 2003.
Gray, John. *Billy Bishop Goes to War: A Play*. Vancouver: Talonbooks, 1981.
Groening, Laura Smyth. *Listening to Old Woman Speak: Natives and alterNatives in Canadian Literature*. Montreal and Kingston: McGill-Queen's University Press, 2004.
Passchendaele. Dir. Paul Gross. Alliance Films, 2008.
Gwyn, Sandra. "Putting a Human Face on the Tragedy of War." Review of *No Man's Land*, by Kevin Major. *Toronto Star*, 1 July 1995, G13.
———. *Tapestry of War: A Private View of Canadians in the Great War*. Toronto: HarperCollins, 1992.
Halbwachs, Maurice. *The Collective Memory*. Trans. Francis J. Ditter, Jr., and Vida Yazdi Ditter. New York: Harper and Row, 1980.
Harrison, Charles Yale. *Generals Die in Bed*. 1930. Hamilton: Potlatch Publishers, 1974.
Hastings, Tom. "'Their Fathers Did It to Them': Findley's Appeal to the Great War Myth of a Generational Conflict in *The Wars*." *Essays on Canadian Writing* 64 (1998): 85–103.
Hayes, Adrian. *Pegahmagabow: Legendary Warrior, Forgotten Hero*. Huntsville: Fox Meadow Creations, 2003.
Hodgins, Jack. *Broken Ground*. Toronto: McClelland and Stewart, 1998.
Holmes, Nancy. "'In Flanders Fields'—Canada's Official Poem: Breaking Faith." *Studies in Canadian Literature* 30, no. 1 (2005): 11–33.
Hulan, Renée. *Northern Experience and the Myths of Canadian Culture*. Montreal and Kingston: McGill-Queen's University Press, 2002.
Humphries, Mark Osborne. "The Horror at Home: The Canadian Military and the 'Great' Influenza Pandemic of 1918." *Journal of the Canadian Historical Association* 16, no. 1 (2005): 235–60.

Hutcheon, Linda. *The Canadian Postmodern: A Study of Contemporary English-Canadian Fiction*. Toronto: Oxford University Press, 1988.
Huyssen, Andreas. *Twilight Memories: Marking Time in a Culture of Amnesia*. New York and London: Routledge, 1995.
Hynes, Samuel. *A War Imagined: The First World War and English Culture*. London: Pimlico, 1990.
Itani, Frances. *Deafening*. Toronto: HarperCollins, 2004.
Jack, Donald. *It's Me Again*. 1975. Sackville: Sybertooth, 2007.
———. *That's Me in the Middle*. 1972. Toronto: McClelland and Stewart, 2001.
———. *Three Cheers for Me*. 1962. Toronto: McClelland and Stewart, 2001.
Janes, Daniela. "Truth and History: Representing the Aura in the *Englishman's Boy*." *Studies in Canadian Literature* 27, no. 1 (2002): 88–104.
Joyes, Kaley. "Regenerating Wilfred Owen: Pat Barker's Revisions." *Mosaic: A Journal for the Interdisciplinary Study of Literature* 42, no. 3 (2009): 169–83.
Kamboureli, Smaro, and Roy Miki, eds. *Trans.Can.Lit: Resituating the Study of Canadian Literature*. Waterloo: Wilfrid Laurier University Press, 2007.
Kamboureli, Smaro, and Robert Zacharias, eds. *Shifting the Ground of Canadian Literary Studies*. Waterloo: Wilfrid Laurier University Press, 2012.
Keenan, Dennis King. *The Question of Sacrifice*. Bloomington: Indiana University Press, 2005.
Kennedy, David. *Elegy*. London and New York: Routledge, 2007.
Kerr, Kevin. *Unity (1918)*. Toronto: Talonbooks, 2002.
Kertzer, Jonathan. *Worrying the Nation: Imagining a National Literature in English Canada*. Toronto: University of Toronto Press, 1998.
Keshen, Jeffrey A. "The Great War Soldier as Nation Builder in Canada and Australia." In *Canada and the Great War: Western Front Association Papers*. Ed. Briton C. Busch. Montreal and Kingston: McGill-Queen's University Press, 2003. 3–26.
Kevra, Susan. "Indigestible Stew and Holy Piss: The Politics of Food in Rodolphe Girard's *Marie Calumet*." *Essays on Canadian Writing* 78 (2003): 110–36.
Klovan, Peter. "'Bright and Good': Findley's *The Wars*." *Canadian Literature* 91 (1981): 58–69.
Koepke, Melora. "Canadian History on a Skewer." Review of *A Secret Between Us*, by Daniel Poliquin, *Vancouver Sun*, 6 October 2007.
Kowaluk, Lucia, and Steven Staples, "Introduction." In *Afghanistan and Canada: Is There an Alternative to War?* Ed. Kowaluk and Staples. Montreal: Black Rose Books, 2009. xi–xvi.
Kroetsch, Robert. "Disunity as Unity: A Canadian Strategy." In *New Contexts of Canadian Criticism*. Ed. Ajay Heble, Donna Palmateer Pennee, and J.R. (Tim) Struthers. Peterborough: Broadview Press, 1997. 355–65.
Kuester, Martin. "'A Mythic Act of Possession': Constructing the North American Frontier(s) in Guy Vanderhaeghe's *The Englishman's Boy*." In *New Worlds: Discovering and Constructing the Unknown in Anglophone Literature*. Ed. Martin Kuester, Gabriele Christ, and Rudolf Beck. Munich, Germany: Vögel, 2000. 272–92.

———. *Framing Truths: Parodic Structures in Contemporary English-Canadian Historical Novels*. Toronto: University of Toronto Press, 1992.
Kuitenbrouwer, Kathryn. "Lusignan on the Loose." Review of *A Secret Between Us* by Daniel Poliquin, *Globe and Mail*, 3 November 2007, D16.
Langhelle, Carol. *The Counterfeit and the Real in Jack Hodgins' The Invention of the World*. Lund: Nordic Association for Canadian Studies, 1992.
Laurence, Margaret. *A Bird in the House: Stories*. Toronto: McClelland and Stewart, 1970.
———. *The Diviners*. Toronto: McClelland and Stewart, 1988.
Leed, Eric. *No Man's Land: Combat and Identity in World War I*. Cambridge: Cambridge University Press, 1979.
Lill, Wendy. *The Fighting Days*. Vancouver: Talonbooks, 1985.
Lloyd, David W. *Battlefield Tourism: Pilgrimage and the Commemoration of the Great War in Britain, Australia, and Canada, 1919–1939*. Oxford: Berg, 1998.
Lukács, Georg. *The Historical Novel*. Trans. Hannah Mitchell and Stanley Mitchell. London: Merlin Press, 1965.
MacLennan, Hugh. *Barometer Rising*. 1941. Toronto: New Canadian Library, 1989.
Major, Kevin. *No Man's Land*. Toronto: Anchor, 1995.
Massicotte, Stephen. *Mary's Wedding*. Toronto: Playwrights Canada Press, 2002.
MacDonald, Ann-Marie. *Fall on Your Knees*. Toronto: Alfred A. Knopf, 1996.
Macfarlane, David. *The Danger Tree: Memory, War, and the Search for a Family's Past*. Toronto: Vintage Canada, 2000.
McCrae, John. "Disarmament." In *In Flanders Fields and Other Poems*. New York: G.P. Putnam's sons, 1919. Project Gutenberg. Web. 20 September 2013.
———. "In Flanders Fields." In *Canadian Poetry from World War I: An Anthology*. Ed. Joel Baetz. Toronto: Oxford University Press, 2009. 81–82.
McKay, Ami. *The Birth House*. Toronto: Random House, 2007.
McKay, Ian, and Jamie Swift. *Warrior Nation: Rebranding Canada in an Age of Anxiety*. Toronto: Between the Lines, 2012.
McKenna, Andrew J. *Violence and Difference: Girard, Derrida, and Deconstruction*. Champaign: University of Illinois Press, 1992.
Monkman, Leslie. *A Native Heritage: Images of the Indian in English-Canadian Literature*. Toronto: University of Toronto Press, 1981.
Mountain-Horse, Mike. *My People, the Bloods*. Standoff: Blood Tribal Council, 1979.
New, W.H. "Review: Ice Crystals." *Journal of Modern Literature* 23, nos. 3–4 (2000): 565–73.
Nonnekes, Paul. *Northern Love: An Exploration of Canadian Masculinity*. Edmonton: Athabasca University Press, 2008.
Novak, Dagmar. *Dubious Glory: The Two World Wars and the Canadian Novel*. New York: Peter Lang, 2000.
Otto, Peter. "Rereading David Malouf's *Fly Away Peter*: The Great War, Aboriginal Dispossession, and the Politics of Remembering." *Australian Literary Studies* 24, no. 1 (2009): 35–51.

Ouditt, Sharon. "Myths, Memories, and Monuments: Reimagining the Great War." In *The Cambridge Companion to the Literature of the First World War*. Ed. Vincent Sherry. Cambridge: Cambridge University Press, 2005. 245–60.

Ouellet, Francois. "Le roman de 'l'être-écrivant' entre l'amonymat et la reconnaissance: entretien avec Daniel Poliquin." *Voix et Images* 27, no. 3 (2002): 404–20.

Palmateer Pennee, Donna. "Imagined Innocence, Endlessly Mourned: Postcolonial Nationalism and Cultural Expression in Timothy Findley's *The Wars*." *ESC: English Studies in Canada* 32, nos. 2–3 (2006): 89–113.

———. "Literary Citizenship: Culture (Un)Bounded, Culture (Re)Distributed." In *Home-Work: Postcolonialism, Pedagogy, and Canadian Literature*. Ed. Cynthia Sugars. Ottawa: University of Ottawa Press, 2004. 75–85.

———. *Moral Metafiction: Counterdiscourse in the Novels of Timothy Findley*. Toronto: ECW Press, 1991.

Peritz, Ingrid, and Shawna Richter. "'It Was Quite Different Than Years Before.'" *Globe and Mail*, 12 November 2004, A7.

Pirie, Bruce. "The Dragon in the Fog: 'Displaced Mythology' in *The Wars*." *Canadian Literature* 91 (1989): 70–79.

Plantos, Ted. *Passchendaele*. Windsor: Black Moss Press, 1983.

Poliquin, Daniel. *A Secret Between Us*. Trans. Donald Winkler. Vancouver and Toronto: Douglas and McIntyre, 2007.

———. *In the Name of the Father: An Essay on Quebec Nationalism*. Trans. Donald Winkler. Vancouver and Toronto: Douglas and McIntyre, 2000.

Poole, Michael. *Rain Before Morning*. Madeira Park: Harbour Press, 2006.

"Population by Selected Ethnic Origins, by Province and Territory (2006 Census) (Canada)." *2006 Census of Population*. Statistics Canada, 28 July 2009. Web.

Prescott, John F. *In Flanders Fields: The Story of John McCrae*. Erin: Boston Mills Press, 1985.

Reddish, Michael G., ed. *Apocalyptic Literature: A Reader*. Peabody: Hendrickson Publishers, 1995.

"Remembrance Vignette." Veterans Affairs Canada. 20 September 2013. Web. http://www.veterans.gc.ca/eng/video-gallery/video/9044.

Rhodes, Shane. "Buggering with History: Sexual Warfare and Historical Reconstruction in Timothy Findley's *The Wars*." *Canadian Literature* 159 (1998): 38–53.

Richler, Noah. *What We Talk about When We Talk about War*. Fredericton: Goose Lane Editions, 2012.

Ricoeur, Paul. *Memory, History, Forgetting*. Trans. Kathleen Blamey and David Pellauer. Chicago and London: University of Chicago Press, 2004.

Rigelhof, T.F. "Subversion à la Günther Grass." Review of *A Secret Between Us* by Daniel Poliquin. *Books in Canada* 36, no. 6 (2007): 10–11.

———. "War Is Hell, Novel Is Brilliant." Review of *Three Day Road* by Joseph Boyden, *Globe and Mail*, 23 April 2005, D6.

Rutherdale, Robert Allen. *Hometown Horizons: Local Responses to Canada's Great War*. Vancouver: UBC Press, 2004.

Sallans, Herbert G. *Little Man.* Toronto: Ryerson Press, 1942.
Schaub, Danielle. "Caught Between Desire to Live and Sense of Duty: Traumatized Narrative in Alan Cumyn's *The Sojourn.*" In *Building Liberty: Canada and World Peace 1945–2005.* Ed. Conny Steenman-Marcusse and Aritha Van Herk. Groningen: Barkhuis Press, 2005. 253–76.
Sherry, Vincent. "Introduction." In *The Cambridge Companion to the Literature of the First World War.* Ed. Sherry. Cambridge: Cambridge University Press, 2005. 1–11.
Shore, Randy. "Canadian Soldiers Lend Authenticity to War Movie." Interview with Paul Gross, *Vancouver Sun,* 17 October, 2008, D1.
Siemerling, Winfried, and Sarah Phillips Casteel, eds. *Canada and Its Americas: Transnational Navigations.* Montreal and Kingston: McGill–Queen's University Press, 2010.
Simard, Jean. *Mon fils pourtant heureux.* Montréal: Cercle du Livre de France, 1956.
Stacey, Robert David. "'State of Shock': History and Crisis in Hugh MacLennan's *Barometer Rising.*" In *National Plots: Historical Fiction and Changing Ideas of Canada.* Ed. Andrea Cabajsky and Brett Josef Grubisic. Waterloo: Wilfrid Laurier University Press, 2010. 53–66.
Stone, Jay. "Canadian War Epic Suffers from Sentimentality." Review of *Passchendaele,* dir. Paul Gross, *Vancouver Sun,* 17 October 2008, D9.
———. "Paul Gross's War Epic Began with a Story from His Grandfather." Interview with Paul Gross, *The Gazette,* 11 October 2008, E2.
Struthers, J.R., ed. *On Coasts of Eternity: Jack Hodgins' Fictional Universe.* Lantzville: Oolichan Books, 1996.
Sugars, Cynthia, and Gerry Turcotte. "Canadian Literature and the Postcolonial Gothic." In *Unsettled Remains: Canadian Literature and the Postcolonial Gothic.* Ed. Sugars and Turcotte. Waterloo: Wilfrid Laurier University Press, 2009. vii–xxvi.
Swan, Mary. *The Boys in the Trees.* New York: Henry Holt, 2008.
———. *The Deep: A Novella.* Erin, ON: Porcupine's Quill Press, 2002.
Szklarski, Cassandra. "'Passchendaele' Grim but Realistic." Review of *Passchendaele,* dir. Paul Gross, *Telegraph-Journal,* 17 October 2008, D1.
Tector, Amy. "A Righteous War? L.M. Montgomery's Depiction of the First World War in *Rilla of Ingleside.*" *Canadian Literature* 179 (2003): 72–86.
Thiessen, Vern. *Vimy.* Toronto: Playwrights Canada Press, 2007.
Thompson, Eric. "Canadian Fiction of the Great War." *Canadian Literature* 91 (1981): 81–96.
Thomson, Alistair. "The Anzac Legend: Exploring National Myth and Memory in Australia." In *The Myths We Live By.* Ed. Raphael Samuel and Paul Thomson. London: Routledge, 1990. 73–82.
Thomson, R.H. *The Lost Boys: Letters from the Sons in Two Acts, 1914–1923.* Toronto: Playwrights Canada, 2002.

Trotter, David. "The British Novel and the War." In *The Cambridge Companion to the Literature of the First World War*. Ed. Vincent Sherry. Cambridge: Cambridge University Press, 2005. 34–56.
Tumanov, Vladimir. "De-Automatization in Timothy Findley's *The Wars*." *Canadian Literature* 130 (1991): 107–15.
Urquhart, Jane. *The Stone Carvers*. Toronto: McClelland and Stewart, 2001.
———. *The Underpainter*. Toronto: McClelland and Stewart, 1997.
Vance, Jonathan F. "A Game of Ghosts." *Canadian Literature* 179 (2003): 129–31.
———. *Death So Noble: Memory, Meaning, and the First World War*. Vancouver: UBC Press, 1997.
Vanderhaeghe, Guy. *Dancock's Dance*. Winnipeg: Blizzard, 1996.
Vauthier, Simone. "The Dubious Battle of Storytelling: Narrative Strategies in Timothy Findley's *The Wars*." In *Gaining Ground: European Critics on Canadian Literature*. Ed. Robert Kroetsch and Reingard M. Nischik. Edmonton: NeWest Press, 1985. 11–39.
Warnock, John W. "What Is Canada Promoting in Afghanistan? A Brief History of Its Role." In *Afghanistan and Canada*. Ed. Lucia Kowaluk and Steven Staples. Montreal: Black Rose Books, 2009. 37–51.
Watkin, William. *On Mourning: Theories of Loss in Modern Literature*. Edinburgh: Edinburgh University Press, 2004.
Webb, Peter. "Occupants of Memory: War in Twentieth-Century Canadian Fiction." Ph.D. diss., University of Ottawa, 2007.
———. "'At War with Nature': Animals in Timothy Findley's *The Wars*." In *Other Selves: Animals in the Canadian Literary Imagination*. Ed. Janice Fiamengo. Ottawa: University of Ottawa Press, 2007. 227–44.
Wiersema, Robert. "Four Cures for 'Premise Fatigue.'" Review of *Banana Kiss* by Bonnie Rozanski, *Globe and Mail* 24 December 2005, D10.
Williams, David. *Media, Memory, and the First World War*. Montreal and Kingston: McGill–Queen's University Press, 2009.
———. *Imagined Nations: Reflections on Media in Canadian Fiction*. Montreal and Kingston: McGill–Queen's University Press, 2003.
Winter, Jay. *Remembering War: The Great War Between Memory and History in the Twentieth Century*. New Haven: Yale University Press, 2006.
———. *Sites of Memory, Sites of Mourning: The Great War in European Cultural History*. Cambridge: Cambridge University Press, 1995.
Wyile, Herb. *Anne of Tim Hortons: Globalization and the Reshaping of Atlantic-Canadian Literature*. Waterloo: Wilfrid Laurier University Press, 2011.
———. "*Windigo* Killing: Joseph Boyden's *Three Day Road*." In *National Plots: Historical Fiction and Changing Ideas of Canada*. Ed. Andrea Cabajsky and Brett Josef Grubisic. Waterloo: Wilfrid Laurier University Press, 2010.
———. *Speaking in the Past Tense: Canadian Novelists on Writing Historical Fiction*. Waterloo: Wilfrid Laurier University Press, 2007.
———. *Speculative Fictions: Contemporary Canadian Novelists and the Writing of History*. Montreal and Kingston: McGill–Queens University Press, 2003.

———. "Dances with Wolfers: Choreographing History in the Englishman's Boy." *Essays on Canadian Writing* 67 (1999): 23–52.

Yardley, Marion Jeanne. "Writing the Great War: Language and Structures in English-Canadian Prose Narratives of World War I." Ph.D. diss., York University, 1989.

York, Lorraine. *Front Lines: The Fiction of Timothy Findley.* Toronto: ECW Press, 1991.

Young, Alan R. "The Great War and National Mythology." *Acadiensis* 23, no. 2 (1994): 155–66.

———. "L.M. Montgomery's *Rilla of Ingleside*: Romance and the Experience of War." In *Myth and Milieu: Atlantic Literature and Culture 1918–1939*. Ed. Gwendolyn Davies and Carrie MacMillan. Fredericton: Acadiensis, 1993. 95–122.

———. "'We Throw the Torch': Canadian Memorials of the Great War and the Mythology of Heroic Sacrifice." *Journal of Canadian Studies* 24, no. 4 (1990): 5–28.

Zacharias, Robert. "'Some Great Crisis': Vimy as Originary Violence." *Shifting the Ground of Canadian Literary Studies.* Ed. Smaro Kamboureli and Zacharias. Waterloo: Wilfrid Laurier University Press, 2012. 109–28.

Index

Acland, Peregrine, 7, 85
Afghanistan, 29, 167–68, 171, 189n23
Alderson, General Edwin, 95
All Else Is Folly, a Tale of War and Passion (Acland), 7, 85
Allward, Walter, 87, 91, 105, 111, 112, 114, 115, 116. *See also* art; *Stone Carvers, The*; Urquhart, Jane; Vimy memorial
anachronism, 18, 19, 35, 38, 96, 101. *See also* Cumyn, Alan; morphine
And We Go On (Bird), 95, 104
anti-war fiction: narrative, 12, 37, 100, 104; paradox of, 9, 37, 86, 88, 164. *See also Broken Ground*; Cobley, Evelyn; "In Flanders Fields"
anxiety, 16, 17, 62, 124; cultural context of, 6, 20, 24, 125, 160; and difference, 130; lack of autonomy and, 25; paradox of, 9, 37, 86, 88, 164; and voice of the dead, 5, 29, 55. *See also* stability
apocalypse, 6, 62–64, 72–74. *See also Barometer Rising*; *Broken Ground*; *Deafening* archivist (or researcher) in historiographic metafiction, 6, 10, 47, 51, 86, 92, 93, 116

art, 101, 105, 115. *See also* artists; Cumyn, Alan; memorial, war; soldier-artist; Urquhart, Jane
artists, 60, 86, 87, 93, 101–4, 105–16; as war outsiders, 87. *See also* art; Cumyn, Alan; soldier-artist; Urquhart, Jane
Atwood, Margaret, 9, 65, 91
audience: assumed Anglo-Canadian identity of, 131; and commemorative art, 114, 116, 117; contemporary, 4, 159; and *Dancock's Dance*, 33, 35, 36, 39; and *Mary's Wedding*, 43–44, 45; and performance, 174n 17; and *Unity (1918)*, 134, 139; and *Vimy*, 125, 126, 131, 132
Avery, Donald, 122

Barker, Pat, 87, 93, 94, 98, 100
Barometer Rising (MacLennan), 6, 7, 16, 59, 60, 62, 81, 182n14
Basilières, Michel, 155, 156
Becker, Annette, 2
Bird, Will, 95, 104
Bourke, Joanna, 97
Boyden, Joseph, 1, 6, 19, 21, 23, 120, 124, 139–49; reclaiming

marginalized history, 125, 140, 149.
    See also Three Day Road
Brandon, Laura, 101, 103
British reimaginings of WW I, 12, 13, 93, 94, 98
Broken Ground (Hodgins), 6, 21, 24, 26, 57–59, 61–72, 74, 79, 82, 83, 110, 153, 163, 166, 170; cultural backgrounds of settlers, 65; false climax in, 73; as inquiry into national self-imagining, 72; plot, 57; returned soldiers in, 62, 65; similarity to *The Wars* (Findlay), 66; subversion of apocalyptic narrative, 62; wrong direction as theme, 63, 68–69, 71. *See also* community; desertion
brotherhood, 25, 86, 104, 108, 117, 149. *See also Famished Lover, The*; masculinity; *Three Day Road*
Brydon, Diana, 10, 22, 24, 25, 86, 88, 114

Cabajsky, Andrea, and Brett Josef Grubisic, 88, 91, 124
Canadian identity, 6, 38, 53, 132
Canadian values, 4, 5, 12, 15, 20, 168, 170, 183n59
Chadwick, Ethel, 154–56
Child, Philip, 7, 85
Churchill, Caryl, 138
citizenship, 6, 24, 25, 28, 39, 60, 125, 132, 160, 166
civic activity or participation, 7, 16, 24, 25, 37, 41, 55, 117, 125, 159
class issues: *Dancock's Dance*, 38–40; *The Sojourn*, 98–101, 117
Coates, Donna, 15, 51, 165, 194n8
Cobley, Evelyn: and combatant fiction, 37, 86, 87, 94, 95, 104; complicity, 8, 12; and postmodern literature, 89; soldier narratives, 37, 153, 158; and war outsider, 112; and *The Wars*, 8, 9, 86–88. *See also* Cumyn, Alan; Itani, Frances; Poliquin, Daniel; Urquhart, Jane; Vanderhaeghe, Guy
codes of honour. *See* honour, codes of
Colavincenzo, Marc, 89, 90, 92
Coleman, Daniel, 35, 39
collective memory: conflict with history, 19, 26, 53; and Jay Winter, 2; loss of, 150; and Maurice Halbwachs, 2, 3; shift in, 16; of war, 5, 6, 9, 23. *See also* memory; remembrance
collective sacrifice. *See* sacrifice, collective
collective, idea of Canadian, 6, 15, 22, 23, 24, 26, 61, 116, 119–25, 160; in *A Secret Between Us*, 159; in *Three Day Road*, 140, 142, 148, 150; in *Unity (1918)*, 136, 138, 139; in *Vimy*, 130–32
coming of age as nation, 8, 12, 15, 58, 81, 138. *See also Deafening*; myth; war
commemoration, 5, 8, 13–15, 23, 42, 47, 51, 87, 111, 114, 140, 144; and art, 86, 87, 106; commemorative art, 86, 87, 101, 106, 114, 115; current national performances of, 28, 29
communication, 22, 46, 62, 81, 83, 102, 108, 112, 124, 133; gulfs in, 44, 70, 74, 75
community, 25, 65–66; and communal activity, 83; creation of, 71, 92, 93, 115–16; duty and service in, 16, 47, 105; as mediating historical meaning, 115; and myth, 116; romance of national, 73; stability of, 117; and voice of the dead, 30, 55. *See also Broken Ground*; *Deafening*; Other, the; returned soldiers; sacrifice
condolence letter, 153–54
Cook, Tim, 10, 45, 68–69, 92, 96, 98, 130, 176n59, 180n75, 190n43, 190n57

cultural nation, 58, 72, 83
Cumyn, Alan, 2, 6, 10, 21, 25, 44, 71, 79, 85–87, 91–105, 163; anachronistic sensibility in, 96; comparison with Jane Urquhart, 106–7, 110–11, 113, 116–17; differs from Barker, 94. See also Famished Lover, The; Sojourn, The

Dancock's Dance (Vanderhaeghe), 4, 24, 28, 33, 34–41, 52; abuses of power in, 41; Dancock as hero, 39; inversion of Canadian identity in, 38; plot, 28, 34. See also honour; sacrificial narrative
dead, the, 2, 23, 24, 29–33, 47–48; deaths as socially meaningful, 150. See also sacrifice
dead, impersonating voice of. See prosopopoeia; voice of the dead
Deafening (Itani), 6, 23, 44, 57, 65, 73–82; focus on Anglo-Canadian, middle-class community, 74; Great Fire as apocalyptic episode, 73; historical details in, 73; Jim as emblematic figure in, 81; plot of, 58; returned soldiers in, 65; as straightforward Bildungsroman, 58
Deep, The (Swan), 5, 21, 23, 33, 44, 47–54; as ahistorical, 47; format of, 49; as radical, 28–29; review of, 53. See also prosopopoeia
deheroicizing, 91
de Man, Paul, 30, 33; threat of logical disturbance, 30, 41, 43
desertion, 6, 58, 69, 114, 153, 164; in Broken Ground, 62–72; difference produced by anxiety, 130; hostility towards, 137; resistance to, 25; respect and tolerance of, 15, 127, 131, 132, 147, 160; sexualizing of, 137–39; social, 81, 122, 127. See also immigrants; Other, the
divisions, war-generated, 122–23

Dobson, Kit, 22, 127, 182n15
double narrative: evolution of, 8; as ironic, 146; structural and figurative, 141–43; of war's meaning, 6; in The Wars, 11
dream space: in "Mary's Wedding," 28, 42–44, 50; as ahistorical, 44; in The Deep, 50, 166; Duffy, Dennis, 123
duty, 4, 15, 33, 47, 75–76, 81, 96–97, 101, 117, 165–66

elegy: collective, 29; elegiac or sacrificial narrative, 41, 50, 54; erasure, 72, 112, 115–16; failure of, 46–48; and fear of erasure, 29; as genre, 30–31;
essential nation, paradigm of, 60, 61, 65

family, 52, 59, 61, 77, 100, 117, 145–48
Famished Lover, The (Cumyn), 79, 86, 87, 92, 93–105; family history and mythology in, 92; POW experience in, 25, 94; setting, 79; veteran experiences in, 21. See also soldier-artist
Findlay, Len, 127, 147
Findley, Timothy, 7, 26, 89; avoids complicity with war agenda, 87; metafictional strategies of, 90–91; and narrative reconstruction, 88; primary concern, 67; researcher in, 47; take on WW I, 8, 11, 20–21, 89. See also Hutcheon, Linda; metafiction, historiographic; Wars, The
fire, 57, 62–64, 73–74, 102, 129. See also apocalypse; Broken Ground; Deafening
First Nations, communities, 125; contributions to Canada's WW I effort, 22, 140, 177n97; in Three Day Road 139–50; in Vimy 128, 129, 131

First Nations trench life, 37, 79, 94
First World War, 16; as cataclysmic event in drama and fiction, 5; as catastrophic and dehumanizing, 11; challenge to mythic status, 153; as having moral merit, 72; as site for fashioning collective Canadian identity, 6; as site of uncomplicated national progression, 24
First World War literature and literary criticism, 7–12, 23–24. *See also* anti-war fiction; historical fiction; historical metafiction
First World War, mythology of, 5, 6, 29, 61, 66, 160
First World War, remembrance of, 22, 71, 117, 169; Australian, 13–15; British, 11; and participation in, 116
Fisher, Susan R., 9, 16–18, 173, 185
Flanders Fields. *See* "In Flanders Fields"
forgetting, 109, 114–16; and morphine, 19; process of, 93; as state-informed, strategic, 102
forging the nation, 6, 20, 57–62, 73, 142, 144
Francis, Daniel, 20, 62
francophone: as marginalized, 21; participation in war, 121, 128, 132; response to war, 105, 125, 128, 157; as soldier, 125, 131, 156. *See also* Poliquin, Daniel; *Secret Between Us, A*; Theissen, Vern; *Vimy*
Frye, Northrop, 65
Fussell, Paul, 44, 53

garrison mentality, 65
genealogical nation, paradigm of, 81; continuity of in Boyden, 149; in Hodgins and Itani, 59
Generals Die in Bed (Harrison), 7, 16, 85, 95, 175; backlash against, 9, 104
genius loci, 60, 65, 66, 82. *See also* Volk

ghosts, 28, 30; and personal loss, 48
Giller Prize, 151, 155, 173n2
God's Sparrows (Child), 7, 85
Goldman, Marlene, 23, 48, 62, 72
Granatstein, J.L. (Jack), 17, 121, 179n44
Groening, Laura, 140, 142, 147
Gross, Paul, 161–67, 169. *See also Passchendaele*
Group of Seven, 101, 103
Grubisic, Brett Josef, and Andrea Cabajsky, 88, 91, 124
Gwyn, Sandra, 9, 119, 128, 156. *See also Tapestry of War*

Halbwachs, Maurice, 2, 3, 48
Halifax Explosion of 1917, 7, 62
Harrison, Charles Yale, 8–9, 36, 79, 85, 87, 95; *Generals Die in Bed* as a memoir/memorial, 88. *See also Generals Die in Bed*
Hastings, Tom, 11
healing, 110, 114, 140–41, 147–48, 169
heroism, personal, 86, 163, 165, 166, 169
historians, 11,12, 15, 92, 119–25, 134. *See also* Cook, Tim; Granatstein, J.L.
historical drama, 4, 5. *See also Dancock's Dance*; *Mary's Wedding*; *Vimy*
historical fiction: anachronistic sensibility in, 18, 35, 72; and British novels, 80; to establish connections, 35; features of, 123; focus on those left out of traditional history, 72; historical figures in, 42, 91, 125, 139, 154; impossibility of totalizing picture, 123; and literary criticism, 123; relationship between history and fiction, 61; relationship to traditional history, 90, 91; revisionist, 11, 142; sacrificial narrative in, 41; shifting political goals of, 124; survey of Canadian, 89, 123–25. *See also* anti-war

fiction; historical drama; historical novel; historiographic metafiction
historical literature. *See* historical fiction
historiographic metafiction, 63, 82, 117; ambivalence about re-creation process, 106; archivist in, 6, 86, 92; definition, 88–89; examples of, 61; and gaps in history, 105; skepticism in, 88, 90. *See also* Hutcheon, Linda
historiography, 8, 55, 64
history: and community making, 17, 93; historical record, 26; idea of progression in, 145; moral merits of events, 72; and myth, 89–90, 115; as objective, 91, 144; productive use of discursively marginalized past, 72, 125, 140, 149; as thematic framework, 34, 43–44, 90–91, 105
Hodgins, Jack, 21, 24, 26, 57–72, 83; approach in contrast with Itani, 82; critical of idea of war's moral merit, 58, 72; parodies, 64; use of ironic metaphor, 65–66. *See also Broken Ground*; desertion
Holmes, Nancy, 29–32, 40
homogeneity, idealization of cultural, 23, 25, 120, 123, 136, 144–45, 160
honour, 37, 38, 147; codes of, 28, 33, 41, 52, 97; thematic examination of, 35; in Vanderhaeghe, 37. *See also* masculinity
Hughes, Munitions Minister Sam, 95, 96
Hulan, Renée, 98
Humphries, Mark, 133
Hutcheon, Linda, 88–90
Huyssen, Andreas, 2–3
Hynes, Samuel, 13, 99, 101

immigrants, 65, 73, 122; experiences, 122; German, 36, 38, 162; as outsiders, 136
incompetence: military and political, 21, 69; of officer class, 35, 36, 95, 97

"In Flanders Fields" (McCrae), 2, 19, 27, 40; analysis of, 29–30; anti-war position of critics, 12; as elegy, 33; last stanza, 30, 31; Preston Manning's use of, 31; pro-war sentiment in, 29. *See also* sacrificial narrative
influenza. *See* Spanish influenza
insider and outsider, war, 44, 49, 81, 85–118, 163. *See also* soldier-artist; soldier-poet
insider, war, 36, 83; as embodiment of national spirit, 58; experiences of, 112; and personal trauma, 106, 109; as "truth teller," 93
intergenerational conflict, 11, 100
Invention of the World, The (Hodgins), 64
Itani, Frances, 23, 57, 58, 73–83, 148; contrast with Hodgins, 61, 65, 82; conventional plot patterns in, 75, 78; conservative interpretation of war, 59, 80; duty and sacrifice, 79; and genealogical paradigm of nation, 78; inversion of apocalyptic narrative, 73; thematic focus on developing "life" of the nation, 75; war's moral value, 82. *See also Deafening*

Johnston, Basil, 140
Joyes, Kaley, 94

Keenan, Dennis, 31, 32, 40
Kennedy, David, 31
Kermesse, La. See Secret Between Us, A
Kerr, Kevin, 1, 6, 120, 124, 132–37; belief in collective, 139; interest in social effects of talk, 135; Note on Events, 133–34; "othering" of Sunna, 137; retrospective sacrificial narrative, 121. *See also Unity (1918)*
Kertzer, Jonathan, 60, 61, 82, 182
Keshen, Jeff, 121
Kevra, Susan, 157

Koepke, Melora, 152, 155
Kroetsch, Robert, 127
Kuester, Martin, 89, 92
Kuitenbrouwer, Kathryn, 151

legacy of war, 20–21
literary response to First World War, 7, 16, 18
Lloyd, David W., 13–15
Lost Boys, The (R.H. Thomson, 2001), 1, 16
Lukács, Georg: historical novels vs. historical dramas, 4, 5

Macfarlane, David, 9
MacLennan, Hugh, 6, 59, 60. *See also Barometer Rising*
Major, Kevin, 1, 19
marginalized communities, 21, 22, 61, 121, 144, 149, 177n97; and historic fictions, 74; and history, 90, 124, 125, 140, 149, 151. *See also* First Nations; immigrants; Other, the
Mary's Wedding (Massicotte), 5, 28, 33, 42, 52; Charlie, 42–44, 67–68; dramatic analysis only of, 4; elegiac mode of the play, 44; Flowerdew (Flowers), 42, 44, 46, 47; plot, 28, 42; romance in, 52
masculinity, 98–101; Australian, 15; Canadian contrasted to British, 98; Canadian notions of, 100–101; conceptions of order and honour, 41, 52, 97; identity and soldiers' brotherhood, 108, 117; male bonding in wartime, 97, 98; and notion of imaginary father figure, 100–101; and service to community, 105; threatened by domesticity, 99
mask imagery, 28, 30, 33, 48; in *Broken Ground*, 71–72; of dead soldier in *Dancock's Dance*, 40–41; as haunting, 40

Massicotte, Stephen, 1, 5, 28, 33, 42–44, 47. *See also Mary's Wedding*
McCrae, John, 2, 5, 24, 27, 53; apologists for, 30; envisioned contract, 50; pro-war stance, 29–31; and prosopopoeia, 27, 31. *See also* "In Flanders Fields"
McGinnis, Dickin, 134
McKenna, Andrew, 32
memorial artist, non-combatant, 103
memorials, war, 15, 50, 111–12, 122, 165. *See also* commemoration; soldier-artist; *Stone Carvers, The*; Vimy memorial
memory: as act of defiance, 43; autobiographical, 3; boom, 43; cultural, 12; as effort made among collective, 2; establishing a unified social, 18–19; of war insider, 107; of witness, 107
metafiction, post-historiographic, 85–93; and contemporary Canadian First World War novel, 91; historical data in, 105. *See also* Wyile, Herb
morphine, 19, 87, 108, 141, 145–46, 177n85; and forgetting, 19; literal and metaphorical use of, 108
Morton, Desmond, 121
Moses, Daniel David, 140
Mottram, Ralph Hale, 87
Mountain-Horse, Mike, 129
mourning, 15, 31, 42, 47, 50, 65, 85, 113, 115, 141
myth: of Canada's special role, 117, 144; of Canadian character, 4; of Canadian collective, 4, 6, 120–21, 124–32, 138; of essential nation, reinforced, 61; of heroic sacrifice, 55, 115–16; and history, 115; of honourable soldier, 158–59; of intergenerational conflict, 11; national, 26, 58; of national progress, 6, 58, 143; of national

unity, 58, 116, 130; as trick, 4; of war's moral merit, 66. *See also* First World War, mythology of; sacrifice; *Vimy*; Williams, David
mythmaking process, 126, 143
myth of national origin, 12, 17–18, 20–21, 49, 57

narrative: of "disillusioned subaltern," 13; of British adaptability, 80; of intimacy across war-torn cultural and experiential divides, 117; of meaningful sacrifice, 126, 136; of nationhood as "protean," 82; of a pointless war death, 36; of progress, 83; of sacrifice, 136; of war's constructive effect, 6, 13
nation: concepts of, 5, 6, 23, 57–85; as born in war, 13–14, 17–18, 46, 132; national character, 15, 20, 29, 60, 159
national self-fashioning, 3, 14, 23, 48, 72, 160
national unity, paradox of, 5, 12, 58, 124, 127
New, W.H., 71
No Man's Land (Kevin Major, 1995), 1, 19
Nonnekes, Paul, 100
nostalgia, 12, 20, 22, 49, 54, 61, 92; celebration, 55; for a particular cultural code, 160; as puzzling, 120; view of war, 83
Novak, Dagmar, 39, 86, 163

Old Men, theme of, 99, 100. *See also* intergenerational conflict
Other, the, 124–25, 128, 137, 138, 144; and Canadian collective, 119; Canadians, 119, 124
Otto, Peter, 15
Ouditt, Sharon, 13, 80, 93, 94, 98

pacifism, 29, 51, 75, 77, 133, 167. *See also* anti-war fiction

Palmateer Pennee, Donna, 10–12, 24, 80, 165, 167, 168
Papineau, Talbot, 156
Passchendaele, 161–63; reviews for, 162
past, remoteness of, 123
peacekeeper myth, 17–18, 168
Pegahmagabow, Francis, 139, 191
Poliquin, Daniel, 21, 24, 120, 125, 150–59; characters based on real people, 128, 156; complex relationship with francophone Canada, 157; influenced by Gwyn, 155; skewering of sacred myths, 125, 159; and work of recovery, 150. *See also Secret Between Us, A*
postmodernism, 6, 10–11, 35, 72, 74, 88–92, 105
post-war mythologizing of, 110
premise fatigue, 1, 170
Prescott, John, 28, 178n6
Prewett, Frank, 35
progress, 48, 74, 81. *See also* apocalypse
prosopopoeia, 5, 23, 27–55, 68; and anxiety, 29; definition, 27, 48–49; in "In Flanders Fields," 27, 28, 30
Rain Before Morning (Poole), 2
rehabilitation of First World War: as metaphor for civic participation, 24; moral merit of, 71; war as code of lost ideals, 41
remembrance: of artist vs. witness, 116; as collective effort, 2; by contemporary authors, 18; the dead, 47; as different for war outsider and war insider, 106; forms of, 9, 16, 49; function of, 48; historical, 16, 48, 121; and mythologizing, 116; practice of, 48, 55, 150; process of, 33; as term, 3; and witnessing, 155. *See also* First World War, remembrance of; nostalgia; prosopopoeia

remembrance, collective, 33, 72, 82, 93, 124, 126, 135, 150, 151, 157, 169; effort of, 1–6; on national scales, 17; social function of, 64; stakes, 9
responsibility, shared vocabulary of, 91
returned soldiers, 34, 63, 65–67, 72, 99, 133, 135, 152; government failure to care for, 110; Land Settlement Act, 63; rootlessness, 68. *See also Broken Ground; Deafening; Famished Lover, The; Stone Carvers, The*
Ricoeur, Paul, 26, 169
Rigelhof, T.F., 10, 151, 152, 155
romance, 46, 60, 70, 73–74, 75–76, 176n48; romance narrative, 85, 162, 163–64
Ross rifle, 96, 98
Ross, W.W.E., 36
Rutherdale, Robert, 122

sacrifice: as concept, 5, 161; as glorious sacrifice, 163; as noble, 46, 105
sacrifice, collective: as myth, 115–16, 122–23. *See also* Vance, Jonathan
sacrificial hero, 55
sacrificial narrative, 5, 27–33; affective response to, 5; and community process, 135; contemporary, 41; as destabilizing, 34–41; failure of, 48; in "In Flanders Fields," 33; of subaltern disillusion, 41; traditional military, 35
Sassoon, Siegfried, 10, 87, 94, 176n68
Schaub, Danielle, 94
Secret Between Us, A (Poliquin), 2, 21, 24, 125, 150–59; Giller Prize nomination, 151; impersonating history, 150; plot, 120; reviews, 151; satiric tone, 151–52
Sherry, Vincent, 13
skepticism, 82, 139, 159
Sojourn, The (Cumyn), 10, 44, 51, 71, 86–87; battlefield setting of, 79; soldier-artist in, 92, 93–105; use of family history and mythology, 92. *See also Famished Lover, The*; soldier-artist
soldier: difficulty of adjusting to civilian life, 99; francophone, 125; homogenizing force of image, 160; mythic status of, 12, 14–15, 153, 158–59; return home, 110; trope of being shot for cowardice, 68–69, 128, 154
soldier-artist, 86, 93, 93–105, 103; and British paradigms, 101–102; and British soldier-poet, 87; as truth teller, 102; work as war memorial, 103; in works of Alan Cumyn, 93–105
soldier-author, 37, 40
soldier-poet, 35, 44, 86, 93; theme of war insiders and outsiders, 44, 137
Soldier Settlement Act, 21, 63, 72
Spanish influenza, 42, 120, 124, 132–37, 190n42; casualties, 135; as "communicable" disease, 134–35; contamination and, 134; as forgotten, 150; origins of, 134; and rhetoric of battle, 136. *See also Dancock's Dance; Unity (1918)*
stability, 47, 82, 91, 92, 110: of community, 72, 117; and historical record, 91, 105; and masculinity, 98; of mimesis, 75; and national collective, 20, 160; and national history and character, 82. *See also* anxiety and nations
Stone Carvers, The (Urquhart), 14, 21, 23, 105–16, 113; forgetting in, 93; as historiographic metafiction, 86; plot of, 87. *See also* art; memorial; soldier-artist
subalterns: disillusionment of, 13, 39, 41, 97; experience in Cumyn's novels, 106
Sugars, Cynthia, and Gerry Turcotte, 23, 48

suicide, 49, 51–54, 87, 109. *See also Deep, The; Underpainter, The*
Swan, Mary, 5, 21, 23, 28, 47–54; and the dead, 33; pessimism of, 50; use of prosopopoeia, 47, 48. *See also* dead, the; *Deep, The*; prosopopoeia

Tapestry of War (Sandra Gwyn), 128, 154
Thiessen, Vern, 14, 21, 23, 120, 124, 125–32; acknowledgements in *Vimy*, 127; Historical Notes, 129. *See also Vimy*
Thompson, Eric, 7–9, 11, 85, 86
Thomson, Alistair, 15
Thomson, R.H., 1, 16
Three Day Road (Boyden), 1, 19, 21, 23, 124, 139–49; and collective Canadian identity, 6, 14; conscience, 141; national mythology, 144; plot, 120; resurrection, 145; sacred identity, 147; trickster figure in, 145. *See also* First Nations trench life

Trotter, David, 80, 94, 104
Turcotte, Gerry, and Cynthia Sugars, 23, 48

Underpainter, The (Urquhart), 18, 23, 86, 87, 91, 105; Augusta's tale, 107
Unity (1918) (Kerr), 6, 21, 124, 132–37; discourse and social effect, 136; dramatic analysis only of, 4; fear of difference in, 137; Note on Events in, 133–34; plot, 120; prologue, 136; similarities to *Dancock's Dance*, 132
unity, conceptions of, 5, 75, 136

Urquhart, Jane, 18, 21, 23, 86, 115–17; avoidance of self-reflexivity, 91; critique of artist's detachment, 109; depictions of artists, 86; focus on Afghanistan, 171; historical research by, 91; interview with Wyile, 90, 93, 186, 186n28; use of history as "inspiration," 105. *See also The Stone Carvers; The Underpainter*
usable past, construction of, 19, 55, 122, 124. *See also* historians
us vs. them, 116–25. *See also* collective; First Nations; francophone; immigrants; insider and outsider, war; Other, the

Vance, Jonathan, 9, 19–21, 66, 104, 122, 159; and *Death So Noble*, 66, 95; narrative of pointless war death, 36; review of *The Deep*, 53; war in terms of utility, 110, 122
Vanderhaeghe, Guy, 24, 28, 33–41, 47, 52, 97; and British soldier-poet narrative, 36; critique of sacrificial narrative, 40; honour and dishonour in, 37–38; interview with Wyile, 34; prosopopoeia, version of, 34; use of history, 34. *See also Dancock's Dance*
Vauthier, Simone, 10, 11, 88
Vimy (Thiessen): and Allward, Walter, 105; characters in, 128; as dramatic analysis, 4; individual and collective memory in, 126; myth of unified experience in, 125–32; mythologizing of war's function, 127, 132; playwright's note, 126; plot, 120, 130; Vimy memorial, 15, 109
Vimy Ridge, 120; narrative about, 14; in *A Secret Between Us*, 151; in *The Stone Carvers*, 87; in *Three Day Road*, 143; in *Vimy*, 124, 125, 130, 132
Volk, concept of, 60, 65, 71, 82

war: agenda, 87; British story of, 13; and discursive conventions, 153; experience of, 13–14; as genealogical crisis, 76; as hell, 79;

human cost of, 23; as a kind of courtship, 45, 47; legacy, 20–21; making sense of, 116; and male bonding, 97–98; as necessary stage or crucible, 61; as productive, 12, 54, 58, 68; as reluctant coming of age, 12; as symbolic, 52; as unifying influence, 14, 123; as waste, 111. *See also* First World War; First World War, rehabilitatation of

war fiction: British combat fiction, 80; combatant fiction, 9, 86, 94; commemorative impetus in, 8; critical assessment of, 10, 87–91; narratives, 21, 153; as novels, 9, 94–95; as realistic, 85; war insider and outsider. *See* insider and outsider, war

Wars, The (Findlay), 16, 26, 47, 86, 88, 90; analysis of, 7; as anti-war, 86; as culminating Canadian First World War novel, 88–91; as historiographic metafiction, 6, 86–91; literary criticism of, 7–11; narrative strategies of, 10; Watkin, William, 31. *See also* mourning

Wiersema, Robert, 1, 161
Williams, David, 17, 18, 20, 57, 59, 60
windigo, 142, 145, 148
Winter, Jay, 2, 3, 16, 42, 43, 48, 163
witness, 107, 108, 114; contrasted with commemorator, 108; experience of, 116; and truth telling, 93
women: appropriate work for, 113; as muses for male soldiers, 113; pacifist stances of, 51; as sacrificing mothers, 194n8; value of women's work, 22, 136; as war participants, 50, 51, 113, 127, 194; war work, 51; work on home front, 137. *See also* mourning
Wyile, Herb: analysis of Canadian historical fiction, 19–20, 72, 124, 142, 170; examination of dialogue, 90; interview with Joseph Boyden, 139; interview with Jane Urquhart, 90, 93; interview with Guy Vanderhaeghe, 34, 37

York, Lorraine, 11
Young, Alan R., 111

Zacharias, Robert, 14, 15

www.ingramcontent.com/pod-product-compliance
Lightning Source LLC
Chambersburg PA
CBHW071816080526
44589CB00012B/808